Painting Popular
DUCK DECOYS

16 Full-Color Plates & Complete Instructions

by
ANTHONY HILLMAN

DOVER PUBLICATIONS, INC. · New York

To Dave and Nancy Rhodes

Copyright © 1989 by Anthony Hillman.
All rights reserved under Pan American and International Copyright Conventions.

Published in Canada by General Publishing Company, Ltd.,
30 Lesmill Road, Don Mills, Toronto, Ontario.
Published in the United Kingdom by Constable and Company, Ltd.,
10 Orange Street, London WC2H 7EG.

Painting Popular Duck Decoys: 16 Full-Color Plates and Complete Instructions
is a new work, first published by Dover Publications, Inc., in 1989.

Manufactured in the United States of America
Dover Publications, Inc.
31 East 2nd Street
Mineola, N.Y. 11501

Library of Congress Cataloging-in-Publication Data

Hillman, Anthony.
Painting popular duck decoys :
16 full-color plates and complete instructions /
by Anthony Hillman.
p.   cm.
ISBN 0-486-26100-X
1. Decoys (hunting)—Painting.   I. Title.
ND1575.H55   1989
745.593'6—dc20   89-34093
CIP

Introduction & Instructions

After you have carved a duck decoy, or purchased an unfinished carving, you will want to give it enough natural coloring to attract wild birds in the field, or—especially if the decoy was created for display rather than field use—you may want to color it in greater, more realistic detail. However you choose to paint your decoy, any time you spend in doing the job accurately and carefully will be well rewarded by years of lasting pleasure.

There is no one correct way to paint a decoy; each painter develops an individual style. First, however, you should study these instructions very carefully, especially if you have never painted a woodcarving before. I have included many tips that will be helpful in painting any wildfowl carving. In particular, the step-by-step guide to painting the male and female Ruddy Ducks (Plates 2 and 3) will give you a good idea of how to proceed with the 14 other decoys illustrated in the plates (which give profiles and top views of 9 species of ducks—males and females of 7 species, plus two for which no separate illustration of the female is needed).* I have also provided a list of the colors of paint you will need to paint the 14 decoys not described in detail.

Of course, no color picture can be a substitute for close observation of a living bird. Every care has been taken, however, to make the 16 color plates in this book the next best thing—illustrations of great usefulness to the decoy painter. The top views are, I believe, unique in this type of publication, and have been carefully created with the needs of decoy painting in mind. And even the profiles include areas that do not appear even in the best bird-identification manuals.

Although these plates are the best painting guide available in book form and should be studied closely, the beginner cannot expect to be able to duplicate complex duck coloration without some practice. Seldom can the exact color desired be squeezed right from a tube of paint. Many colors can be created only by the blending of pigments—and don't be afraid to experiment—but even basic colors vary depending on the type of paint (acrylics, oils, etc.) and the manufacturer.

Don't let this intimidate you. Study the instructions, plates and other sources carefully, and practice mixing and applying paints, but also do not be afraid to draw upon your own creativity. Discovering your own "recipes" is part of the fun of decoy painting. There is, I repeat, no one way to paint a decoy. Gradually you will develop a personal style that you will be proud of.

Research Your Subject

Before you begin painting, it is essential to study your subject carefully. Learn the different topographical features of a duck (see Figure 1). This will help you remember where to apply the proper colors and markings. Feather shape and size often determine the color pattern, especially on females of dabbling-duck species, and therefore determine how you apply paint to your decoy.

---

*The female Cinnamon Teal is almost identical in plumage with the female Blue-winged Teal (see Plate 12 of my *Painting Duck Decoys*, Dover 24810-0), and the male and female Fulvous Whistling Duck are identical in plumage.

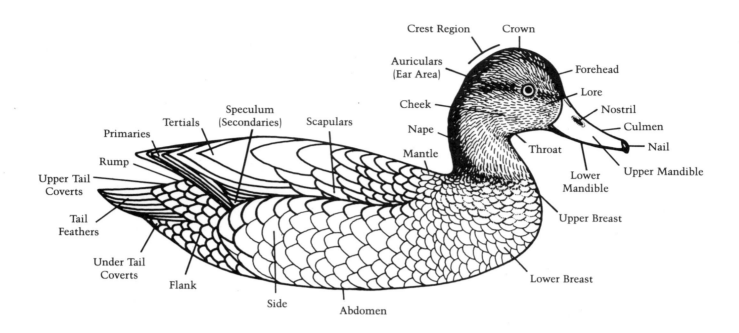

Fig. 1. TOPOGRAPHY OF A DUCK

Study the color illustrations on Plates 1–16 in this book. These plates, which include both profiles and top views, may be removed from the book so that the appropriate one can be placed beside your carving and referred to as you paint. Supplement the plates with color photographs and, wherever possible, live or preserved specimens. Thorough research is important; study skins are invaluable but sometimes difficult to obtain. If you are studying preserved specimens, double-check against the illustrations for the proper coloration of the bill and any fleshy parts represented in your carving, as the colors of live birds fade after death.

Learn to identify the true coloring of your subject. This is not as easy as it sounds. For example, from a distance, the head of the male Common Goldeneye may at first appear simply black. Closer observation will reveal a rich green in the highlights on the fuller areas of the head (mainly the cheek and crown). Making observations like this can be an enjoyable part of painting waterfowl carvings. As you become better acquainted with this aspect of our wildlife, you will note subtle (and not-so-subtle) variations in the colors of plumage based on seasonal change and other factors.

Brushes and Paints

When choosing any art supplies, a good rule to follow is to buy the best, or at least the best you can afford. This rule applies especially to brushes, since the brush is the instrument that gets the paint onto the surface of your carving. A wide variety of brushes is available for any paint medium you use. Figure 2 illustrates some types of brushes I find useful for painting waterfowl. If brushes of the type you desire are not available locally, write for catalogs from some of the major art-supply firms. It will be futile to attempt to paint with inferior brushes.

Through the years I have become partial to sign-painting and lettering brushes. The longer bristles on these brushes hold more paint and make it easier to control long, delicate lines. They also help keep paint from getting up into the ferrule, an important advantage when working with acrylics (for which your brush also should have a soft, white, nylon type of bristle).

The "fan blender" is another useful brush, both for blending colors and for "dry-brush" technique. With this type of brush, I prefer white oil bristles, even for acrylic paints, as the stiffer bristles maintain the proper fan shape.

For applying large, solid areas of color, the larger-size "flats" (brushes with flattened ferrules) are the most useful. These brushes deliver a large quantity of paint while allowing good control where sharp edges are desirable.

In time you will find that some of your brushes are losing their shapes, their hairs twisting in every direction. Save these worn-out tools. Although they may no longer serve the specialized purposes you purchased them for, they can be invaluable for stippling and dry brushing.

Just as different kinds of brushes serve different purposes, different types of paint have different properties and produce different effects. Oil paints have the major disadvantage of taking a long time to dry. This can also be an advantage, however, as it permits colors to be blended to perfection. And if you make a mistake, the area can be wiped clean to start over again. If drying

(Instructions continue after plates.)

Plate 1.   Cinnamon Teal, male.

Plate 2. Ruddy Duck, male.

Plate 3. Ruddy Duck, female.

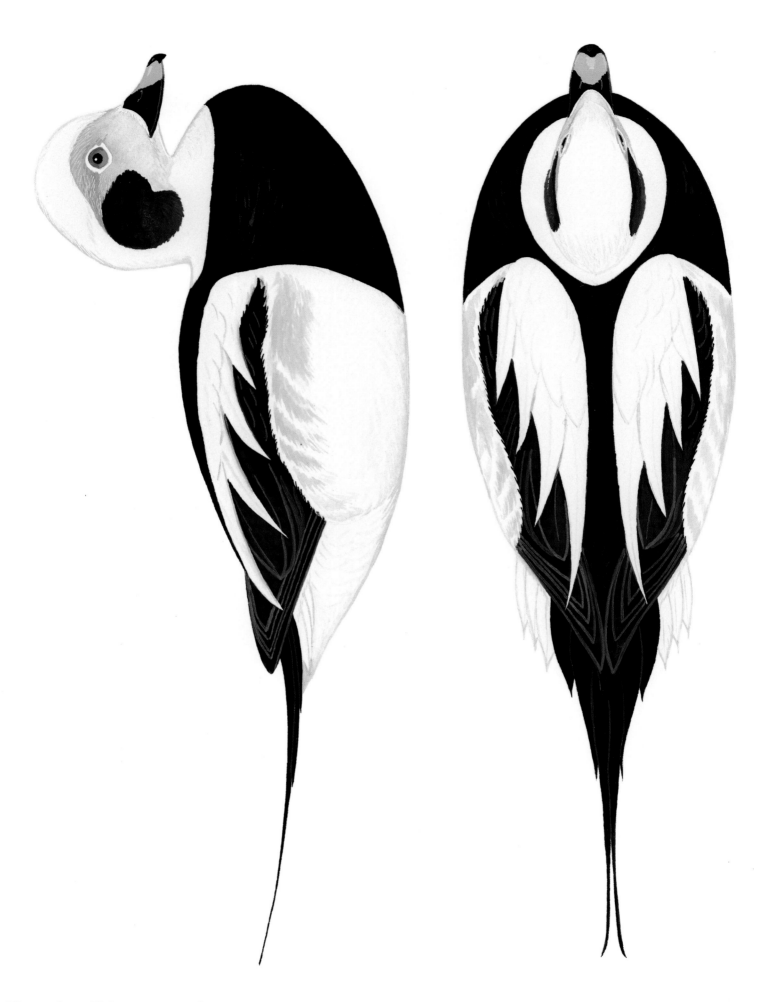

Plate 4. Oldsquaw, male.

Plate 5. Oldsquaw, female.

Plate 6.   Surf Scoter, male.

Plate 7. Surf Scoter, female.

Plate 8. Gadwall, male.

Plate 9. Gadwall, female.

Plate 10. Hooded Merganser, male.

Plate 11. Hooded Merganser, female.

Plate 12.   Common Goldeneye, male.

Plate 13. Common Goldeneye, female.

Plate 14.   Ring-necked Duck, male.

Plate 15. Ring-necked Duck, female.

Plate 16. Fulvous Whistling Duck (sexes similar).

time is of no concern, you may prefer oils, for they produce a rich, almost sensual, gloss that seems to be obtainable with no other medium.

The two basic media for oil paint are turpentine and linseed oil. Turpentine will reduce drying time and deaden the sheen inherent in tube colors. Linseed oil, when added to paint, extends drying time and adds sheen. Several drying agents, such as cobalt drier, are available. Allowing oil paints to stand overnight on absorbent brown paper (like that used to make shopping bags) will drain off some of the linseed oil, as is preferred by some decoy carvers.

Acrylic paint is probably the medium most widely used by carvers of duck decoys. It dries quickly, and brushes can be cleaned in soap and water, making acrylics more convenient than oils for most people. *It is important to remember that for acrylic paints you must use acrylic primer.*

The speed at which acrylic paints dry can be a handicap for the beginner, but practice and familiarization with the medium soon overcome this difficulty. A gel medium, available in art-supply stores, slows drying time when added to tube acrylic paints.

Tube acrylics tend to dry with a slick surface. Given the requirements of decoy painting, this is not necessarily desirable. I use flat exterior house paints as the main colors of my palette. Flat acrylics offer a distinct advantage when you are painting undercoats and thin washes of color, there being less chance of running or puddles of pigment remaining when the brush is lifted off the painting surface. Another advantage is that when additional markings are applied, as in feathering, the flat finish takes the applied color better.

Usually house paints are sold in quart cans. You may find it awkward to work from these directly, but transferring enough paint for several projects to smaller containers works fine. Basic colors available in flat house paints include black and white (from which you can also make gray) and brown. You may use tube colors and tints to achieve reds, blues, yellows, and other colors. This combination of house and tube paints is my personal preference. In any case, remember that it is easier

to make the flat finish of a completed piece glossy (if you desire it) than to tone down a glossy finish to a soft luster.

Selecting Your Colors

Most of the species in this book are diving ducks, of which the males generally have relatively bold, simple color patterns. This high contrast makes these ducks generally easier to paint than "dabbling" ducks (so named because they usually feed near the surface, without diving). The Gadwall, Fulvous Whistling Duck, and Cinnamon Teal are the only dabbling ducks in this book. Along with some of the female diving ducks, they have somewhat subtler, more complicated color patterns than most of the male diving ducks. If you have never painted a decoy before, therefore, it is a good idea to begin with a male diving duck.

For this reason I have provided in detail the procedures for painting the decoy of what is probably the most popular of the species in this book, that of the male Ruddy Duck. Once you have painted a male Ruddy, you may wish to try the female, which is somewhat more difficult. Although she seems nondescript at a distance, the female Ruddy Duck actually has a subtle, interesting color pattern. If you are a beginner at decoy painting or need to refresh your memory, I suggest that you carefully read through the following instructions. Even if you do not intend to paint any Ruddy Ducks, you will familiarize yourself with the kinds of procedures necessary for painting any duck decoy.

The exact colors you use will of course be determined by the particular species represented by your decoy. Following the instructions for the pair of Ruddy Ducks, I have provided a list of specific colors you will need for each duck shown in the other color plates. Remember, you will need to mix lighter and darker shades of several of these colors for contrast and definition of feathers. In other words, once you have, for example, a solid brown base color, create lighter and darker versions of this color by adding to it white, black, or whatever other color is appropriate. As an example of the latter procedure, adding raw sienna to burnt umber will often effectively lighten the burnt umber without using white.

In most cases, you will have to create contrast of colors by mixing. The following basic colors, however, are needed for all or at least most of the species illustrated:

1. White.
2. Black.
3. Burnt umber. (With flat house paints you must check color samples, as each manufacturer may market several brown shades under different trade names. An example is Cook & Dunn's "Cape Cod Brown," an excellent dark brown once a small amount of black has been added.)
4. Burnt sienna.
5. Raw sienna.
6. Payne's gray.
7. Cadmium yellow medium.

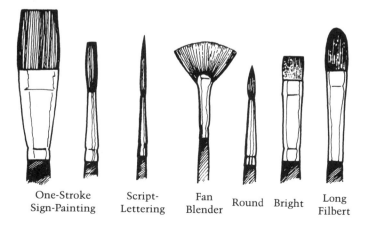

One-Stroke Sign-Painting   Script-Lettering   Fan Blender   Round   Bright   Long Filbert

Fig. 2. TYPES OF BRUSHES

8. Red. (Note: Most tube colors that look like "fire-engine red" are sold under such trade names as "Grumbacher red," "Winsor red," etc. Trade names vary for many other colors as well. Be sure to check color samples before purchasing.)

With the addition of a medium gray (which you may create, of course, by mixing black and white), these colors will provide the painter with the bulk of what he needs. Other colors necessary in smaller quantities include:

9. Thalo blue.
10. Viridian (a type of green).
11. Burnt orange.
12. Indian red or red oxide.
13. Violet.

Besides actual paints, a wide variety of colors is available in tints. The Rich Lux Products Company of Philadelphia puts out an excellent line known as "Minit Tint." The beauty of tints is that, since they contain no hardeners or driers, they have an extremely long shelf life under moderate temperature conditions. Be sure to follow instructions to determine the maximum amount of tint that can be safely used. Applying too much will prevent proper drying.

Metallic acrylic paints are another option available to decoy carvers. A fine job can be done with these paints, but it is a mistake to overuse them. They can create a garish effect where subtle coloring of highlights would be more desirable. Many a good carving has been spoiled by the indiscriminate use of metalflake paints.

Before You Begin

After you have sanded your carving to a smooth finish, it is necessary to seal the wood. Clear wood sealers include lacquer and shellac. Two coats are usually sufficient. Sand between coats with #220 or finer sandpaper. Wood that contains knots needs to be carefully sealed, as the resins in knots will discolor paint.

Once it has been sealed, your carving should be primed. Priming further protects the wood and provides a uniformly pigmented surface to paint on. Remember to use oil-based primer when you are painting with oils, acrylic primer when you are using acrylic paints. When you paint with acrylics, you may want to start with an oil primer and then coat this with acrylic primer. Acrylic primer applied directly to the wood raises the grain, an effect you may prefer. This requires more sanding, but it allows the natural beauty of the grain to show through.

"Kilz," made by Masterchem Industries, is an excellent product that I recommend especially for working decoys. Since this is a primer-sealer, it allows you to prime and seal in one operation, saving you a step. Best of all, it can be covered with either oils or acrylics. When using acrylics, however, it is a good idea to top it with a coat of an acrylic primer.

While brushing on any coat of primer, be sure not to leave ridges or brush marks, the presence of which will make painting of details more difficult later on. After the primer has dried, sand a final time with #220 or finer sandpaper. This will remove any roughness, providing a smooth base to paint over.

NOTE: Read and follow the instructions found on the labels of all primers, sealers and paints you may use. Familiarize yourself with the qualities of each product as well as precautions necessary for their safe use.

Painting Your Decoy—Step-by-Step

Now you are ready to begin painting your decoy. The following detailed procedures for painting male and female Ruddy Duck decoys will give you an idea of how to go about painting any decoy.

To paint the male Ruddy (see Plate 2), first outline the major color areas lightly with a pencil. Define the edges of the crown, forehead, and crest region of the head—what will be painted black. Then outline the cheek patch. Now lightly define the edges of the side feathers on the body where they curve to border the lower wing. Continue by marking the complete edges of the wings and use the top view to guide you in defining the primaries (wingtips). Make sure your marks are accurate.

Using black paint, start painting the top of the head in the area previously marked. Always make sure you have good, solid coverage, but avoid applying too much paint at once, or it will drip or run. Two coats are usually required when using latex paints. Paint the white cheek patches next (or simply leave them white if you used sufficient white primer), being especially careful as you come to the edges of the bill.

Using Indian red or red oxide, paint the neck, breast, and body to the appropriate margins as you have marked them in pencil. Refer also to the color plate and any other reference material you have. Once you have laid down a good, solid base color, use brown to color the wings and tail. Remember, we are only establishing the main color areas at this time. The decoy at this stage should be very simply and boldly patterned, with no feather detail. Before proceeding further, make sure your base colors are dry and they do not look too thin.

Our next step is to add the feather detail, covering one section at a time. I recommend saving the tail and bill for last. That way, if you need to rest the decoy on one end or the other while painting, you will avoid marring any recently applied paint.

Now go on to paint the feather detail on the body. Use burnt umber, with a small amount of black added, for the dark edges over the rust-red body areas. Paint for the lighter highlights can be mixed by adding raw sienna to the red-oxide body color. Use white to break up the straight edge of red oxide where it borders the white portions of the belly and lower breast. Then use burnt umber mixed with white to define the wing feathers. Individual feather barbs may be defined with thin, delicate strokes of burnt sienna. To complete the wing detailing, add black to burnt umber to accent the lower edges of the primary flight feathers. If you wish to detail the feathers on the black crown, as I did, use black lightened with a small amount of white. A very light gray may be used sparingly to suggest feathering around the outer edges of the white cheek areas.

The tail is defined in much the same manner. Use darkened burnt umber to indicate individual tail feathers and raw sienna mixed with burnt umber to lighten edges as desired. The bill color is achieved by mixing white with Thalo blue and adding a minute amount of Payne's gray. The "nail" on the tip is painted black.

Check over your carving and compare what you've done with the color plate. Sometimes it is best to leave the project alone for a short time so that you will be able to view your work with a fresh eye. Subtle mistakes (and real whoppers!) can be discovered this way and corrected. The final result of your efforts should look the same on both sides. The feathers should show enough contrast to look "fluffy" where appropriate. If you are satisfied, you may congratulate yourself on having successfully painted a male Ruddy Duck decoy!

The female Ruddy Duck, less striking in appearance, has a subtle beauty of her own. As with the male, first lightly define in pencil the major divisions of head, cheek, back, wings, and sides. On this bird the wings (except the primaries) and back are the same brown color beneath any details. The primaries are a little darker.

The first paint you should apply after the primer is a light wash of raw sienna to create a buff color in the areas shown in Plate 3. It will be necessary to use a fine-pointed brush where this thin layer of undercolor fades to white on the lower breast, belly, and sides. To soften the edges, it may be desirable to paint white up into the sienna wash.

Now paint the head, nape, back, wings, and tail with a basic coat of brown and allow this to dry. Add the white cheek patch, and when this is dry apply burnt umber with a fine-pointed brush to define the irregular stripe that crosses the cheek. With burnt sienna paint the reddish brown band that extends around the upper breast. Use a light touch!

Continue painting by detailing the edges of the wing feathers with gray. Using the top view as a guide, indicate the fine mottling on the back and tertial wing feathers by applying a mix of raw sienna and a very little burnt umber. On the flanks, sides, and abdomen, indicate darker details with strokes of burnt umber, and lighter details similarly with raw sienna. Details of the crown and crest area may be created by using a mixture of black and burnt umber for the darker streaks, and raw sienna and brown for the highlights. Edge the tail feathers with raw sienna. Finish by painting the bill with Payne's gray lightened with white. Use black paint for the nostrils and the "nail." You can approximate Payne's gray by adding Thalo blue to a white and black mixture, but Payne's gray is also readily available as a tube color and will be useful for painting the bills of several species of ducks, especially the females.

With practice you will acquire familiarity with the effects of different paints, tools, and procedures. Do not strive for speed; it will come on its own. The paint patterns on the plates may be simplified if your decoys are intended only for hunting. On the other hand, if you are interested in accuracy of detail, more research will enable you to improve on these color schemes. Good luck!

For your convenience, the colors of the paints needed for the decoys illustrated on Plates 1 and 4–16 are given below. Remember, however, that pigments vary from manufacturer to manufacturer and with the type of paint. In many cases you will need to experiment with different mixtures to achieve a particular color. Some of the colors listed may be created by mixing others. And you may work out any number of satisfactory substitutions. The following list is intended only as a rough guide.

List of Colors

PLATE 1. Cinnamon Teal, male: Black, white, burnt umber, burnt sienna, raw sienna, Thalo blue, red, cadmium yellow medium, viridian.

PLATE 4. Oldsquaw, male: Black, white, burnt umber, burnt sienna, red.

PLATE 5. Oldsquaw, female: Black, white, burnt umber, burnt sienna, raw sienna, Thalo blue, red.

PLATE 6. Surf Scoter, male: Black, white, burnt umber, burnt sienna, Thalo blue, red, cadmium yellow medium.

PLATE 7. Surf Scoter, female: Black, white, burnt umber, raw sienna, Payne's gray, cadmium yellow medium.

PLATE 8. Gadwall, male: Black, white, burnt umber, burnt sienna, raw sienna, Payne's gray.

PLATE 9. Gadwall, female: Black, white, burnt umber, burnt sienna, raw sienna, burnt orange, Payne's gray.

PLATE 10. Hooded Merganser, male: Black, white, burnt umber, burnt sienna.

PLATE 11. Hooded Merganser, female: Black, white, burnt umber, burnt sienna, red, cadmium yellow medium, Payne's gray.

PLATE 12. Common Goldeneye, male: Black, white, cadmium yellow medium, viridian.

PLATE 13. Common Goldeneye, female: Black, white, burnt umber, burnt sienna, red, cadmium yellow medium.

PLATE 14. Ring-necked Duck, male: Black, white, burnt umber, burnt sienna, Payne's gray, viridian, violet.

PLATE 15. Ring-necked Duck, female: Black, white, burnt umber, burnt sienna, raw sienna, Payne's gray, viridian.

PLATE 16. Fulvous Whistling Duck, male and female: Black, white, burnt umber, burnt sienna, raw sienna, Payne's gray.

Introduction

The cold war was a time of lasting unease in Britain as the great nuclear superpowers continually challenged one another on the international stage – with the threat of global atomic annihilation sometimes drawing a little too close for comfort. Yet the cold war also saw a host of magnificent British-made aircraft take flight as the nation fought to maintain its position on the top-tiers of military might and commercial success.

Some, such as the Hawker Hunter, Avro Vulcan, English Electric Lightning and Hawker Siddeley Harrier, were world-beating fighting machines in their day. Others, such as the Supermarine Swift, proved to be spectacular failures. All were flown by highly skilled pilots, sometimes under the most unusual and demanding of circumstances.

Between the end of the Second World War and the collapse of the Soviet Union, the British aviation industry underwent a dramatic transformation. Every famous manufacturer lost its name along the way as a series of acquisitions and mergers compressed the independent firms into what some see today as a pale shadow of a glorious past, but which others regard as a modern, focused and interconnected industrial sector.

Immediately after the war, massive government spending cuts and order cancellations left companies struggling to make ends meet. Most tussled for the handful of military contracts that were available, some forged ahead with efforts to develop a civil aviation business and others came increasingly to rely on sub-contracting work. The programme to develop Britain's second generation military jet aircraft, after the Gloster Meteor and de Havilland Vampire, made slow progress. Only the sudden beginning of the Korean War and the realisation that the Soviets, with their ground-breaking MiG-15 jet fighter, had stolen a march on the West prompted a belated but significant injection of cash into the defence industry.

Early British jet fighters, such as the Sea Hawk (P6), offered little advantage over first generation types. The more advanced Swift (P20) and Hunter had been in development since before the Korean War but now there was a renewed sense of urgency. Both programmes, however, were bedevilled by teething troubles which, in the case of the Swift, would prove fatal. The Hunter proved its mettle and went on to be a great success worldwide while English Electric – a company without the legacy, and baggage, of being a Second World War 'name' – produced the remarkable Mach 2-capable Lightning (P84).

In 1952, the introduction of the de Havilland Comet changed civil aviation forever. With incredible futuristic looks and a wonderfully quiet and comfortable passenger cabin, the world's first commercial jet airliner was a sensation and left the Americans trailing in its wake. Here was a lifeline for British aircraft manufacturers that could give them their long-sought independence from the capriciousness of government contract work.

Sadly this bright new future quickly dimmed when a series of fatal crashes revealed a fundamental flaw in the Comet's design and the Americans began to catch up. The British manufacturers pressed ahead with a proliferation of airliner projects, including the Vickers VC10 (P42) and Hawker Siddeley Trident (P52), but their bungled procurement would eventually hand the Americans the lead.

The Suez Crisis of 1956 (P30) was a watershed moment in Britain's cold war history. Although it proved politically damaging for Britain in the short term, it resulted in American efforts to rebuild British international prestige and arguably led to the UK-US Mutual Defence Agreement. This, in turn, led to Britain's acquisition of the nuclear submarine technology it needed to replace its fleet of nuclear bombers.

The three V-bombers – the Avro Vulcan (P64 and P74), Handley Page Victor and Vickers Valiant – had been planned as Britain's last line of defence in the event of a nuclear war with the Soviet Union. Their mission under such circumstances was to get airborne before their bases were destroyed, fly into enemy airspace and drop nuclear bombs or fire nuclear cruise missiles at strategically important targets. Thankfully they were never required to do it.

The innovative Hawker Siddeley Harrier (P89) became a surprising British cold war success story. Throughout the 1960s, nearly every aviation company around the world with aspirations to work for the military came up with some sort of design for a vertical take-off and landing fixed-wing aircraft. But only Hawker Siddeley really got it right and the Harrier went on to become an international aviation icon with many variants produced, including the Sea Harrier.

The latter's finest hour undoubtedly came during the Falklands War in 1982 when, flying from HMS *Invincible* and HMS *Hermes*, Sea Harriers shot down 20 Argentine aircraft for no air-to-air losses. The Americans at this time were deeply concerned that the British lacked sufficient aircraft carriers for a successful outcome and offered to lease them one (P104) from which the RAF's Blackburn Buccaneers might have operated at a pinch but again, it never happened. An Argentine Pucará was captured and evaluated by the British after the conflict (P110).

Although the cold war effectively came to an end in 1991, Britain has continued to operate aircraft developed during that period such as the Nimrod (P122) which, though it was based on the de Havilland Comet, first flown in 1949, remained in service until 2011. The VC10 carried on until 2013.

Within this volume you will find a collection of articles concerning incidents, accidents, events, decisions, mistakes, oddities, arguments and above all beautiful British aircraft from the cold war period. Each of the 17 pieces comes with a guarantee of painstaking research carried out by some of the finest aviation historians working around the world today. I hope you enjoy reading these 'cold war stories' as much as I have.

Dan Sharp

Contents

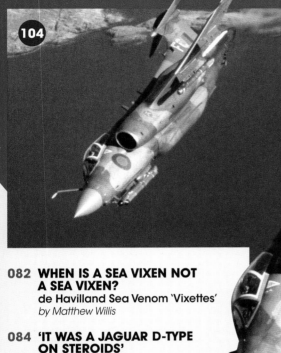

104

★★★★★ Aviation ★★★★★

BRITISH COLD WAR STORIES

The Aviation Historian

'LIKE A D-TYPE ON STEROIDS' BAC LIGHTNING EXPERIENCE

THRILLS & SPILLS WITH THE SCARLET HUNTER

VULCANS PUTTING ON THE STYLE IN LAS VEGAS

CAPTURED ARGENTINE PUCARA ON TEST

THE TRIDENT STORY ★ CIVILIAN HARRIER ★ FALKLANDS CARRIERS ★ SUEZ
DITCHING A NIMROD ★ BEA'S HELICOPTERS ★ HAWKER SEA HAWK
SUPERMARINE SWIFT DISASTER ★ MINI SEA VIXENS

FRONT COVER:
English Electric
Lightning T.5 by
John Fox.

110

118

EDITOR: Dan Sharp

Design: Sean Phillips – atg-media.com

Publisher: Steve O'Hara

Group advertising manager: Sue Keily
skeily@mortons.co.uk

Marketing manager: Charlotte Park

Commercial director: Nigel Hole

Thanks to: Mick Oakey and Nick Stroud

Published by:
Mortons Media Group Ltd,
Media Centre,
Morton Way, Horncastle,
Lincolnshire LN9 6JR
Tel: 01507 529529

Printed by: William Gibbons and Sons,
Wolverhampton

ISBN: 978-1-911276-94-4

MORTONS
MEDIA GROUP LTD

How to build a
Sea Hawk

Using a sequence of official Hawker photographs from a contemporary technical brochure, naval aviation specialist MATTHEW WILLIS takes us through the construction of one of the prototypes of the company's first jet fighter, the P.1040 — which, while dismissed by the RAF, would go on to provide sterling service for the Royal Navy as the Sea Hawk.

The series of photographs presented here shows in detail the construction of a prototype Hawker P.1040, which would become the Sea Hawk naval fighter. These official Hawker images follow the assembly of one of the three prototype aircraft ordered by the Admiralty to Specification N.7/46 – VP401, VP413 and VP422 (probably the second) – in Hawker's experimental workshop during 1947–48, from individual components through to a substantially completed airframe. The photographs are particularly fascinating in showing how Hawker elegantly approached the packaging of a jet engine, this being the first of the company's jet aircraft designs to reach the hardware stage.

Although the N.7/46's technology represented a marked step forward from the company's preceding piston-engined fighters, it is notable that the swept-wing North American XP-86 prototype had already flown in the USA by the time the P.1040 made its maiden flight, rendering it effectively obsolescent – perhaps not surprising considering the three-year period that elapsed between the P.1040's conception

and its first flight. Nevertheless, straight wings would be used on the majority of first-generation naval jet fighters, and indeed the Sea Hawk remained in front-line service into the 1960s in the Fleet Air Arm, and the 1980s in the Indian Navy, partly thanks to Hawker's careful design.

INGENIOUS DESIGN

In 1944, when Hawker began working on its first jet fighter, designated P.1035, the design was closely based on the piston-engined F.2/43 (what would become the Sea Fury). The new design used the same semi-elliptical wing as its propeller-driven stablemate and a straight-through jetpipe for the new Rolls-Royce B.41 (later Nene) centrifugal-flow turbojet engine, much as Supermarine was doing with its "Jet Spiteful" E.10/44 design. However, the long jetpipe threatened to rob a significant amount of power from the engine. Hawker worked with the engine manufacturers to mitigate this by developing a bifurcated exhaust exiting just aft of the wing trailing edge. Hawker's design team was able to fair this into the relatively wide fuselage by creating a thick wing centre-

section into which the air intakes were incorporated, which blended into the thin wing. This also had the benefit of reducing interference drag and creating space for the main undercarriage bays. The improved design was known as the P.1040.

As the design developed, the Sea Fury wings were replaced with straight-tapered mainplanes with a thinner (9·5 per cent thickness/chord ratio) "high-speed" aerofoil section, using updated construction techniques, and which were simpler to manufacture. By this time, all resemblance to the Sea Fury had vanished.

Although the RAF showed little interest in the design, the Admiralty was more enthusiastic, and raised Specification N.7/46 for a naval version of the fighter, issued to Hawker in October 1946. The first aircraft, VP401, was a purely aerodynamic prototype with no armament or naval features. It first flew on September 2, 1947. Two more prototypes were ordered to provide a blueprint for the production aircraft, these being VP413 and VP422. The second prototype flew a year and a day after the first, and the third flew just over a year after that. ●

LEFT: The second Hawker N.7/46 prototype, VP413, photographed by Cyril Peckham after its completion. The type marked a radical change of direction for Hawker, but ultimately proved to be an excellent example of ingenious engineering solutions, remaining in service with the Royal Navy for more than 15 years.
Colin Dodds Collection via author

RIGHT: The first image from the Hawker material shows a pressed light-alloy fuselage frame from the area of the wing-root intakes, illustrating the recesses where ducting will guide air to the Rolls-Royce Nene engine. The frame has been photographed upside-down; when installed in the airframe, the flat inside edge should be at the base. Notches in the outer edges of the frame are to accommodate the fuselage's longerons and stringers. *via author*

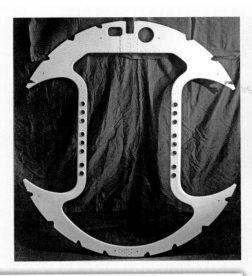

ABOVE: In terms of construction this light-alloy fuselage frame is conventional, although its shape is unusual. The "V" shape in the lower part of the frame was adopted to create space within the fuselage for the main undercarriage bay. The N.7/46's thin wing left less space for the undercarriage than in previous piston-engined designs, while the large-diameter engine and the thicker wing roots required for the intakes left space free just aft of the engine, which Hawker used to house the mainwheels when retracted. The space in the upper half was for a saddle-type fuel tank sitting over the aft end of the engine. The wings were too thin to incorporate fuel tanks. *via author*

ABOVE: With the engine in the centre of the fuselage, the mainspar could not pass directly through, so a ring-frame had "outriggers" attached, taking the loads from the outer wing spars, in this case the rear spar that carried the flaps and ailerons. The central pillar bisecting the ring-frame passed between the two branches of the bifurcated jetpipe that Hawker and Rolls-Royce developed for the N.7/46. The diagonal flanges on the ring-frame indicate the inner surface of the undercarriage bay, of which this frame formed the aft face. The frame seen (from the rear) in this photograph has been placed in the main fuselage construction jig. The fuselage was constructed in three main sections — the central part, as seen here, the nose section and the rear fuselage and tail section. *via author*

ABOVE: The central fuselage further along in its construction in the jig, looking forward. More frames have been added, forming the backbone of the aircraft. This section would eventually contain the engine and its associated intake trunking, the frames with their recesses for which, as in the first photograph, may be seen at the forward end of the assembly. This sub-assembly would also contain the engine exhaust system, the main undercarriage bays and form the wing/fuselage connection. It demonstrated the biggest difference from piston-engine practice in this transitional jet design. *via author*

ABOVE: The forward fuselage section from a port three-quarter view, with the majority of the frames now in place. Armament was included on the second and third N.7/46 prototypes; VP413 was the first to be equipped with the planned four 20mm Hispano cannon in the underside of the nose, two of which may be seen midway along the section. Note the hollow in the frames adjacent to the gun bay to allow clearance for the cannon's blast tubes. The upper half of the sub-assembly is open, as this is where the cockpit will ultimately be sited. *via author*

ABOVE: The same assembly seen from the forward end, now with the skin attached, and the wing root added. This image shows how the intake air was guided from the wing-root intake, the shape indicated by the bracing rods between the fuselage and the large inner wing rib, into the central fuselage to feed the Nene engine's prodigious (for the time) mass-flow requirements. *via author*

ABOVE: The rear fuselage was relatively simple compared with the central and nose sections, both of which had to incorporate a great deal of equipment and house major items such as the engine and cockpit. Here the light ring-frames have been positioned in the jig, running aftwards from left to right. Note the transition from those furthest forward, which are of a broadly circular cross-section, to much thinner oval-section frames at the aft end. The semi-monocoque rear fuselage structure consisted of a total of 15 of these light frames and 16 stringers supporting the skin. *via author*

ABOVE: Rather than the longerons and stringers for the rear fuselage being connected directly to the frames before skinning, a number of pre-formed sections of outer skin with stiffening already attached were built up and fitted to the frames after their assembly. This is the lower fuselage section; but all the skin panels were of similar form, with hatch openings pre-cut, as seen here. *via author*

RIGHT: The forward fuselage has now been joined to the nose section, and skinning has begun. Note the oval-shaped recess behind the trailing edge of the wing root, through which the starboard section of the bifurcated jetpipe exited. The main undercarriage bay is visible beneath the aft part of the wing-root. The sloping bulkhead towards the nose, with the protruding half-circle at the top, would have the pilot's ejection-seat rail attached to it. The half-hoop at the forward end is the aft frame for the windscreen, which was integral to the nose section. The open rectangular panel beneath it incorporated access to the guns' blast tubes. *via author*

ABOVE: The pre-skinned rear fuselage section has now been mated to the central fuselage, and the main structure is complete. The base of the fin was integral with the fuselage, as the tail was of cruciform design with the tailplane mid-mounted on the fin — a compromise between raising it clear of the jetwash and avoiding the higher weight associated with a T-tail. Note the frames of another N.7/46 in their jigs in the background — possibly the third prototype, VP422. *via author*

ABOVE: The finished article — a fine Cyril Peckham study of WF144, the second production example of the Sea Hawk F Mk 1. Only 35 Sea Hawks were produced by Hawker (apart from the prototypes) before production moved to Armstrong-Whitworth at Baginton. This aircraft differed from the prototypes by having square-ended elevators, a redesigned cockpit canopy and a longer arrester hook; otherwise it was very similar, lacking features of later production aircraft such as the "acorn" fairing at the intersection of the fin and tailplane and underwing weapon hardpoints. *via author*

ABOVE: Parts of the characteristic twin jetpipes, central to the N.7/46's design, developed by Rolls-Royce and Hawker specifically for the type. Note how they curve, initially splaying outwards before bending inward to direct the jetflow more in line with the aircraft's axis. The rear of the jetpipe is closest to the camera on the left-hand item (marked "STBD", i.e. starboard) and furthest from the camera on the right-hand jetpipe. *via author*

BELOW: The mainplane structure of the N.7/46, which was a notable advance on the preceding Sea Fury in several respects. The almost total lack of stringers is evident here, with stiffness imparted instead through a thicker-gauge skin, a practice learned from American manufacturers during British engine genius Roy Fedden's mission to the USA during the Second World War. The straight leading and trailing edges simplified manufacturing, while the "high-speed" aerofoil — with maximum thickness at around 40 per cent chord (note how far aft the main spar is) and a 9.5 per cent thickness to chord ratio (compared with 14 per cent for the Sea Fury) — significantly improved performance. *via author*

RIGHT: The Rolls-Royce B.41 engine, known in production as the Nene, was essentially a version of the same company's Welland, scaled-up and improved via lessons learned from the USA's General Electric/Allison J33. The Hawker P.1035/P.1040 was designed around the engine, which became the most powerful jet in production for a spell in the late 1940s. The engine is seen here from the port rear side. A manifold would be attached to the aft end of the engine, to which each jetpipe would be fitted. The jointed tubes at the top of the engine were part of the N.7/46 installation; the sockets at the rear attached to fittings on a ring frame inside which the engine sat. *via author*

BELOW: The fin, with its starboard face skinned, showing its longitudinal and vertical ribs. The slot in the trailing edge housed the rudder's balance tab. This is only the upper part of the fin; as described on the previous page, the lower part was integral with the fuselage and the curvature of the lower edge corresponds to the upper surface of the tailplane. *via author*

ABOVE: An N.7/46 elevator in its construction jig, showing generally similar construction to the mainplanes. Note the elevator's curved outboard end; this feature was only included on the prototypes, and production elevators were square-ended. The forward edge shows the balance and flange for the aerodynamic "seal strip", which prevented air leaking between the upper and lower surfaces of the tailplane. *via author*

BELOW: Although it is not specified in the material, it is likely that the aircraft seen being constructed in the preceding photographs was the second N.7/46 prototype, VP413 — which, unlike the first, included folding wings, catapult spools and full gun armament. The aircraft made its maiden flight on September 3, 1948, after which it went to Boscombe Down for dummy deck assessment trials. It was then flown on to HMS Illustrious, aboard which it is seen here, for take-off, landing and general handling trials. *via author*

Acknowledgements
The author would like to thank Colin Dodds for his help with the preparation of this article.

The **Sea Hawk** remained in front-line service into the **1960s** in the Fleet Air Arm, and the **1980s** in the Indian Navy, partly thanks to **Hawker's careful design.**

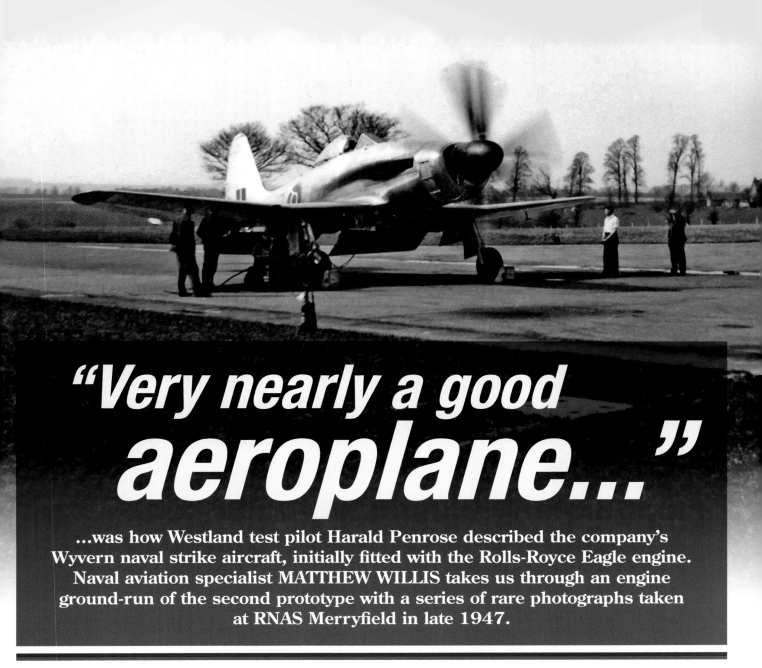

"Very nearly a good aeroplane..."

...was how Westland test pilot Harald Penrose described the company's Wyvern naval strike aircraft, initially fitted with the Rolls-Royce Eagle engine. Naval aviation specialist MATTHEW WILLIS takes us through an engine ground-run of the second prototype with a series of rare photographs taken at RNAS Merryfield in late 1947.

The series of photographs presented here, taken by an unknown photographer and from the collection of the late John Havers, shows part of the early testing programme for the Westland Wyvern naval strike fighter. The Wyvern suffered a particularly protracted development, owing to the complexity of the aircraft and the number of new elements combined into one package, not to mention changes of powerplant. As such, it is a

particularly fascinating glimpse into the first months of a programme that would last more than six years before the aircraft was finally cleared for service use in April 1954.

THE EAGLE AND THE PYTHON

The Wyvern was a large propeller-driven strike aircraft conceived towards the end of the Second World War. Specification N.11/44

was issued on January 1, 1945, solely to Westland, which had been working on various configurations of heavy naval fighter to take advantage of new and more powerful engines then under development.

Westland had developed its initial designs with the large Rolls-Royce Eagle 24-cylinder sleeve-valve engine in mind (including some configurations with a mid-set engine and ▶

TOP: The second Westland Wyvern prototype, TS375, has its Rolls-Royce Eagle sleeve-valve engine run up at RNAS Merryfield, a satellite of RNAS Yeovilton, around the time of its first flight in September 1947. The noise from the massive powerplant and its eight-bladed contra-rotating propeller must have been deafening, and at least two of the bystanders are, quite sensibly, covering their ears!
TAH Archive

RIGHT: As Westland's factory at Yeovil was not suitable for the Wyvern's early test flights, much of its development flying was undertaken from Merryfield. Here we see TS375 in front of a T2 hangar, with engineers working on the complex Rotol propeller. Only the rear blades are yet in place; the apparatus to lift the front blade unit into place may be seen to the left. *TAH Archive*

long shaft-mounted propeller). However, the possibilities offered by the embryonic "propeller turbine" – or turboprop – were becoming apparent, and N.11/44 specified the option of a turboprop instead of the Eagle. The Wyvern would eventually be powered by one of these, namely the Armstrong Siddeley Python (then under development as the ASP), but the first prototypes were powered by the Eagle, almost as experimental as the turboprops, and which incorporated numerous new design features for the company.

The first N.11/44 (it was not formally known as the Wyvern until early 1947), serial TS371, first flew in December 1946. The flight took place at Boscombe Down rather than Westland's own test airfield at Yeovil, probably because Boscombe Down's considerably greater space and long concrete runway offered greater safety and practicality than the small grass runway at Yeovil for such a large, powerful and complex aircraft. After a tethered engine run on December 16 that year, Westland's chief test pilot Harald Penrose took TS371 into the air. It was not until September 10, 1947, however, that the next prototype, TS375, made its maiden flight.

These photographs show a tethered engine run by TS375, around the time of its first flight. These procedures were not always straightforward with the Wyvern. During a later tethered run with the engine eventually chosen for service use, the Python, the aircraft slipped its bonds and jumped forward, whereupon the propeller completely destroyed the engine manufacturer representative's 1929 Armstrong Siddeley saloon. Fortunately, nothing so dramatic appears to have taken place on this occasion!

BEST OF THE BREED?

Wyvern TS375 was central to Westland's development of the aircraft, especially after the loss of TS371 in late 1947. It was retained by Westland until March 1949 when it went to the Aeroplane & Armament Experimental Establishment (A&AEE) at Boscombe Down for handling trials, being fitted with an ejection seat in June 1950. It was also fitted with features under development for service aircraft, such as a dihedral tailplane and outer-wing airbrakes.

By the late 1940s Rolls-Royce wished to concentrate on jet engines, and the Eagle never really underwent anything more than preliminary development before it was axed.

Most of the engines built were installed in the six prototype and seven "production" Wyvern TF.1s. The turboprop alternatives were the Rolls-Royce Clyde and as already mentioned, the Python, and trial aircraft fitted with these engines were initially designated TF.2 regardless of engine. (Some sources refer to the Clyde-engined examples as TF.2As, but this appears to have been unofficial.)

The Eagle-engined Wyverns, designated TF.1 (for Torpedo Fighter, a classification later changed to S for Strike) were in many ways the most impressive of the entire breed, outperforming the later Python-engined variants in top speed – 456 m.p.h. (734km/h) as against 383 m.p.h. (616km/h); rate of climb – 2,900ft (883m)/min versus 2,350ft (716m)/min; range – 1,180 miles (1,900km) versus 910 miles (1,465km) and ceiling – 32,000ft (9,800m) as against 28,000ft (8,500m). However, the Python-engined S.4 did have the edge in cruising speed – 348 m.p.h. (560km/h) versus 295 m.p.h. (475km/h) and speed at sea level – 383 m.p.h. (616km/h) as against 365 m.p.h. (587km/h), the TF.1 offering its best speed at 23,000ft (7,000m).

The Python, a very bulky engine originally developed for large bombers, required significant alteration of the Westland fighter's airframe, including a longer, deeper nose to accommodate the engine, a taller mid-fuselage to raise the cockpit and improve the pilot's view, and a much larger fin and rudder to retain directional stability.

Possibly the most promising Wyvern, however, was the sole example powered by a Rolls-Royce Clyde two-spool turboprop. The Clyde was smaller, lighter and easier to install in the Wyvern Mk 1 airframe than the Python, and more powerful, but, despite its considerable promise, Rolls-Royce again decided to curtail work to concentrate on pure jet engines. This would prove to be premature and Rolls-Royce would soon re-enter the turboprop market. The single Clyde Wyvern, VP120, accrued a mere 50hr of flying time and ended its life as a crash-barrier test airframe. In the meantime, the loss of the Clyde and the Eagle left the Wyvern with the least suitable engine, which took considerable work to render fit for purpose.

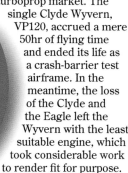

*Wyvern TS375 was central to Westland's **development** of the aircraft, especially after the loss of **TS371** in late 1947.*

ABOVE: This photo of TS375 from the rear highlights the Youngman flaps, seen extended in the "cruise" setting. This type of flap had proved itself on the wartime Fairey Barracuda and Firefly, acting as a slotted flap for take-off and landing or as an auxiliary aerofoil to increase wing area and efficiency to extend endurance in cruising flight. *TAH Archive*

ABOVE: Seen here from the front in "clean" configuration, with flaps retracted, TS375 did not have folding wings or any armament fitted; the first two prototypes were purely aerodynamic and systems test vehicles. The first prototype, TS371, was lost in a fatal crash little more than a month after TS375 first flew. *TAH Archive*

OUT OF TIME

Interest in the Eagle-engined aircraft dwindled quickly. An initial order for 20 production-standard Mk 1s was cut to ten and then cancelled after seven had been built. After their trials careers they faded from view and were disposed of sooner or later. One is believed to have been buried at RNAS Sultan, Gosport. Some of the "production" Mk 1s never even flew, including VR137, which went to Cranfield as an instructional airframe. By 1966 it was the only complete Wyvern in existence, all production aircraft having been scrapped or lost in accidents. This aircraft,

now on display at the Fleet Air Arm Museum at Yeovilton, is similar in most respects to TS378 or TS380 (as seen ABOVE), as a fully navalised machine representative of a service aircraft had the Eagle-powered version progressed. It has also been restored to its original bare-metal finish, although such was the lack of interest in it when it was completed that it never even received any markings. ●

Acknowledgments
The author would like to thank Robin Carter of the Wyvern Project, and TAH thanks the late John Havers and Richard and Bettina Havers, for their help with the preparation of this article.

The Wyvern project is an active tribute to all those who helped to develop, fly and maintain the Westland Wyvern, and has been collecting Wyvern remains, information and images for 25 years; for more info visit www.facebook.com/Westland.Wyvern.S4/

ABOVE: With a strap placed around its rear fuselage. TS375 is prepared for a tethered engine test run. Only a few early test Eagles had been built before 15 examples of the 3,500 h.p. Eagle 22 were produced by Rolls-Royce, largely for the Wyvern test programme. The prominent gills in the forward part of the cowling are the outlets for hot air passing over the intercoolers, which were arranged in a semi-annular fashion around the reduction gear. *TAH Archive*

ABOVE: A different Wyvern and possibly a different location – the aircraft is probably the third or fourth of the original six prototypes. Of the Eagle-powered machines, only TS378 and TS380 appear to have worn the post-war Admiralty colour scheme of Extra Dark Sea Grey over Sky as seen here in this group shot. The location is hard to establish, although it may be Merryfield or even Rolls-Royce's aerodrome at Hucknall. The gentleman in the white shirt and spectacles is believed to be Dennis Edkins, Wyvern designer Teddy Petter's assistant. *TAH Archive*

BELOW: The test crew assembles for the tethered engine run, and the Wyvern is fuelled from a small Brockhouse-type bowser. The battery trolley has also been plugged in. Note the square carburettor intake under the nose, wedged between the annular intercooler intakes, and the staining along the forward fuselage from the exhaust. *TAH Archive*

The South Bank Show

In July 1952 JOHN STROUD was granted free access to document the BEA Helicopter Experimental Unit's trial flights in and out of a diminutive landing area located among the remains of the previous year's Festival of Britain, on the south bank of the Thames next to Waterloo station.

For two weeks in the summer of 1952 occupants of the numerous offices that fringed the south bank of the River Thames became accustomed to the sight – and not inconsiderable sound – of a pair of helicopters buzzing and whirring their way to a makeshift landing area a few short steps away from bustling Waterloo station. With the remains of the previous year's Festival of Britain still being dismantled – most notably Ralph Tubbs's impressive 365ft-diameter 93ft-tall Dome of Discovery –

British European Airways (BEA) was keen to make use of this prime real-estate a stone's throw from the heart of the capital, virtually in the shadow of the Houses of Parliament just across the river.

London County Council (LCC), which occupied County Hall, immediately adjacent to the Festival site, was less keen, however. It consistently raised objections to the idea of a permanent "rotorstation" on the grounds of noise pollution and safety concerns – both reasonable enough – and also had its own

agenda to establish a home for the National Theatre and an exhibition space, as well as offices, alongside the only permanent survivor of the previous year's celebrations: the Royal Festival Hall.

Since the advent of the practical helicopter in the 1930s, its unique characteristic as a mode of transport – the ability to travel the shortest distance between two points and land without the provision of a long runway – has proven attractive for those interested in providing a form of mass transport capable

OHE JOHN STROUD ARCHIVE
One of Britain's most respected aviation journalists and authors, John Stroud (born April 3, 1919) joined Imperial Airways aged 14. Six years later he became a freelance aviation writer and in 1963 was appointed General Editor of the definitive Putnam series of aeronautical books. Also a talented photographer, John continued to contribute articles to the British aviation press until his death in March 2007. In 2014 a substantial part of John's archive, including numerous rolls of previously unseen 35mm film, was acquired by A Flying History Ltd and forms the basis of this regular *TAH* series.

of inserting passengers directly into the urban fabric.

With this in mind BEA quickly seized the opportunity afforded by the availability of a vacant suitable landing ground in the centre of the city to request permission to conduct helicopter trials in and out of the South Bank site. With permission granted, one of the BEA Helicopter Experimental Unit's four-seat single-engined Sikorsky S-51s, G-AJOV, made a trial flight along the Thames on Monday March 17, 1952, from London Airport (Heathrow), tracing a route over Hounslow Heath, Richmond Park, Barnes Common, Hurlingham and Battersea Park. From there it continued downstream at low altitude past Blackfriars Bridge to Tower Bridge before returning the way it had come.

With the approaches satisfactorily tested and surveyed for potential obstructions, and noise tests completed on the ground, further permission was obtained to begin landing trials on the former Festival site.

On Monday July 28, 1952, the head of the BEA Helicopter Experimental Unit (HEU), Wg Cdr R.A.C. "Reggie" Brie, took off from Gatwick in S-51 G-AJOR, and, after passing over Barnes Common and Hurlingham, followed the Thames to alight at the South Bank site on the first day of two weeks of helicopter trials in and out of the city centre. On hand for at least some of the trials was freelance aviation reporter and photographer John Stroud; he was asked to investigate by weekly aviation magazine *Flight*, the

Stamford Street offices of which were a 10min walk away.

Two days later another flight into the South Bank site was made, this time using one of the Bristol Type 171 Mk 3 prototypes, G-ALSR, which the HEU had leased from the manufacturer for evaluation the previous year. It was planned that both machines would be used to make flights in and out of the site and over the Houses of Parliament at a height of 500ft in order to assess noise levels in the chambers of both Houses. Noise measurements would also be made in the offices of County Hall.

TO THE LORDS BY WHIRLYBIRD

On the following Thursday, July 31, history was made with the arrival of the first peer to fly to a House of Lords debate by helicopter. With perhaps more than one eye on publicity, BEA's chairman, Lord Douglas of Kirtleside (aka Marshal of the Royal Air Force William Sholto Douglas), flew in from Northolt in G-ALSR to attend a debate across the river. According to His Lordship, he had allowed himself 2min to walk from his office at Northolt, west of London, to the helicopter, in which pilot Capt J.A. "Jock" Cameron was waiting; another 10min from take-off to touchdown at the South Bank site;

2min for rotor rundown and a final 2min to Westminster by car – a total of 16min. He did, however, find another 15min to extol the virtues of the downtown city heliport to the band of journalists that had been posted to cover his arrival. "I think we shall have really big helicopters coming into London in five to ten years", he predicted. Accom-panying Douglas were BEA's deputy chairman, Sir John Keeling, and the director of the airline's helicopter development unit, Dr G. Hislop.

The future of the South Bank site as a rotorstation appeared promising, although when asked in the House of Commons in early July 1952 about whether a final decision on the matter had been made, Reginald Maudling, junior minister for the Ministry of Aviation, replied that "it would be misleading the public if the impression were given that the regular operation of helicopters to a point in the Metropolitan area is likely to be possible in the very near future".

In its August 1, 1952, editorial, *Flight* continued to express its support for the concept of city-centre heliports, but voiced concern that "it does not require flights in and out of the South Bank site to prove that experienced pilots can land a helicopter there, nor need they be made to discover that at the moment it is a rather bad site from the pilot's point of view. ▶

> BEA Helicopter Experimental Unit's four-seat single-engined **Sikorsky S-51s, G-AJOV,** made a trial flight along the Thames on **Monday March 17, 1952**

ABOVE: Two days later Bristol Type 171 Mk 3 G-ALSR was flown in. *John Stroud/A Flying History Ltd*

LEFT: On July 28, 1952, John Stroud was on hand at the former Festival of Britain site on the south bank of the Thames to capture Wg Cdr Reggie Brie landing BEA S-51 G-AJOR in the first of a series of trials. *John Stroud/A Flying History Ltd*

To put a single-engined helicopter down in a confined space surrounded by buildings and obstructions must always entail some risk, not so much to life and limb, but to the aircraft itself". It continued: "As to whether the position of the site near Waterloo Station is convenient for passengers, there is again little to learn from making flights in and out".

The editorial did, however, express satisfaction that the "pilots are quite glad to have a go" and that, although the trials may only yield information of limited value, it did represent "activity, practice and another step in the education of the public in preparation for helicopter services, which it is hoped are not now many years distant". The trials continued, with John Stroud being allowed free access to capture the regular comings and goings at the South Bank site. The testing was completed on August 11, most of the flying having been undertaken by Capts Cameron and J.G. Theilmann, with Wg Cdr Brie supervising.

In October 1952 BEA published its annual report and announced the corporation's plans to acquire new premises in central London to replace its Kensington Air Station, which, according to Lord Douglas, was "bursting at the seams". After protracted negotiations with the LCC, it was decided to develop a corner of the South Bank site as a terminal – and if BEA got its way, a possible focal point for its prospective network of inter-city helicopter services. The LCC, however, made it very clear that any further trials or experimental services

It was decided to develop a corner of the South Bank site as a terminal – and if BEA got its way, a possible focal point for its prospective network of inter-city helicopter services.

ABOVE: Sikorsky-built S-51 G-AJOR, named Sir Owen in BEA service, was one of four operated by the airline in the early days of its helicopter fleet, and was powered by a single vertically-mounted 450 h.p. Pratt & Whitney R-985 Wasp Junior B4 radial piston engine. This example served with BEA until it was sold to Autair Helicopters in July 1953. *John Stroud/A Flying History Ltd*

BELOW: Up, up and away — Brie lifts G-AJOR over the river towards the imposing sight of Whitehall Court on the northern bank of the Thames. *John Stroud/A Flying History Ltd*

ABOVE: With the remains of the futuristic Dome of Discovery in the background, Reggie Brie brings G-AJOR into the South Bank site. Brie had long been an advocate of the helicopter for city-centre operations, and had suggested floating landing platforms in the Thames as far back as the late 1930s. *John Stroud/A Flying History Ltd*

RIGHT: Following his initial flights in and out of the South Bank site, Brie (holding hat) left the flying to Capts "Jock" Cameron (left) and J.G. Theilmann (flying the S-51). *John Stroud/A Flying History Ltd*

would be subject to further negotiation. A seven-year lease was granted and the plans for the new complex, to be known as Waterloo Air Terminal, were approved.

THE SOUND AND THE FURY

With construction of the new terminal under way, the results of the test flights of the previous summer were carefully scrutinised. At the request of a London newspaper, scientific-instrument manufacturer Dawe Instruments Ltd of Ealing was engaged to take objective sound readings of the noise level of a BEA S-51 landing at the South Bank site in March 1953. Calibrated in decibels (dB), Dawe's instrumentation was used to take readings both inside County Hall and in the streets of the local environs. Four take-offs by the S-51 were made, with the readings in

a first-floor office of County Hall reaching a maximum of 79dB during take-off, dropping to 56dB as the chopper passed overhead, before settling at the usual level of around 42dB. Dawe put this in perspective by revealing that its own offices on the first floor of a Piccadilly office building were recorded at 82dB the same afternoon with no helicopter activity, just the usual boom of traffic.

Despite these tests suggesting that noise would not present a major obstacle to the establishment of helicopter services to and from the new terminal, which was officially opened on May 19, 1953, the LCC nevertheless continued to be resistant to the idea. It stated in the autumn of 1953 that plans were afoot to build a new collection of buildings for the arts and at least one high-rise office block, intended to be the international headquarters of the Shell Petroleum Company. Interestingly, the LCC encouraged investigating the use of the roof of Waterloo train station as a potential heliport site; essentially, "get it off our front lawn and into the remit of the Railway Executive". Plans for an enormous flat roof to be put on the station were put forward, but the idea was never adopted.

By the end of 1953 the notion of a Heathrow—South Bank helicopter shuttle service was very much back on the agenda, with a route along the river being stipulated, along with float-equipped helicopters in case of ditching. By the summer of 1954 plans for such a service were gathering

pace, *Flight* reporting in its June 25 issue that "the relaxation of flight restrictions for helicopters flying over London, the immediate use of the South Bank site for landings and take-offs and plans for a scheduled BEA service to London Airport next year were all part of the encouraging news which came to the notice of Londoners a week ago". The report went on to state that BEA had been authorised to buy two new Westland-Sikorsky WS-55s, which, once they had obtained their Certificates of Airworthiness, would be introduced on the service on an experimental basis. The previous week a WS-55 operated by Westland in Royal Navy colours had paid a visit to the site in a proof-of-concept trial, and the following month Belgian national airline Sabena made a demonstration flight from Brussels city centre to the South Bank in 2hr 48min with an S-55, beating BEA's Elizabethan service between Brussels and the Waterloo Air Terminal by 40min.

In May 1955 trials using BEA's WS-55 G-ANUK, looking somewhat ungainly with floats and a Vokes silencer, were performed

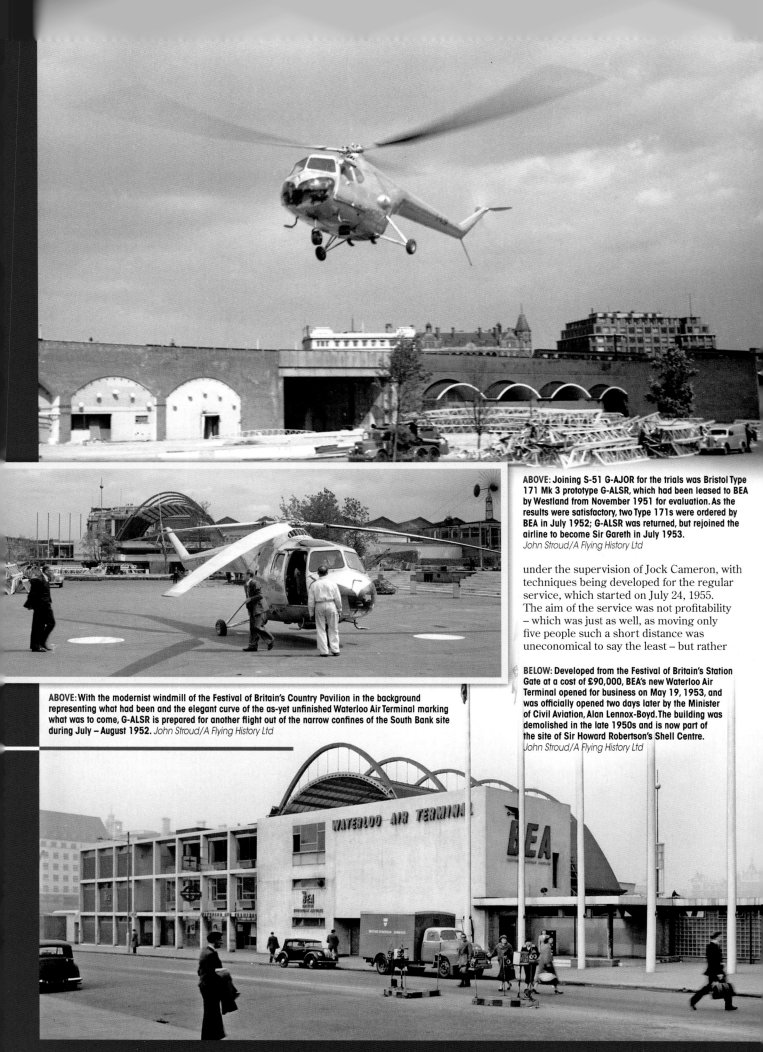

ABOVE: Joining S-51 G-AJOR for the trials was Bristol Type 171 Mk 3 prototype G-ALSR, which had been leased to BEA by Westland from November 1951 for evaluation. As the results were satisfactory, two Type 171s were ordered by BEA in July 1952; G-ALSR was returned, but rejoined the airline to become Sir Gareth in July 1953.
John Stroud/A Flying History Ltd

under the supervision of Jock Cameron, with techniques being developed for the regular service, which started on July 24, 1955. The aim of the service was not profitability – which was just as well, as moving only five people such a short distance was uneconomical to say the least – but rather

ABOVE: With the modernist windmill of the Festival of Britain's Country Pavilion in the background representing what had been and the elegant curve of the as-yet unfinished Waterloo Air Terminal marking what was to come, G-ALSR is prepared for another flight out of the narrow confines of the South Bank site during July – August 1952. *John Stroud/A Flying History Ltd*

BELOW: Developed from the Festival of Britain's Station Gate at a cost of £90,000, BEA's new Waterloo Air Terminal opened for business on May 19, 1953, and was officially opened two days later by the Minister of Civil Aviation, Alan Lennox-Boyd. The building was demolished in the late 1950s and is now part of the site of Sir Howard Robertson's Shell Centre.
John Stroud/A Flying History Ltd

ABOVE: An aerial view of Waterloo Air Terminal (note the BEA coaches in the parking area) and the landing area in 1955, when the airline began regular scheduled helicopter services to and from Heathrow. County Hall is at bottom right, and Stamford Street, home to Flight's offices, runs towards the top of the picture from the railway bridge.
John Stroud/A Flying History Ltd

to gain experience of helicopter operations into city-centre sites, with a view to expanding BEA's inter-city network. Indeed, the vast majority of the new service's passengers used it as an extended sightseeing opportunity rather than as a true shuttle service from Heathrow to the centre of town and vice versa.

By May 1956 the experiment had run its course and after the carriage of 3,833 passengers the service was closed, the last flight taking place on May 31. The 351ft (107m)-high Shell headquarters proposed for the site by the LCC was duly built in 1961, with the construction of the famously brutalist collection of arts buildings on the South Bank site beginning a few years later.

The moment for the helicopter to become as much a part of the London landscape as

the red double-decker bus had passed; and, although privately-owned helicopters are still very much a regular sight over the Thames, thanks to the heliport opened at Battersea in the mid-1970s, mass helicopter use failed to materialise and revolutionise urban travel. For those 1950s BEA executives who dreamed of ever-larger helicopters delivering ever-higher numbers of passengers into the heart of the city centre, the future proved to be a letdown. ●

Nick Stroud

Acknowledgments
The Editor would like to thank Colin Higgs and Jo Ware at A Flying History Ltd (www.aflyinghistory.com) for their help with this regular series.

BEA'S SOUTH BANK HELICOPTER SERVICE, JULY 1955–MAY 1956

British European Airways' experimental scheduled helicopter service between Waterloo Air Terminal and London (Heathrow) Airport began on July 24, 1955 and operated until May 31, 1956. The fares charged were £1 15s 0d per person single and £3 10s 0d per person return. Four round trips per day were operated as below:

Heathrow	Depart	1000hr	1200hr
Waterloo	Arrive	1013hr	1213hr
Waterloo	Depart	1015hr	1215hr
Heathrow	Arrive	1028hr	1228hr
Flight No	**BEH53/52**	**BEH57/56**	
Heathrow	Depart	1300hr	1500hr
Waterloo	Arrive	1313hr	1513hr
Waterloo	Depart	1315hr	1515hr
Heathrow	Arrive	1328hr	1528hr
Flight No	**BEH59/58**	**BEH63/62**	

RIGHT: Westland-Sikorsky WS-55 G-ANUK alights in front of County Hall in 1955. Even if all eight trips a day were full, BEA would still make a loss of £322.
John Stroud/A Flying History Ltd

ABOVE: The Supermarine Type 535 research aircraft, serialled VV119, was essentially the prototype of what would develop into the Swift, and was used memorably in the filming of David Lean's The Sound Barrier. *TAH Archive*

High anxiety:
the Supermarine Swift & Britain's first post-war procurement crisis

Digging deep into the archives, PROFESSOR KEITH HAYWARD FRAeS uses official papers and contemporary documents to examine the 1955 White Paper on the supply of military aircraft, issued at a time when it was becoming increasingly clear that the nation's much-vaunted new high-altitude interceptor was falling far short of expectations.

BELOW: A characteristically superb portrait of the first pre-production Swift, WJ960, by the doyen of aviation photographers, Charles E. Brown. This production prototype was essentially similar to VV119 but with longer-span ailerons. Built at Hursley Park, the aircraft made its maiden flight on August 1, 1951, from Boscombe Down.
TAH Archive

"A grave position has arisen affecting the Swift single-seat fighter under construction by Vickers Supermarine".[1] So began a secret memorandum to the Churchill Cabinet in February 1955. There had been growing internal concern about the progress of the Swift, acquired to defend UK airspace against high-level bombing attack.[2] But this stark statement gave notice of what was arguably the first major post-war crisis in UK aircraft procurement.

Although the sorry tale of the Swift would dominate official concerns during the early to mid-1950s, it should be better viewed as symbolising a wider set of issues and problems affecting UK Cold War military aircraft projects. There were also some unequivocal technical and operational successes – the English Electric Canberra and the "V-bombers", for example – but in general, the military procurement crisis of 1955 was symptomatic of a more fundamental struggle to come to terms with developing and procuring the more complex aircraft of the jet age.

SWIFT – FOCUS OF A CRISIS

The first production Swift F.1, WK194, made its maiden flight on August 25, 1952. It was also the last British production aircraft to hold a world air speed record, which Supermarine test pilot Mike Lithgow achieved

ABOVE: Supermarine test pilot Lt-Cdr Mike Lithgow in Swift F.4 WK198 on his arrival at RAF Idris in Libya in September 1953, where he set a new world air speed record. No doubt Supermarine's management was delighted to have broken the previous record set by Hawker Hunter WB188 only three weeks previously.
Philip Jarrett Collection

on September 26, 1953, when he set a new record of 735.7 m.p.h. (1,185km/h) in WK198 at Castel Benito in Libya. The Swift formally entered RAF service with No 56 Sqn in February 1954. The type was found to be uncontrollable at high speeds and, if anything, the modified F.2 was even worse than the F.1.[3]

The Swift was ordered in seven variants; the F.1, F.2., F.3 and F.4 interceptors, the FR.5 and FR.6 photo-reconnaissance versions and the F.7, which was to be equipped with radar-beam-riding *Blue Sky* air-to-air missiles.[4] The type garnered little praise from the RAF, but as all 25 of the F.3s had been built, the Service had no alternative but to accept them (all became instructional airframes only), as well as the 40 F.4s originally ordered (although only eight were built as such).

By the time the Swift's shortcomings had be-come clear, its immediate cancellation would have cost some £21 million; completing the production order would cost £24.5 million (equivalent to some £425 million today).[5] Procurement of the FR.5 and (ultimately unbuilt) FR.6 variants would incur additional costs. Further costs would be incurred by procuring aircraft to replace the troubled fighter. In total, the Swift programme was to have cost £45 million (£851 million).[6] The idea of – at best – writing off more than three-quarters of a billion pounds in today's money was a daunting prospect, and attention turned to how best to announce this and explain the failure.[7] There were also strategic industrial reasons to protect the Supermarine design team.[8]

While the Swift was perhaps the worst example of cost overrun and poor performance, there were other programmes worrying the government; developments of the Gloster Javelin, for example, regarded as "our most important aircraft after the V-bombers". Designed to intercept Russian nuclear-armed bombers, the Javelin was fundamental to the strategic defence of the UK. Since it was an Allied asset, procurement was partly financed by the USA. But as the Minister of Supply noted, the so-called "Thin-Wing Javelin" (TWJ) project might "never become a satisfactory fighting machine" unless more money was spent on development and at the cost of a "serious delay".[9]

By 1956 the TWJ's development problems were easing, but its in-service date had slipped to 1961, two years later than planned. The Minister of Supply was far from complimentary. "I have little confidence in the Gloster Company, which is one of the weakest in the industry" – a view which would anticipate a later, more fundamental, review of the UK aerospace industry.[10]

In public, throughout 1954, news of UK military aviation progress was upbeat. The SBAC airshow at Farnborough in September was its usual parade of British aircraft; the Swift generated sonic booms to widespread satisfaction. However, in line with usual British practice, actual performance and other data was closely guarded.[11] Earlier that year, the Minister of Supply, Duncan Sandys, announced satisfactory progress on the Swift and that its introduction, "with its superb flying performance and terrific firepower, is a milestone in the progress of Britain's air defence" and was "greatly impressed" generally with the state of the military programme.[12]

Out of the public eye, however, officials were less sanguine; the UK was falling behind the Americans and the Russians, and without a massive increase in resources and some radical changes to the shape of

the domestic aircraft industry, the gap would widen still further. As a comparative review put it only a year or so later, "It is unlikely that we [will] close, or even hold steady, the performance gap between British and American aircraft in the foreseeable future".[13] In short, towards the end of 1954, there was a growing official consensus that something had to be done to improve the way in which the UK ordered and developed its military aircraft. This embraced ministry organisation and procedures and, increasingly, the structure and efficiency of the domestic industry.

THE 1955 WHITE PAPER
Any hopes that the problems affecting the supply of military aircraft could be kept secret were rapidly fading as the problems with a number of projects began to leak. Questions in the House of Commons about the rate of progress in supplying military aircraft were growing in frequency, as were "unofficial reports" about the limitations of the Swift's high-altitude performance.[14] There were also a number of uncomfortable ▶

BELOW: Swift F.1 WK198 was modified to become the prototype Mk 4 (given the company designation Type 546), and is seen here on a test flight before Mike Lithgow's assault on the world air speed record. The Mk 4 introduced a variable-incidence tailplane, which, it was hoped, would alleviate the type's notable pitch-up characteristics. *TAH Archive*

The **Swift** was ordered in seven variants; the **F.1**, **F.2.**, **F.3** and **F.4** interceptors, the **FR.5** and **FR.6** photo-reconnaissance versions and the **F.7**.

ABOVE: The Gloster Javelin FAW.1 all-weather interceptor entered RAF service in February 1956, having suffered from its own considerable development problems. A "thin-wing" development of the type was planned, for which components and sub-assemblies were completed, but the project was ultimately cancelled in the summer of 1956. *TAH Archive*

headlines in national newspapers, as in September 1954 when the *News Chronicle* asked *"Where are the Planes?"*.

By the new year the Cabinet had decided that the Government had to come clean about the nature and extent of the crisis – as far as it was politically safe so to do. In January 1955 the Cabinet agreed to publish a White Paper, *The Supply of Military Aircraft*.[15] But given

growing press speculation, there was also a question of how to announce its publication and to manage the subsequent Parliamentary debate. As the Chancellor of the Exchequer, R.A. Butler, noted: "Care would be needed in presenting to the public the Government's decisions on future production of the Swift aircraft". On the one hand, it was "important to avoid any impression that the programme

of Swift production had been a total failure". On the other hand, as the future of these aircraft was still far from certain, the Government "would be well advised to say nothing which it might latter have to retract".[16] Some of the blame could be shifted on to the previous administration, which had misjudged the need for a second generation of fighter aircraft, but there were limits to this strategy;

as one Minister would later observe: "The record is not a happy one. The situation which we inherited in 1951 was not good, but we can no longer hide behind the sins of omission of our predecessors. Candour compels me to say that I do not think the record in the last 3½ years has been satisfactory".[17]

In the event, the White Paper was something of a classic piece of Whitehall drafting. At its core was the Swift fiasco, but surrounding it was a much lengthier explanation of post-war aircraft development and the military exigencies that had led to the concurrent development and production of both the Hawker Hunter and Swift and other fighter aircraft, as well as a description of its successes (largely the V-bomber programme and the Canberra). There was also a forward look aimed at modernising the system by which complex military aircraft were to be developed and procured in the future.

The White Paper described the immediate post-war period as being characterised by a combination of strategic uncertainty and economic austerity.[18] Developing a British atomic bomb and the means to deliver it had a clear priority, but spending on conventional weapons would be curtailed both for reasons of economy and to allow time for new technologies, such as the jet engine, to mature. This principle was enshrined in the "Ten-Year Rule", which assumed no major conflict for Britain within the decade and which in 1948 had led to the cancellation of a number of fighter projects that would have superseded the Meteor and Vampire.

Combined with some inherent conservatism on the part of Government scientific advisors, decisions were also taken to proceed cautiously with a number of research projects, which had the dual purpose of keeping design teams in business but deferring procurement. In total, there were 26 active research projects during this period, costing just under half a billion pounds out of a total aircraft spend of £34 billion, which to a Commons Select Committee, did not "seem to be excessive".[19] This had little negative effect on the strategic-bomber programme, as a protracted development of the delivery system would be in step with building the atomic bomb. But the impact on UK fighter aircraft was more serious. First, it delayed development of supersonic concepts; secondly, when the UK was involved in a serious shooting war, its fighter aircraft were inferior to both its allies and its adversaries.

This strategic complacency was shattered first by the Berlin crisis of 1948, and more seriously by the outbreak of the Korean conflict in 1950, which triggered a massive British rearmament programme, forcing the purchase of more already obsolete British jet fighters and Canadair-built F-86 Sabres. More importantly, the emergency led the Ministry of Supply (MoS) to order promising designs "off the drawing board", which entailed a commitment to production in the early stages of development and well before any major technical problems emerged. The Hunter and Swift were assigned this accelerated status.[20] With so many projects rushed into production, however, severe bottlenecks resulted. The adoption of a "Super Priority" scheme proved to be no panacea, as so many projects were awarded this status. While the Hunter experienced a number of serious problems during its expedited development, some of these had been partly resolved by 1953, and the shapely fighter went on to become one of Britain's most successful military aircraft.[21] The Swift did not.

DISAPPOINTMENT AND DISASTER

Having outlined these development issues, the 1955 White Paper then sketched briefly the history of the Swift programme, describing how, despite the development of four variants, the aircraft was still unable to meet its specification, with an overall performance described as "dis-appointing". Other problematic aircraft such as the Javelin were given less attention. In some respects, the Javelin was a more significant programme that began to go wrong during this period.[22] Later, the Ministry would tell a House of Commons Select Committee that it would be "wrong to say that the whole [Swift] aircraft was a disaster", and claimed that the problems were due to the "exceptional nature of the circumstances surrounding the Swift and the decision to develop it so quickly". However, the Commons Select Committee later reported that the Ministry should have cut its losses earlier than it did.[23]

The remainder of the White Paper focused on the future. In the first place, an "adequate programme of research and the necessary capital facilities for such a programme are vital for success". Plans were in train for such a programme with the Ministry and industry collaborating.[24] It noted that many ▶

Adequate programme of ***research*** *and the necessary* ***capital facilities*** *for such a programme are vital for* ***success***.

BELOW: The Swift F.1 served with only one unit, No 56 Sqn, with which it entered service in February 1954 at Waterbeach in Cambridgeshire. Nearest the camera is WK208, lost after it became uncontrollable on May 13, 1954. All Swifts were grounded for two months as a result. *TAH Archive*

ABOVE: The Swift F.3 variant – the first of which, WK247, is seen here – was similar to the F.1 and F.2 but introduced reheat for its Rolls-Royce Avon engine. All 25 F.3s ordered were built, but none entered squadron service. All except WK248, which went to the College of Aeronautics, were instructional airframes by the end of 1956. *TAH Archive*

of the problems had derived from the increasing complexity of modern aircraft.[25] Significantly, past practice of developing aircraft equipment separately from the airframe was no longer valid. Henceforth the approach would be based on an integrated "weapons system" concept. Ideally, "the complete responsibility for co-ordinating the various components of the system should rest with one individual – the designer of the aircraft".[26]

Some of these concepts had in fact begun to percolate around the UK procurement establishment in 1954. Much of the groundwork was performed by an MoS working party dedicated to the theme of speeding up aircraft production. This included extensive consultations with British aircraft manufacturers. A key issue was the bottlenecks caused by building too few prototypes. Ministry thinking turned to ordering aircraft as pre-production "Development Batches", although there were concerns about how exactly this would further the early stages of development and whether it might complicate the transition to production models. The English Electric P.1 (developed into the Lightning) was the first example of a Development Batch contract.[27]

Overall, the sentiment that something more radical had to be tried was strongly evident in these official discussions.

Involving industry earlier in the formulation of operational requirements was another item on the agenda. In the event, the current approach was felt to be satisfactory, as long as the concept of weapons-systems development was driven home. However, more could be done to discuss with industry broad background issues, giving access to appropriate technical and research studies on emerging defence trends that could inform the requirements process.[28]

It was a difficult sell. The MoS was caustic about the Air Staff's informal relations with companies and the way it tended to allow "an arbitrary selection" of firms to discuss future requirements. This had been applied to discussions on a future supersonic fighter. These were "almost entirely related to the aircraft vehicle. Thereby they misled many firms into doing a great deal of work which is now shown to be virtually useless ...any work by the aircraft designer on a knowledge of the performance of the aircraft vehicle alone is largely wasted. We have to educate the Air Staff, the industry and indeed ourselves to think in future in terms of a complete weapons system and no longer of an airframe alone".[29]

Ministry officials also debated whether the weapons-system approach implied the selection, as it did in the USA, of a "prime contractor" responsible for designing and integrating the entire system. This would certainly challenge the established system

of "embodiment loan", whereby equipment was procured and developed separately, with only general characteristics available to the platform design team. While this situation was increasingly untenable, the Ministry was reluctant to accept such a radical change, that a lead contractor should increasingly take responsibility for "co-ordinating" work between airframe and equipment designers.[30]

The White Paper went on to observe that the extended development period needed for a modern aircraft carried with it the threat of obsolescence. This underlined the need for adequate research as well as effective relations between procuring ministries and industry. To speed up the process, the White Paper announced that aircraft would no longer move from proto-type to pre-production variant, but would be procured in Development Batches, as initially proposed by the 1954 MoS working party.[31] It was also considered desirable that design innovation might proceed in "shorter steps". In short, these changes might imply greater initial expenditure but better "economy of the nation's resources and an increase in its preparedness at any point".[32]

The Blackburn NA.39, Gloster's improved Thin-Wing Javelin and further development of the Lightning were initial candidates for this new approach. The need for a more integrated view of development was perhaps best illustrated by the Hunter's engine-surge/gun

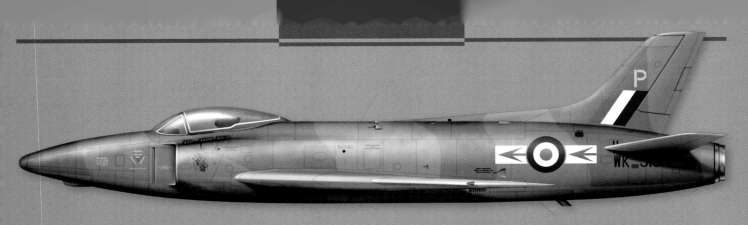

ABOVE: Swift FR.5 WK315 served with No 79 Sqn, which replaced its Meteor FR.9s with the variant in June 1956, operating the Swift in the fighter-reconnaissance role in Germany until the end of December 1960. Artwork by Juanita Franzi / Aero Illustrations.

Juanita Franzi / Aero Illustrations © 2019

problem. As Prime Minister Anthony Eden later put it, the Hunter was "a melancholy story. What will happen to our name and fame when all of this is known, as I fear it must be among our allies? I hope everything is being done to avoid similar troubles being found at a later stage in the development of our next fighters".[33] However, the failure to sort out the exact relationship between companies and procurement ministries would be an important contributory factor in the next serious procurement crisis – the BAC TSR.2.

THE AFTERMATH

The fate of the Swift still had to be decided. Although a small number of aircraft had entered squadron service, the Air Ministry simply refused to accept the first 25 aircraft and demanded that the cost should fall

> The **Swift F.7** would at least have the radar necessary for the **Blue Sky (Fireflash) missile**, part of the original requirement for a high-altitude interceptor.

entirely on the MoS budget, a demand which was stoutly rejected. There was then what to do with 40 Swift F.4s then in production, out of an original order for 263. It was suggested that they could be used as trials aircraft for engine reheat research. The Air Ministry was reluctant to take the Swift FR.6 as a photo-reconnaissance platform and was angling for more Hunters (and was interested in the Folland Gnat). The Swift F.7 would at least have the radar necessary for the *Blue Sky* (Fireflash) missile, part of the original requirement for a high-altitude interceptor.[34] In the event, only 14 F.7s were built and none entered service with the RAF. They were used as trials aircraft for the Fireflash.

From a Treasury perspective, the primary objective was clear: "If the Swift finally disappears from the

fighter programme, the amount of money lost – which will be substantial – shall as far as possible be minimised".[35] Officials were also quick to reinforce the view that while current exigencies implied a continuing spend on military aircraft, "the warning of a financial limitation should be repeated".[36] There were also warning shots over the White Paper's central proposals for the future. Although the Treasury conceded, with some masterly understatement, that reform was perhaps needed – "there are already good grounds for thinking that we have not had value for all the money expended" – an official observed that "there appears a tendency on the part of the Air Ministry and the MoS to regard the Development Batch procedure as the cure-all in the development and speedy production of efficient aircraft". The NA.39 procurement had been allowed to go forward as a Development Batch, but "we have made it clear that we shall wish to deal with each case on its merits". The shorter-steps approach would also be expensive, and as such, a note of caution would be required in respect of the ►

ABOVE: From nearest to furthest from the camera, the first, second and fifth pre-production examples of the Blackburn NA.39, which would evolve into the Buccaneer. Ordering a pre-production batch, rather than the usual single prototypes, meant that there were sufficient trials aircraft to permit a far more efficient test programme. *TAH Archive*

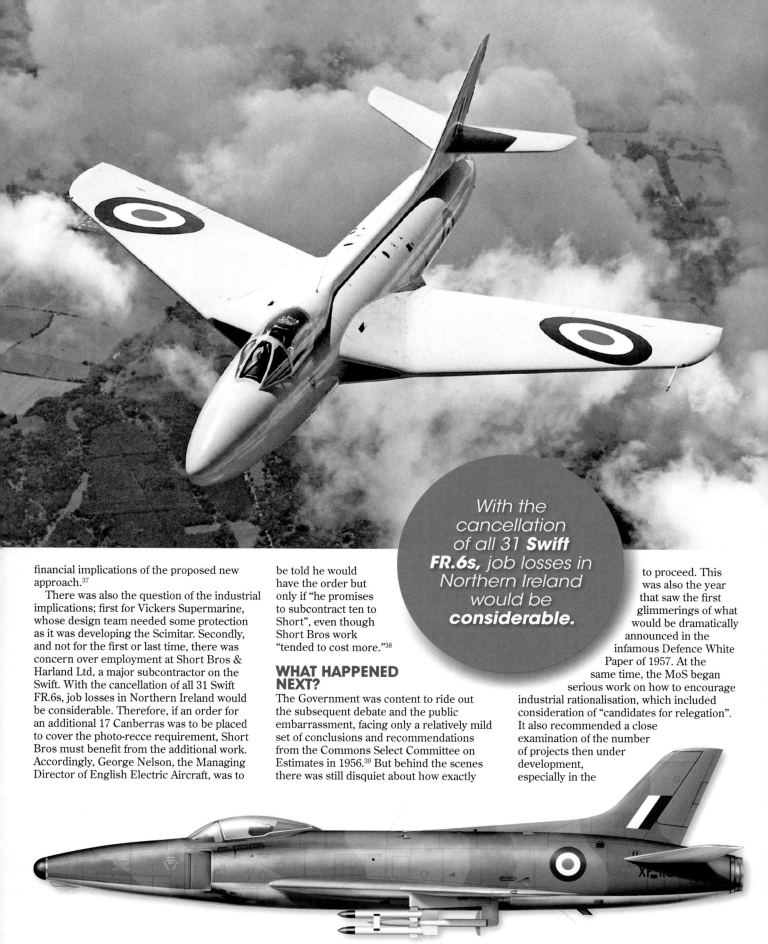

financial implications of the proposed new approach.[37]

There was also the question of the industrial implications; first for Vickers Supermarine, whose design team needed some protection as it was developing the Scimitar. Secondly, and not for the first or last time, there was concern over employment at Short Bros & Harland Ltd, a major subcontractor on the Swift. With the cancellation of all 31 Swift FR.6s, job losses in Northern Ireland would be considerable. Therefore, if an order for an additional 17 Canberras was to be placed to cover the photo-recce requirement, Short Bros must benefit from the additional work. Accordingly, George Nelson, the Managing Director of English Electric Aircraft, was to

be told he would have the order but only if "he promises to subcontract ten to Short", even though Short Bros work "tended to cost more."[38]

WHAT HAPPENED NEXT?

The Government was content to ride out the subsequent debate and the public embarrassment, facing only a relatively mild set of conclusions and recommendations from the Commons Select Committee on Estimates in 1956.[39] But behind the scenes there was still disquiet about how exactly

*With the cancellation of all 31 **Swift FR.6s,** job losses in Northern Ireland would be **considerable.***

to proceed. This was also the year that saw the first glimmerings of what would be dramatically announced in the infamous Defence White Paper of 1957. At the same time, the MoS began serious work on how to encourage industrial rationalisation, which included consideration of "candidates for relegation". It also recommended a close examination of the number of projects then under development, especially in the

ABOVE: Swift F.7 XF118 was one of ten operated by the Guided Weapons Development Squadron at RAF Valley from June 1957 until December 1958, and was used for intensive trials of the Fireflash air-to-air missile, an example of which is seen mounted beneath the wing.
Artwork by Juanita Franzi / Aero Illustrations. *Juanita Franzi / Aero Illustrations © 2019*

LEFT: A magnificent Cyril Peckham study of the prototype Hawker P.1067, WB188, in 1951, the year in which the shapely fighter made its maiden flight. The Hunter, as it became, was the Swift's main rival for the high-altitude interceptor role. It too suffered from development problems, but went on to become a world-class success. *TAH Archive*

ABOVE: The English Electric P.1A prototype, WG760, made its first flight on August 4, 1954, and was the basis for the Lightning, the RAF's first true supersonic fighter, capable of exceeding the speed of sound in level flight. The Lightning would be one of the few survivors of the radical changes in procurement policy during the 1950s. *TAH Archive*

light of the new ballistic and other missiles for both attack and defence.[40]

The immediate post-war security environment generated a whole set of uncertainties, including technological trends affecting military aviation. Equally, with so much priority afforded to the nuclear weapons programme and creating the associated bomber force, it was little wonder that the Labour Government adopted a conservative and financially prudent approach to conventional aircraft development (the cautious approach to manned supersonic flight perhaps being more arguable). The rapid deterioration in the UK's security environment, culminating in the Korean conflict and rapid rearmament, forced a number of procurement expediencies, which in retrospect seem ill-judged and poorly implemented. These emergency measures undoubtedly contributed to the problems in the supply of military aircraft experienced during 1954–56.

The House of Commons Select Committee was prepared to forgive mistakes made under the stress of events, although it was influenced by some carefully disingenuous official evidence. The machinery had revealed some weaknesses, but "it would not be fair to those concerned [to say] that a great deal had not been achieved". The system had produced "some of the finest aircraft in the world" and, on balance, had achieved this with economy. The programme had been over-ambitious, and more scrutiny of projects would be essential in the future. Failure to do so "may well place the whole programme in jeopardy".[41]

What the committee and the MoS could not fully appreciate was that aircraft procurement had already been affected by the pernicious problems of rising "inter-generational" costs and the issues associated with managing increasingly complex combat aircraft. When combined with an ambitious programme sustained by a weak and dispersed industrial base, the structural and organisational weaknesses of the procurement system were all too apparent. The response was a series of reforms that on the one hand reflected some of the new realities of weapons-systems development, as well as triggering a necessary, if belated, rationalisation of the aircraft industry.

The problem of rising project costs and the appropriate way of managing complex defence programmes would not go away, and by the early 1960s the UK government faced a succession of procurement crises, the most problematic being a survivor of the Sandys White Paper, the TSR.2. Looking back on the 1955 White Paper, it is now evident that the UK had embarked on a long and unforgiving road of procurement reform, trying to create a system that would deliver effective weapons on time and close to the original estimated costs – still a work-in-progress. ●

REFERENCES

1. Aircraft Production: the Swift, Memorandum by the Secretary of State for Air and the Ministry of Supply, February 10, 1955; The National Archives (TNA) CAB/129/73
2. A Report by the Committee on Defence Policy, submitted to the Cabinet, July 24, 1954; TNA CAB/129/69
3. See www.airvectors.net/avsuper.html; TNA CAB/129/69
4. This was the Fairey Fireflash, Britain's first air-to-air missile
5. The figures in parenthesis are 2015 values, and assume an average inflation rate of two per cent per annum
6. TNA CAB/129/69, op cit
7. TNA CAB/128/28. Minutes of Treasury Meeting February 28, 1955, TNA T225/378
8. TNA CAB/129/69, op cit. Second Report from the Select Committee on Estimates, Session 1956–57, The Supply of Military Aircraft, House of Commons Paper 34 (HC 34), paras 28–31
9. Report from the Minister of Supply to the Prime Minister, July 9, 1955. TNA PREM 11/806
10. Memo to Prime Minister from Minister of Supply, May 28, 1956, TNA PREM 11/1712
11. Flight's annual review of military aircraft also gave the impression of satisfactory progress with the Hunter, Swift and Javelin. The Fairey Gannet was also experiencing severe problems during development. In May 1954 Sir Roy Fedden, a leading UK industrialist, expressed grave concern at the rate of progress in UK aircraft developments. See Flight, May 21, 1954, p643; June 25, 1954, pp822–823; September 17, 1954, passim
12. Flight, April 2, 1954, p386
13. Even the Dassault Mystère IVB was felt to be superior to the Hunter. See memoranda from Secretary of State for Air to the Prime Minister, January 1, 1955, and February 7, 1956. TNA PREM 11/06. Secretary of State for Air to the Prime Minister, February 7, 1956, TNA AIR 20/8572
14. See reports in Flight regarding Parliamentary debates; December 31, 1954, p920 and February 11, 1955, pp162–163
15. The Supply of Military Aircraft, HMSO, February 1955, House of Commons Command Paper (Cmnd) 9388
16. Minutes of Cabinet meeting, February 22, 1955, TNA Cab/128/28
17. June 23, 1955, TNA PREM 11/806
18. See Keith Hayward, The British Aircraft Industry, Manchester 1989, pp59–63. See also statement by George Ward, Under Secretary of State for Air, Hansard, March 18, 1952, col 2106
19. HC 34 op cit, paras 15–20. In a flash of déjà vu, one can cite a modern procurement chief describing this as the "conspiracy of optimism"
20. Some of the challenges of ordering "off the drawing board" were described by a Hawker executive, including finding enough firms to make the jigs required for production when all manufacturers were claiming the same level of preference. Flight, May 7, 1954, p597
21. Prime Minister memorandum to Minister of Supply, August 23, 1956. TNA PREM 11/1712; Flight, April 2, 1954, p386
22. The Javelin was planned to be the heart of the UK's air defence against the Soviet bomber force and its procurement was partly funded by the USA as an Allied asset. By 1955 it too was behind schedule with inadequate performance compared to its intended adversaries. Later in 1955 the Government announced a slow-down in Javelin production, denying that there were any serious problems in developing the aircraft fully to operational standards. See memoranda to the Prime Minister, June 3 and 23, 1955. TNA PREM 11/806; Cmnd 9388, op cit paras 30–35; Flight, July 15, 1955, p72
23. HC 34 op cit, paras 39–45
24. Cmnd 9388 op cit, paras 44–46
25. HC 34 op cit, paras 62–65. Minutes of the Defence Committee of the Cabinet, May 31, 1956, TNA PREM 11/1712
26. Cmnd 9388 op cit, para 47
27. Ministry of Supply memorandum Speeding Up Aircraft Production, March 1, 1954, TNA AVIA 65/31
28. Ibid
29. Ibid
30. HC 34 op cit, para 104
31. Cmnd 9388 op cit, paras 48–62
32. Ibid, paras 62–63
33. August 16, 1956, TNA PREM 11/1712. It would be nearly two more years before modifications to Hunters in service and in production would be completed
34. TNA T225/378, February 28, 1955
35. TNA T225/378, February 10, 1955
36. Ibid
37. TNA T225/378, July 9, 1955
38. TNA T225/378, February 28,1955; TNA CAB/128/27 and TNA PREM 11/1712
39. HC 34 op cit, passim
40. Ibid, paras 107–115
41. Ibid, para 131

Suez:
The Egyptian perspective. Baptism of war

In examining one of the most geopolitically significant conflicts of the Cold War period, Middle East military aviation specialist TOM COOPER uses official Egyptian documentation – a great deal of which has only come to light in the past decade – to provide the most accurate account yet published of the nation's aerial activities during the Suez Crisis of 1956.

While most accounts of the so-called "Suez Crisis" of 1956 published in the West have been presented from the British, French or Israeli perspective, this feature is based on official Egyptian documentation. This includes the Egyptian Air Force's Eastern Command War Diary and interviews with members of the Egyptian forces which participated in the conflict, notably Air Vice-Marshal Gabr Ali Gabr EAF, who flew Vampires during the Crisis before becoming an official EAF historian in the 1980s. Much of the information herein updates what has previously been published in sources such as the excellent Wings Over Suez (Grub Street, 1996), Dr David Nicolle's article Suez: The Other Side in Air Enthusiast Issue No 111 (May/June 2004) and Arab MiGs: Vol 1 (Harpia Publishing, 2009), co-written by this author and Dr David Nicolle.

ORIGINS OF THE CRISIS

Many Western sources maintain that Egypt's decision in the mid-1950s to order Soviet-designed Mikoyan-Gurevich (MiG) fighter jets was a primary reason for the outbreak of hostilities in the Middle East in 1956. From the Egyptian point of view, the genesis of the conflict is much more complex.

In 1952 the Free Officers Movement – a group established in the armed forces of Egypt and Sudan in the immediate post-war period – staged a coup d'état against King Farouk of Egypt, who was exiled, with all power being vested in the Revolutionary Command Council (RCC). Motivated by nationalism, the new regime was a hotbed of hopes and plans, one of which was a desire to improve Egypt's relations with Great Britain and the West in general, but to do so from a standpoint of equality.

BELOW: The Egyptian Air Force was the first Middle East air arm to operate jet-powered aircraft, Gloster Meteors forming a considerable part of its early jet fighter force. The first of its F.4 variants, a trio of which is seen here over the Pyramids of Giza, was delivered to Cairo at the end of October 1949. *Philip Jarrett Collection*

ABOVE: In early 1950 the EAF received a total of 12 denavalised Hawker Sea Fury FB.11s, diverted from production for the Fleet Air Arm. This example, serial "703", set a speed record on its ferry flight from Blackbushe in the UK to Almaza, near Cairo, in February 1950, Hawker's Assistant Chief Test Pilot Neville Duke taking 6hr 32min 10sec. *TAH Archive*

To the frustration of the RCC – especially its emerging leader and then President of Egypt, Gamal Abdel Nasser – relations with Britain failed to improve, owing to London's reluctance to treat the Egyptians as equals. Peace with Israel, another of the RCC's original aims, also failed to materialise. Although Nasser repeatedly expressed tolerance and respect for Egypt's new neighbour – going so far as to enter secret peace negotiations with the Israeli Prime Minister Moshe Sharett – hawkish individuals around Israel's first Prime Minister, David Ben-Gurion, and the Chief of Staff of Israel's Armed Forces, Moshe Dayan, moved to sabotage such efforts.

Throughout 1954 the Israeli secret services launched a campaign of terrorist attacks on Western interests in Egypt (Operation Susannah etc), while in 1955 the Israeli Defence Force (IDF) undertook a series of escalating raids against Egyptian positions along the ceasefire lines of the 1948–49 Arab-Israeli War.

Such experiences began to change Nasser's priorities. While refusing American military aid offered by President Dwight D. Eisenhower's administration in 1954, by early 1955 Nasser had begun seeking arms from Washington DC and London. The British, already in the process of withdrawing from their military bases in Egypt, turned all such requests down, while the Americans demanded basing rights in Egypt and the latter's membership of the newly-established Central Treaty Organisation (CENTO) in return.

ESTABLISHING A MODERN AIR FORCE

Humiliated by the Israeli cross-border raids, senior Egyptian military officers became keen to modernise and expand all branches of the

ABOVE: Gamal Abdel Nasser, one of the leaders of the overthrow of King Farouk of Egypt in 1952, became the nation's second President in June 1956 at the age of 38. Nasser's commitment to pan-Arab unity made him one of the most powerful leaders in the region — and set him on a collision course with the Western superpowers and the still-young state of Israel.

nation's armed forces. However, the delivery of orders for arms placed by Cairo in the UK were repeatedly interrupted by a series of embargoes. Nowhere was this felt more keenly than with orders for new equipment for the Egyptian Air Force (EAF). Nearly 50 per cent of aircraft ordered for the EAF in 1949 – and more than 90 per cent of aircraft ordered in 1950 – were impounded. Of some 350 aircraft ordered by Egypt by 1953, only 12 Gloster Meteor F.4s, 12 Meteor F.8s, four Meteor T.7s, one de Havilland Vampire FB.5, 20 Vampire FB.52s, a few Vampire T.55s, 18 Supermarine Spitfire F.22s, 12 Hawker Sea Fury FB.11s, nine Avro Lancaster B.Is and nine Handley Page Halifax A.IXs were delivered; barely a third.

Another embargo prevented Egypt from establishing a production line for licence-built Vampires at a newly constructed factory at Helwan, south of Cairo, despite expensive machinery having been paid for and put in place. This left the EAF with no alternative but to order 58 Vampires from Italian company Aermacchi in 1953, all of which were delivered by September 1955, but only under the guise of deliveries to Syria.

The supply of spare parts was equally intermittent and unpredictable, wreaking havoc with the EAF's training and expansion programmes, at a time when it was placing great emphasis on recruiting and training new pilots. The result was that while British intelligence reports confirmed the EAF's recruitment of excellent men with high morale and good general discipline, the air force was unable to undertake regular training or combat operations.

Throughout this period Egyptian military intelligence received regular reports – some true and some unfounded – about uninterrupted deliveries of jet fighters, tanks and other arms to Israel. As a result, the Egyptians unsurprisingly felt unfairly treated by the British and Americans.

From Nasser's perspective, the behaviour of the USA and UK was proof that the Western powers were siding with Israel against Egypt and the Arab world in general. As a result, he began seeking an alternative source of arms.

A RED STAR RISES IN THE EAST

In April 1955 Nasser met Zhou En-Lai, Prime Minister of the People's Republic of China, who explained that Beijing was dependent on Soviet supplies and promised to raise the matter of Egypt's requests for arms with the Soviets. On May 19, 1955, Nasser received a positive reply via the Soviet Embassy in Cairo.

Concerned that the acquisition of Soviet-designed and -built arms might make Egypt overly dependent on Moscow, Nasser offered the USA and the UK one last chance. Believing that the Egyptian President was trying to play them off against the Soviets, London and Washington responded with veiled threats. Left with no choice and alarmed by another series of Israeli raids on Gaza and Khan Yunis – added to Egyptian military intelligence reports about the latest delivery of French-built Dassault Ouragan and Mystère IVA fighter jets to Israel – Nasser decided to proceed with the Soviet arms deal.

As the talks reached an advanced stage, the Egyptian and Soviet delegations met in Prague, Czechoslovakia, to handle the last few details. Among other points it was agreed that the entire operation would be run through the Czechoslovakian government, borne out of both parties' common interest in not antagonising the Western powers further. On September 27, 1955, Nasser publicly announced the Egyptian-Czech Arms Deal, stressing that its main purpose was "for defence, not for aggression".

The Czechoslovakians gave the arms deal the codename Operation 105, which stipulated the delivery of 80 single-seat MiG-15bis and six two-seat MiG-15UTIs, to be built by the Avia factory, in addition to 45 Ilyushin Il-28 light bombers, 20 Il-14 transports and 55 advanced trainers and helicopters produced in the Soviet Union. The first MiGs arrived by ship in Alexandria on October 1, 1955, and were transported by truck to nearby Dekheila Air Base (AB) for assembly and post-delivery test flights by Czechoslovakian personnel. A team led by Maj Josef Medun, including two pilots, five technicians, two doctors, two interpreters and a cook, then began the business of converting Egyptian pilots on to the MiGs.

Reports about the increased flow of French arms to Israel during the winter of 1955–56 prompted Nasser to negotiate two additional orders for military equipment. The first of these was placed in November 1955 and specified the delivery of 16 warships and three submarines. The other was concluded in May 1956 and, among other items, provided for the delivery of 24 examples of the more advanced MiG-17F.

By this time the Czechoslovakians had launched Operation 104, which related to the sale of 20 MiG-15bis and four MiG-15UTIs to Syria. For the sake of simplicity, all were delivered to Alexandria, where they were assembled and test-flown at Abu Sueir AB (now known as Abu Suwayr). As two groups of Syrian pilots were already undergoing training in Egypt – one at the Flying College at Bilbeis, while the other was in the process of converting to Meteors – the decision was made to convert them on to the MiGs in Egypt.

A second group of Czechoslovakian advisers, led by Maj-Gen Jan Reindel and including three pilots, two technicians and an interpreter, arrived in Egypt in May 1956 to provide the conversion course for the Syrians. However, after the Syrian students had completed their ground course, their flying training proceeded slowly owing to repeated Egyptian failures to provide the necessary fuel. Thus all 24 Syrian MiGs were still at Abu Sueir in October 1956 but with no crews to fly them.

THE NATIONALISATION OF THE CANAL

Seeing large orders for Soviet arms as evidence of Egypt drifting into the Soviet sphere of influence, the USA and Britain withdrew ongoing financial aid for construction of the proposed Aswan High Dam. Keen to save

> The **first MiGs** arrived by ship in Alexandria on October 1, 1955, and were transported to **Dekheila** for assembly and **test flights.**

BELOW: Egypt's first two Meteors — F.4 serial "1401" (nearest camera) and T.7 two-seat trainer "1400" — over the Gloucestershire countryside before their delivery to Egypt, where they arrived on October 27, 1949. By the time the Suez Crisis erupted the EAF had received 12 F.4s, six T.7s, 12 F.8 fighters and six NF.13 nightfighter variants. *Philip Jarrett Collection*

EGYPTIAN AIR FORCE ORDER OF BATTLE, OCTOBER 29, 1956

UNIT	BASE	EQUIPMENT	REMARKS
Central Command — HQ: Almaza			
No 1 Sqn	Almaza	18 x MiG-15bis & 12 x MiG-17F	CO Sqn Ldr Hinnawy; some aircraft at Kabrit
No 2 Sqn	Cairo West	20 x Vampire FB.52	12–14 aircraft operational; some aircraft at Fayid
No 3 Sqn	Almaza	20 x C-47/Dakota	—
No 4 Sqn	Dekheila	Misc light aircraft	—
No 7 Sqn	Almaza	20 x C-46	—
No 8 Sqn	Inchas	12 x Il-28	CO Wg Cdr Kamal Zaki; only four crews qualified; most aircraft at Cairo West, combined with No 9 Sqn
No 9 Sqn	Inchas	12 x Il-28	CO Wg Cdr Hamid Abdel-Ghafar; only four crews qualified; most aircraft held in reserve at Cairo West, combined with No 8 Sqn
No 10 Sqn	Almaza	5 x Meteor NF.13	—
No 11 Sqn	Almaza	C-47/Dakota & Il-14	—
Il-28 OTU	Luxor	20 x Il-28s & Il-28Us	Operational Training Unit
Eastern Command — HQ: Ismailia			
No 5 Sqn	Fayid	8 x Meteor F.8	CO Sqn Ldr Mohammed Hilmi; unit originally based at el-Arish but withdrawn and apparently absorbed into No 40 Fighter Training Unit (FTU)
No 20 Sqn	Cairo West	12 x MiG-15bis & Kabrit	CO Sqn Ldr Mohammed Nabil al-Masry; in process of conversion to MiGs
No 30 Sqn	Deversoir & Kabrit	15 x MiG-15bis	CO Sqn Ldr Nazih Khalifa; fully operational
No 31 Sqn	el-Arish	Vampire FB.52s	CO Sqn Ldr Baghat Hassan Helmi; unit withdrawn from el-Arish; Vampires sold to Saudi Arabia, pilots under-going ground course on MiG-15; most served with No 40 FTU during Suez War
No 40 FTU	Fayid	8 x Meteor F.4; 2 x Meteor NF.13; 10 x Vampire FB.52	CO Sqn Ldr Salah ad-Din Husayn; incorporated Nightfighter Flight with Meteor NF.13s; some sources refer to this unit as No 10 Sqn
MiG OTU	Kabrit	12 x MiG-15bis, 10 x MiG-15UTI	Included 20 x MiG-15bis and 4 x MiG-15UTI ordered by Syria, crews still undergoing ground training
EAF Flying College — HQ: Bilbeis			
Elementary Flying School		15 x Heliopolis Gomhouria (Egyptian licence-built Bücker Bestmann); 25 x Chipmunk; 20 x T-6/Harvard	
Advanced Flying School		15 x Spitfire F.22; 8 x Sea Fury FB.11; 20 x Fiat G.55; 7 x Yak-11	

the development of this crucial symbol of Egyptian modernisation, Nasser was left with no alternative but to nationalise the Suez Canal, which he announced on July 26, 1956. Although Nasser guaranteed that all stockholders in the Universal Suez Ship Canal Company would be paid the full price of their shares according to that day's closing price on the Paris Stock Exchange, the British and French governments immediately denounced the decision as a flagrant violation of international law, while the USA immediately blocked all Egyptian assets abroad. Within days, Paris had opened negotiations with London and Tel Aviv for a joint invasion of Egypt.

Egyptian military intelligence soon received numerous reports of Anglo-French forces massing on Cyprus, Malta and at various bases in North Africa, but Nasser could not believe that the Western powers would launch an invasion. He changed his mind through September and ordered the Egyptian General Command to develop defence plans. Correctly assessing that any invasion would start with an all-out attack on its air bases, the EAF's C-in-C, Air Vice-Marshal Sidqi Mahmoud Sidki, ordered his units to prepare plans to disperse their aircraft to the greatest number of airfields possible, and then provide support for Egypt's ground forces.

The threat of a possible invasion thus caught the EAF midway through its conversion from British to Soviet combat aircraft; indeed, the fluid status of most of Egypt's flying units resulted in often contradictory foreign intelligence estimates of the EAF's combat strength. British assessments were massively exaggerated, while those of the French were rather more understated, and broadly similar to those prepared by Soviet advisers in Egypt at the time.

According to Egyptian records, the EAF entered the conflict with only 76 operational combat aircraft. It was found that high

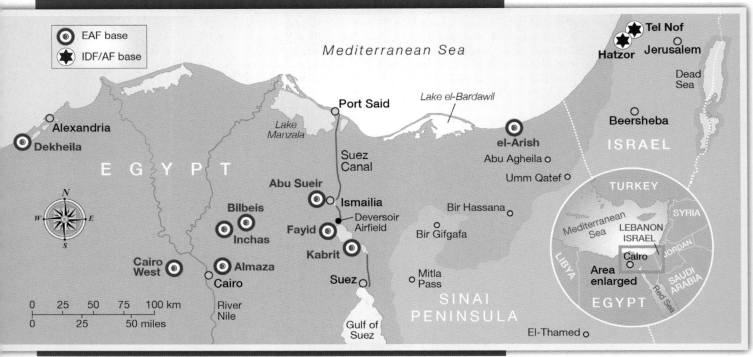

landing speeds and other peculiarities of the new Soviet-designed aircraft caused problems for EAF pilots accustomed to more forgiving British types. Indeed, some 17 MiGs were seriously damaged or lost in accidents during 1955–56. Although many were repaired and returned to airworthy status by Egyptian and Czechoslovakian technicians, only 64 MiG-15bis and MiG-15UTIs were deemed serviceable for the three EAF operational MiG squadrons and one operational training unit (OTU) as of October 29, 1956; roughly half of these were operational at any given time. Nevertheless, with 60 pilots having successfully converted to the new type before hostilities broke out, Egypt's MiG-15 squadrons were better-staffed than Israel's recently re-equipped Ouragan and Mystère units.

Of greater concern for the EAF's senior officers was the unsatisfactory status of stockpiles of spares, weapons and droptanks, although this was expected to improve significantly with additional Soviet deliveries, and once all personnel had completed their conversion courses. For similar reasons, the Egyptians were not overly concerned about the comparatively poor condition of most of their remaining British aircraft either. Indeed, on October 25, 1956, Cairo donated five surplus Vampire FB.52s to Jordan. The first Egyptian batch of 12 MiG-17Fs from May 1956 order arrived in Egypt in early October, with another delivery expected in the middle of the following month. The factory-fresh aircraft were quickly integrated into the EAF's No 1 Sqn, and six pilots had converted to the new type by October 29, 1956 (see EAF order of battle on facing page).

ISRAEL STRIKES

For the Egyptians, the Suez conflict began with an Israeli para-drop to the east of Jebel Heitan (also known as the Heitan Defile) in ▶

Two Israeli Meteor F.8s were attacking the Egyptian 1st Armoured Brigade marching on Bir Gifgafa when they were intercepted by four (some reports say six) Egyptian MiG-15s.

ABOVE: Egyptian ground staff manœuvre a highly realistic wooden MiG-15 decoy into a badly damaged hangar at an unidentified air base in Egypt during the Suez conflict. Scores of these convincing mock-ups were destroyed by French and British pilots, who would return to base claiming to have despatched rows of neatly parked MiGs. *Dr David Nicolle Collection via author*

BELOW: Along with the Meteor, the de Havilland Vampire formed the backbone of the EAF's early jet fighter force, 21 British-built examples being supplemented by nearly 60 Italian-built FB.52s. Here a pair of EAF Vampires is seen in Turkey during their ferry flights in 1951. *Dr David Nicolle Collection via author*

the Sinai Peninsula during the afternoon of October 29, 1956. This Israeli operation exploited the fact that 12 Vampires of No 31 Sqn EAF – a unit usually deployed at el-Arish AB, only 30 miles (50km) from the Israeli border – had been sold to Saudi Arabia in early October, and its pilots were undergoing conversion to the MiG-15 at Fayid AB, north-east of Cairo. Reacting to the Israeli invasion, the EAF was ordered to attack the paratroopers near Jebel Heitan in co-operation with Egyptian ground forces, and to find and destroy any Israeli ground units advancing over the border into Sinai.

Shortly after dawn on October 30, four Egyptian Vampires of No 2 Sqn EAF, led by Sqn Ldr Bahgat Hassan Helmi, were sent from Fayid to reconnoitre along the Mitla Pass, 30 miles east of Suez. Owing to a blanket of thick fog over the pass, the Vampires continued eastwards for 95 miles (150km) until they spotted an Israeli armoured column approaching el-Thamed. As a result, four MiG-15s were scrambled as a first line of defence, two of the MiGs strafing the column to inflict heavy damage.

At 0915hr, as the fog cleared over the Mitla Pass, the other two MiG-15s attacked Israeli paratroopers near Jebel Heitan and damaged one Piper Super Cub (s/n 47) on the ground. Several flights of Meteor F.8s of No 5 Sqn and Vampires of No 2 Sqn, all based at Fayid, launched attacks, causing extensive casualties and destroying numerous vehicles – but missing the Super Cub in which Moshe Dayan had reportedly just arrived to inspect the situation.

In response to the Egyptian air strikes,

Two Israeli Meteor F.8s were attacking the Egyptian 1st Armoured Brigade marching on **Bir Gifgafa** *when they were intercepted by four (some reports say six)* **Egyptian MiG-15s.**

ABOVE: Three of the EAF's newly-operational Czechoslovakian-built MiG-15s overfly Cairo during a demonstration of Egyptian air power in September 1956. A dozen of No 1 Sqn's recently-introduced fighters provided the Egyptian public with a view of their nation's state-of-the-art front line of defence. *Tahsin Zaki Collection via author*

formations of Mystères and Ouragans began appearing over the battlefield, two of the former attacking an Egyptian infantry battalion on its way to the Mitla Pass. As additional EAF Meteor F.8s swooped down on the Israeli paras, a pair of Mystères appeared, but were engaged by Egyptian MiGs. Neither side lost any aircraft in this first air combat of the conflict.

Further north, at 1530hr, two Israeli Meteor F.8s were attacking the Egyptian

1st Armoured Brigade marching on Bir Gifgafa when they were intercepted by four (some reports say six) Egyptian MiG-15s. One Meteor withdrew and returned to base, while the other fell into a spin after a droptank failed to release. Egyptian military intelligence later reported that the Israeli pilot recovered at very low altitude to make a forced landing at his unit's base at Hatzor.

In the late afternoon, some 13 Israeli jets – six Mystères, two Meteors and five

ABOVE: A poor quality but rare photograph of EAF pilots running to their MiGs during a scramble in early October 1956. The MiG-15bis was an improved version of the original MiG-15, incorporating an uprated engine and a strengthened structure to permit higher speeds.
Nour Bardai Collection via author

Ouragans – appeared in the skies over the Mitla Pass before continuing for the EAF base at Kabrit. Although supposedly ordered not to cross the Suez Canal, the six Mystères dived from 20,000ft (6,100m) to attack six MiG-15s of No 20 Sqn as they were taking off on a sortie against an Israeli column near Bir Hassana. One MiG-15 was shot down while climbing after take-off, its pilot ejecting safely, but Flt Lt Hussein Sidki claimed one Mystère IVA as shot down in return, although Israeli sources claim it was only damaged and returned to Hatzor.

Considered as an attack on Kabrit AB, this action was deemed by the Egyptians to be a provocation, and on the night of October 30 the EAF ordered a series of attacks on Israeli air bases by Ilyushin Il-28s of Nos 8 and 9 Sqn, despite their crews having only just finished converting to the twin-engined jet bombers. Two Il-28s each were launched to attack the airfields at Hatzor and Tel Nof, but both sorties proved

ineffective. The Egyptians were satisfied, however, concluding that over the course of 80 sorties flown during the day, in addition to causing heavy losses to Israeli ground troops, EAF pilots had shot down an Israeli Mystère IVA and destroyed a Super Cub on the ground, while Egypt's ground-based air defences had shot down an Israeli Meteor and two North American P-51D Mustangs.

Expecting an escalation of fighting, EAF Eastern Command launched an all-out effort on October 31, beginning at dawn, when four Vampires of No 2 Sqn, led by Sqn Ldr Helmi, took off from Fayid to strike Israeli forces near the Mitla Pass. While changing from a tight two-pair vic formation to echelon for ground attack, they were jumped by Mystères, two of the Vampires being shot down. Helmi was killed, but Plt Off Ahmad Hassan Farghal baled out and was captured. Flight Officer Wa'il Afify was wounded when his Vampire was hit, after which he attempted to return

to Kabrit but crashed five miles (8km) west of the Mitla Pass. Pilot Officer Gabr Ali Gabr managed to fire off a burst at one of the Mystères before the Israeli accelerated away, the Egyptian returning safely to Kabrit.

LEARNING THE HARD WAY

It had been an expensive lesson for the EAF, and orders were put in place that all further Meteor and Vampire operations were to be closely escorted by MiGs. The majority of Egyptian strikes that morning hit the Israeli paras in the Mitla Pass, before action switched to the northern and central regions of the Sinai around noon, in response to Israeli air strikes there.

Throughout the morning, Egyptian Army troops had put up heavy and accurate anti-aircraft fire, downing two Israeli North American Harvards over Abu Agheila in the early morning and damaging two Meteors over Umm Qatef. ▶

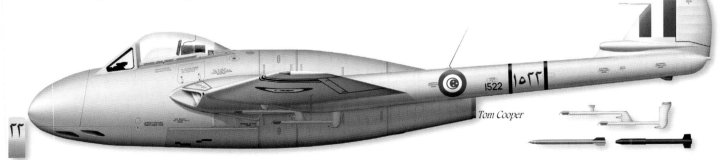

ABOVE: Vampire FB.52 "1522" was built by de Havilland and given standard EAF markings. Note the last two Arabic numerals of the serial repeated on the nosewheel door. By 1956 most EAF Vampires were fitted with launch rails for 3.5in Sakr unguided rockets. *Artwork by Tom Cooper © 2019*

ABOVE: Delivered at the end of 1955, Egypt's Il-28 twin-jet bombers were deployed to three units, Nos 8 and 9 Sqns based at Inchas, and the Il-28 Operational Training Unit at Luxor. This unidentified example was photographed at Almaza in 1957 during an exhibition celebrating the 25th anniversary of the formation of the Egyptian Air Force. *Philip Jarrett Collection*

When a pair of Israeli Ouragans attempted to attack the Egyptian 1st Armoured Brigade near Bir Gifgafa, they were intercepted by four MiG-15s, led by Sqn Ldr Nazih Khalifa, which were on their way to attack an Israeli column north-east of Bir Hassana. Khalifa damaged two enemy jets in a short clash: one managed to return to Hatzor, while the other was forced to make a belly-landing in the desert. On the way back to Kabrit AB, Khalifa's formation shot down an Israeli Piper Cub over the Mitla Pass.

Another MiG flight was less fortunate. During an attack on Israeli tanks east of Abu Agheila, the MiG-15 flown by young EAF pilot Abd al-Rahman Muharram was damaged by groundfire. While returning to base, he was jumped by two Mystères, sustaining heavy damage to the starboard wing. Muharram evaded his pursuers by descending to low altitude, but was finally forced to ditch his MiG

in the shallow waters of Lake el-Bardawil. While the pilot escaped back across the Suez Canal, his aircraft was found by the Israelis, who promptly turned it into a major propaganda coup; photographs of Muharram's MiG being inspected by Israeli pilots can be found in nearly all accounts of the Suez conflict.

Around noon, two flights of Syrian-owned MiG-15bis from Abu Sueir were heading towards Abu Agheila when they ran into two sections of Mystères north of Bir Hassana. The MiG flown by Plt Off Fuad Kamal was hit and entered a spin, forcing the pilot to eject. The other flight continued unhindered and attacked the Israeli ground troops, causing more losses.

At 1330hr one of three two-aircraft sections of MiG-15s from Abu Sueir were over central Sinai when an Ouragan formation was spotted below. Diving towards the Ouragans, Plt Off Farouk el-Ghazzawy shot down one Israeli fighter, but was in turn

> *When Israeli paras advanced into the "saucer" of the **Mitla Pass** in the afternoon, they were subjected to repeated air strikes from **MiG-15s, Meteors, Vampires, Il-28s** and even ageing Egyptian **Sea Furies** and **Spitfires.***

hit by the other. The Egyptian pilot nursed his MiG back to Abu Sueir, where he was able to make a safe landing.

Half an hour later, another MiG flight intercepted two P-51s that had been damaged by anti-aircraft fire of the 1st Armoured Brigade and shot one of them down (contrary to Israeli records, which cite only one loss owing to aerial combat, a Cub, during the entire Suez conflict). Elsewhere, Egyptian anti-aircraft fire damaged 16 other Israeli fighter-bombers (including two Meteor F.8s and a Mosquito FB.6 that were forced to make emergency landings) and shot down several P-51s. Furthermore, when Israeli paras advanced into the "saucer" of the Mitla Pass in the afternoon, they were subjected to repeated air strikes from MiG-15s, Meteors, Vampires, Il-28s and even ageing Egyptian Sea Furies and Spitfires.

The EAF had completed 120 combat sorties by the early evening of October 31, having lost three MiG-15s and three Vampires. Its pilots claimed one Mystère, two Ouragans, one Mustang and one Cub as shot down. Furthermore, Egyptian ground troops claimed four more Mustangs, one Mosquito and two Harvards.

At this point, the EAF High Command was informed that Republic F-84F Thunderstreaks in Israeli markings had

ABOVE: MiG-15bis serial "1972" was one of 64 of the original 80 examples still in operational service with the EAF in October 1956, about half of which were serviceable on the outbreak of hostilities. All were left in natural metal and carried roundels in six positions as well as black stripes around the rear fuselage and inboard of the wingtips. *Artwork by Tom Cooper © 2019*

been involved in the attacks on the 1st Armoured Brigade. Knowing that the IDF/AF had suffered heavy losses that day, the Egyptians were convinced that they were some way towards achieving air superiority over the Sinai. Emboldened, and to maintain pressure, the EAF sent four Il-28s for another attack on Israeli air bases that night. One of the twin-engined bombers, flown by Sqn Ldr Mustafa Helmi, crashed on take-off, killing the crew, but Wg Cdr Hamid Abdel-Ghafar bombed Tel Nof before returning safely to Inchas – only to find his base under attack by RAF bombers. The two Il-28s that attacked Hatzor missed their targets, but managed to evade interception by Israeli Meteor NF.13 serial "52", which was on patrol that night.

ENTER THE MUSKETEERS

On the evening of October 30 a joint ultimatum had been issued by the French and British, stipulating the cessation of all hostilities on both sides, on threat of Anglo-French forces intervening "in whatever strength may be necessary to secure compliance". The fighting continued the next day, however, resulting in air strikes on Egyptian air bases by RAF bombers that evening, as mentioned above. This was a profound shock to many EAF personnel, many of whom still considered the British to be their friends and allies. Nevertheless, the EAF High Command issued an order for the dispersal and evacuation of aircraft. Nine Il-28s and one Il-14 were flown to Jeddah in Saudi Arabia, with a refuelling stop at Luxor,

where they were photographed by an IDF/AF Mosquito, while No 1 Sqn EAF hid 24 of its MiGs by covering them with camouflage nets in a scrapyard outside Almaza on October 31.

With few Egyptian pilots qualified for night flying and a poor early-warning radar network, the EAF was hopelessly outmatched by an armada of RAF bombers during the night of October 31. Only Sqn Ldr Husayn and his wingman got airborne in a pair of Meteor NF.13s to claim a Vickers Valiant as damaged, but the bomber, B.1 XD819 of No 148 Sqn, actually came away untouched.

At dawn on November 1, six MiG-17s of No 1 Sqn were launched from Almaza, Flt Lt Sayd el-Qadi claiming damage to one of the RAF's reconnaissance Canberras; his superiors, however, subsequently deemed his ▶

ABOVE: By early October 1956 the first batch of MiG-17Fs had been delivered to Egypt and rushed into service with No 1 Sqn at Almaza. Although only six EAF pilots had converted on to the type (a substantially improved MiG-15 with an afterburning engine) by the outbreak of the Crisis, they flew numerous combat sorties during the conflict. *Shalabi el-Hinnawy Collection via author*

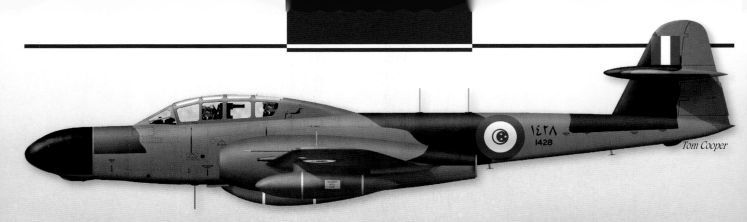

ABOVE: The only combat aircraft in EAF service to wear camouflage during the Crisis were the five Meteor NF.13s still in service with No 10 Sqn at Almaza, including "1428", as seen here. The nightfighters were painted in Medium Sea Grey and Dark Green and wore the standard roundels and fin flashes, but no fuselage or wingtip black stripes. *Artwork by Tom Cooper © 2019*

report untrustworthy and punished him. Led by Sqn Ldr Shalabi el-Hinnawy, four of the MiG-17s flew a strike on well-camouflaged Israeli paras near the Mitla Pass.

All six of these aircraft and one Il-28 were to be destroyed on the ground at Almaza during successive air strikes undertaken by British and French fighter-bombers. At least four MiGs were destroyed at Cairo West, and about a dozen at Abu Sueir. However, most of the EAF's jets were evacuated to airfields in Upper Egypt or stretches of straight highway in the Nile Delta, while at least ten EAF MiG-15s and three Syrian MiG-15UTIs were flown to Syria. In their place, scores of extremely realistic wooden dummies were subsequently claimed as destroyed by British and French fighter-bomber pilots. In contrast, because there were not enough crews to evacuate all the Il-28s, and most of the training aircraft were left parked in the open, Inchas and Bilbeis suffered much more.

For the next few days, the EAF ceased operations and limited itself to waiting for the prospective ground invasion. Day after day of continuous aerial bombardment, however, began to take a serious toll on

ABOVE: Squadron Leader Shalabi el-Hinnawy, Commanding Officer of No 1 Sqn EAF during the Crisis, was the leading Egyptian fighter pilot of the conflict, and is seen here in the cockpit of one of the 12 Meteor F.8s delivered to the EAF in the early 1950s. He would go on to become the Commander-in-Chief of the Egyptian Air Force during 1967–69. *Shalabi el-Hinnawy Collection*

the morale of the Egyptian military and its leaders, but the situation suddenly improved on November 5, when it became known that London and Paris were under increasing pressure from the USA and Soviet Union to withdraw their forces from the conflict, neither of the latter superpowers seeing any favourable geopolitical outcomes from it. In light of this development, Flt Off Nabil Kamil flew a single sortie in a MiG-15bis over Port Said on November 6, even if only to demonstrate that the EAF was still active. By the following morning, a United Nations-negotiated ceasefire was in effect.

THE FINAL TALLY

From the Egyptian perspective, the conflict did not end on November 7, 1956, but lasted another 120 days, by which time the Anglo-French forces had completed their withdrawal from Egypt, and the Israelis had withdrawn from the Sinai Peninsula (on March 6, 1957).

From the EAF's point of view, the conflict had caused significant damage to its air bases, but not the crippling losses claimed by the British, French and Israelis. For

ABOVE: Adorned with the black and yellow "Suez stripes" painted for identification purposes on British and French aircraft during the conflict, seven English Electric Canberra B.6s of No 12 Sqn RAF await the next political move at RAF Luqa on Malta in late September 1956. The aircraft would take part in the Anglo-French Operation Musketeer a few weeks later. *TAH Archive*

example, the British reported no fewer than 105 MiG-15s and -17s as destroyed, whereas by the end of the nine-day conflict 32 EAF MiG-15bis and at least six MiG-17Fs remained fully serviceable.

While the French reportedly destroyed 20 Il-28s during a single strike against Luxor airfield on November 2, they actually accounted for only six on that occasion. The Egyptians managed to evacuate safely 37 examples of the twin-jet bomber. Similarly, Egyptian personnel losses were kept at an absolute minimum; only two EAF pilots are known to have been killed during the conflict. Once UN peacekeepers had been deployed to Egypt to separate the belligerents, the EAF returned its evacuated aircraft to Egypt and continued to build up its strength with the addition of more MiG-17Fs from Czechoslovakia.

Generally, Egyptians concluded that the Suez conflict had culminated in a clear-cut victory for Egypt, as Cairo had achieved its political objectives in becoming the de facto owner of the Suez Canal, with the exclusive right to operate it without any interference or objection. For Britain and France, their last gasps of colonialism in the Middle East were an unqualified disaster with far-reaching geopolitical consequences. Instead of removing Nasser, it was the British and French leaders, Anthony Eden and Guy Mollet respectively, that had been ousted by the summer of 1957. Indeed, Egypt's international prestige grew enormously and Nasser became the undisputed figurehead of Arab nationalism until his death from a heart attack in 1970.

Although commonly portrayed as the nominal "winner" of the conflict – at least in terms of materiel it recovered from the Sinai – Israel's involvement in the tripartite plot destroyed any chance of a negotiated settlement with Arabs for another 20 years. ●

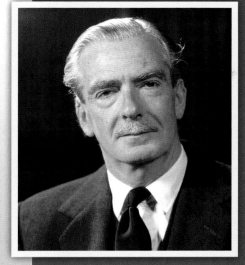

ABOVE: The three Musketeers — from top to bottom; British Prime Minister Sir Anthony Eden, whose reputation was severely damaged by his handling of the Suez Crisis...

ABOVE: ...Guy Mollett, France's Prime Minister from February 1956...

ABOVE: ...and David Ben-Gurion, Israel's Prime Minister, with whom Eden and Mollet conspired in secret to attack Egypt.

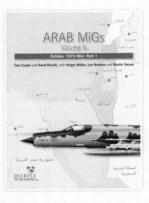

FOOTNOTE

Tom Cooper is a co-author of the indispensable Arab MiGs series published by Harpia Publishing, incorporating six volumes detailing the Cold War history of Soviet military aircraft in the Middle East. For more information on the Suez Crisis see Arab MiGs Volume 1: Mikoyan i Gurevich MiG-15 and MiG-17 In Service With Air Forces of Algeria, Egypt, Iraq, Morocco and Syria (ISBN 978-0-982553-9-23, RRP £34.99). For full details of Harpia's extensive book catalogue visit the website at www.harpia publishing.com.

Between the devil & the deep blue sea

Prof **KEITH HAYWARD** FRAeS digs deep into the archives to reveal how all parties involved in the procurement of the Vickers VC10 for BOAC were compromised by the conflicting agendas of airline and industry.

By the mid-1950s the fleet planning of the British Overseas Airways Corporation (BOAC) was in some disarray. Following the series of de Havilland Comet disasters in 1954 and the politically sensitive cancellation of the Vickers V.1000 in 1955, BOAC had thought it could rely on the Bristol Britannia turboprop and the modified Comet 4 to remain competitive on the key North Atlantic routes.[1] Initially, both the airline and the British Government felt that this was a sound strategy. However, by the summer of 1956, with its competitors flocking to order Boeing 707 or Douglas DC-8 jetliners, BOAC was forced to look across the Atlantic.

While there was some official scepticism about the performance promised by the American jets, BOAC requested permission on July 26, 1956, to order 17 (later reduced to 15) Boeings powered by Rolls-Royce Conway engines. As a condition of the deal, however, BOAC was required to look at a British-built solution to its "Eastern" or "Empire" route needs. Ideally, this should be undertaken as a private venture in order to conform to a government policy aimed at reducing – and ultimately ending – direct public support for civil aircraft development.

THE ONLY GAME IN TOWN?

Buoyed by profits from its Viscount turboprop and the promise of a large launch order from BOAC, Vickers – and as became apparent, only Vickers – was prepared to tackle the project under these terms.[2] As future BOAC chairman Sir Matthew Slattery would later observe:

"There was only one company prepared to embark upon such an aeroplane, and that was Vickers. We now get to the stage where you could have any colour so long as it was black. You have got to have a British aircraft, and there is only one possible aircraft. I am quite sure that the Corporation was quite free to make any choice [it] liked."[3]

As the Treasury later noted: "Whether the VC10 was the best aircraft available for BOAC was not questioned at this time".[4] This did not mean that the two were dragooned ▶

BELOW: The rivals — Boeing 707 G-APFI shares ramp space with fellow BOAC aircraft Super VC10 G-ASGA and standard VC10 G-ARVL at Heathrow in October 1967. The American jetliner was perceived to be more cost-efficient to operate, but the Super VC10 ultimately proved more profitable, with much higher load factors on the vital North Atlantic route. *Mike Stroud/TAH Archive*

ABOVE: The Chairman of BOAC in the early days of discussions about what would become the VC10, Sir Miles Thomas, resigned from the Corporation in 1956.

ABOVE: Sir George Edwards, Vickers' Managing Director, joined the company at Weybridge in 1935.

ABOVE: Duncan Sandys, Minister of Aviation during 1959–60.

into partnership; Vickers and BOAC had been discussing this requirement for some months. An outline specification produced by the airline's planning staff called for a design optimised for "hot and high" airfield performance and, given the lower passenger density of these routes, with a capacity smaller than the American jets, which would "best serve the needs of the Corporation".[5] Vickers stated that it could produce a suitable aircraft for BOAC at £1.75m (roughly equivalent to £43m in 2017) per airframe, but on condition that the airline ordered 35 aircraft, later increased to 42 when a transatlantic version was added.

BOAC had hoped to place a smaller initial order, increasing numbers as demand grew. In January 1958 BOAC announced an order for the VC10 in a contract worth £68m (£1.7bn) – at the time the most expensive single order for a British airliner.[6] The size of the order was subject to both external and internal questioning. Outside analysts felt that BOAC had an overly optimistic view of the market. Ministry of Aviation (MoA) officials later conceded that "35 may have been a bit high", but Vickers made it clear that this was the minimum needed to launch the aircraft as a private venture.

The most important factor from the Conservative government's point of view was that it vindicated its private-venture policy, and that the size of the order and Vickers' willingness to pay for its development "were clearly tied together". Even the Treasury could not later find direct evidence of undue Government pressure:

"History suggests that much of the original discussion took place as unrecorded meetings between the [BOAC] Chairman [Sir Miles Thomas until May 1956] and the Minister of Transport & Civil Aviation [Harold Watkinson]. The first the Treasury knew of a potential order was a letter to the Chancellor [Harold Macmillan] dated May 2, 1956, which explained the innovative nature of the design, [which would be] competitive with the Americans, and that Vickers would develop it as a private venture".[7]

In the Treasury's view this was, in retrospect, a very ill-judged step and based on a very narrow assessment of future development potential: "The Government's insistence on a private venture led to a thoroughly uneconomic purchase by the Corporation, by no means fulfilling [its] earlier stated requirements, and at a time when the Corporation, guaranteed with Government funds, was already running at a loss; it was the smallest number for which Vickers would undertake [the project] as a private venture".

Neither the Ministry of Supply (MoS) nor the Ministry of Transport & Civil Aviation (MoTCA) seemed to be too bothered that the design would need further development to be competitive on North Atlantic routes.[8]

In its haste to confirm the deal, Vickers held to a rear-engined clean-wing concept that offered the best answer to the Empire requirement for "hot and high" airfields that might only have semi-prepared runway surfaces, a risk to any podded engine.[9] Sir George Edwards, Vickers' Managing Director, later admitted that if the company

had produced a design for the North Atlantic from the outset, it would have looked like the cancelled V.1000. Soon after the original specification was defined, BOAC accepted some changes to give the aircraft better overall performance. The BOAC Board also overruled a last-minute challenge to the whole project from its Engineering Department.[10] Even with such a large order, Vickers nevertheless assumed a considerable risk, with development costs initially put at £6.25m (£165m); the £1.75m unit price of the first order of 35 aircraft implied an immediate loss of £3m (£67m), which Vickers was expected to make up through exports of the new type.[11] Vickers estimated that it needed to sell a total of 80 VC10s to break even.

For its part, the MoS (under Reginald Maudling) was very pleased with the outcome: "This rep-resents a major step forward in our policy of encouraging the private-sector financing of civil aircraft, and I think that the Government will be able justly to claim great credit for it".[12]

The combination of private-venture development supported by a large domestic order seemed to have worked; it was certainly used as leverage in the debate over British European Airways' order for a new medium-range jet, the de Havilland D.H.121 Trident, which ended up being funded on the same basis as the VC10. [For the full story of BEA's procurement of the D.H.121, see Trident: Britain's Fork in the Road in TAH16.] While the Trident launch attracted much controversy, development of the VC10 moved on without too much initial trouble. This was soon to change. By 1959 the VC10 programme was in difficulty, with Vickers close to ruin.

THE VICKERS FINANCIAL CRISIS OF 1959

In mid-1959 Vickers warned BOAC that the costs of developing the VC10 had increased, and that the airline would have to find the money to cover the difference.[13] Vickers suggested that matters would be improved if BOAC could change its order in favour of a stretched (Super) VC10 more able to compete with the American jets on the North Atlantic route, but the airline was reluctant to take on the even heavier burden of supporting a larger and more expensive version.[14] A 1959 Cooper Brothers audit for the MoS revealed an underestimate of losses on the BOAC order, which were now put at £15m (£312m).[15] In June 1959 Vickers warned of potential difficulties without direct government aid. Speaking at the Vickers AGM, its chairman, Viscount Knollys, argued that "the Government [has] to appreciate and ease the great and disproportionate financial burden borne by Vickers and other companies in private ventures. Without firm and early support by the Government... this country is more likely, sooner rather than some people might expect, to find itself without a real aircraft industry at all."[16]

Vickers' problems had emerged very rapidly; the company had grossly underestimated the costs of developing both the Vanguard turboprop and the VC10. According to Sir George Edwards this was not uncommon in the industry, but in this case the estimates "proved wrong by quite a bit".[17] Boeing and Douglas had also launched a price-cutting campaign, and a fourth competitor – the Convair 880 – had entered the market.[18]

The solution to Vickers' problem, as well as a more general crisis affecting the British aircraft industry, was to encourage rationalisation as the price for government aid.[19] Vickers was already in discussions with de Havilland about a merger when the new and energetic Minister of Aviation, Duncan Sandys, opened his industrial "marriage bureau".[20] (The MoTCA had become the Ministry of Aviation in October 1959.) By December 1959 Vickers and English Electric were close to forming what would become the British Aircraft Corporation (BAC). However, such was the parlous state of Vickers' finances that a full merger depended on the Government giving support to new airliner development – namely the medium-haul VC11 for BEA – and helping out with the costs of the VC10 programme.

Not only had the price Vickers agreed with BOAC for the VC10 been too low – £1.2m (£26m) per aircraft instead of a more realistic £1.4m (£29m) – the non-recurring costs for its development had "reached astronomical figures despite the most stringent controls". This was on top of Vanguard losses, by this time put at more than £7m (£147m).[21] Vickers wanted £15m

(£309m) from the Government for both the VC10 and VC11. Vickers' contribution (new and sunk costs) would total £21m (£441m). The Government would get its money back at a ten per cent rate if 85 VC10s and 110 VC11s were sold.[22]

Sandys was well aware of the need for speed, and understood that if matters were left hanging until February 1960 Vickers' problems could reach breaking point. The MoA felt that a package worth £17.6m (£368m) would suffice. At a crucial meeting with Sandys and his officials, Sir George Edwards suggested that BOAC might be persuaded to drop its Boeings, then due to enter service in April 1960, in favour of the Super VC10. The RAF might also be encouraged to use a VC10/Super VC10 hybrid, with the standard VC10's short fuselage and the wings, tailplane, undercarriage and extra fuel capacity of the Super. However, the officials challenged Edwards' assertion, citing BOAC's obligation to act commercially, and estimated that the total financial call (including the cost of Boeing sales) would amount to £28.2m (£588m).[23] Sandys nevertheless agreed to include some direct support for the Super VC10 in the new

arrangements for civil aircraft support, which were agreed by the Cabinet in January 1960.

Sandys admitted that the VC10 was hardly a "promising civil project", but the decision to support it was taken "mainly on the ground that it is necessary to tide Vickers over [its] present difficulties in order to prevent [it] going out of the civil business, and in the hope of greater success with future civil projects, when a group of sufficient strength has been created". The new policy would include a launch-aid scheme for civil aircraft developments and the concentration of contracts among the merged groups.[24] The new consortium, BAC, and a second group, Hawker Siddeley Aviation (including de Havilland), would now form the core of the UK airframe industry, and manufacturers of future civil aircraft could apply for government launch aid.

RESTRUCTURING THE BOAC ORDER
BOAC was now under strong pressure to help the rationalisation process by reshaping the VC10 contract. This entailed taking at least ten of the longer-range Super VC10s at £2.7m (£58m) per aircraft. Sandys implied that a Vickers bankruptcy would cost BOAC £6m (£125m) in lost progress payments. In 1960 the incoming BOAC chairman, Sir Matthew Slattery, asked for some time to consider the options, but was forestalled by his predecessor, Sir Gerard d'Erlanger, who agreed to a new contract, signed that June, for 35 standard and ten Super VC10s, before the handover.[25]

> The new consortium, **BAC**, and a second group, **Hawker Siddeley Aviation** (including de Havilland), would now form the core of the **UK airframe industry**.

BELOW: Encouraged by healthy sales of its Viscount turboprop airliner, Vickers began discussions with BEA in 1953 about a successor which would be larger, faster and offer better economics. The prototype Vanguard made its first flight in 1959, but only 44 would be built. Seen here is second production example G-APEB, named Bellerophon. *TAH Archive*

ABOVE: The prototype VC10, G-ARTA, nears completion at Weybridge in late 1961 or early 1962. Structurally the VC10 exploited the integral machining techniques adopted for production of the Vanguard's wing panels, and the use of fuselage hoop frames and inner wing members was a direct carry-through from Vickers' earlier V.1000. *BAE Systems via Brooklands Museum Trust*

There is no direct evidence of exactly how much pressure Sandys applied to d'Erlanger, but BOAC "bent over backwards to meet the Minister's wishes", and a Treasury official learned in the strictest confidence that below Board level there "was considerable doubt within the Corporation as to the wisdom of ordering the Super VC10".[26] Treasury officials were left in no doubt that the Minister "will not accept that this order for [the] Super VC10 is in any degree open to question".[27]

The RAF was rather less of a pushover when asked to take on the VC10 as a military transport; the Air Council was not as "amenable" as BOAC, and made a decision to buy "independently and in [its] own time".[28] Sandys claimed that he was equally concerned about the financial health and welfare of both the airline and aircraft industries, but as a House of Commons Select Committee later reported, "BOAC's confidential documents show

ABOVE: Beside a model of the Super VC10 as originally envisaged, with tiptanks and 28ft (8.5m) fuselage stretch, the BOAC contract for 35 standard and ten Super VC10s is signed on June 23, 1960. Left to right: N.H. Jackson, Director, Vickers; Sir George Edwards; K.H. Staple, Secretary, BOAC and Charles Abell, chief engineer, BOAC. *BAE Systems via Brooklands Museum Trust*

that the rehabilitation of Vickers and [its] merger... [were] constantly on the minds of BOAC's Board, and particularly of Sir Gerard d'Erlanger, in the discussions that followed". The new team of Slattery and Sir Basil Smallpeice admitted that it was "a bit of a gamble".[29]

In April 1961, despite internal concerns about the VC10's unfavourable operating costs compared to those of the 707 or DC-8, BOAC agreed to a restructured order comprising three more 707s, 15 standard and 30 Super VC10s, the latter now a scaled-down design. This would cost an additional £6.3m

(£131m), taking the total VC10 cost up to £101.4m (£2.1bn).

The Treasury sourly noted that the BOAC case seemed to indicate that "an expansion of traffic was planned to meet the problems created by the delivery of new aircraft, rather than the other way round". Press reports argued that BOAC may already have been in the position of having to sell off some of its DC-7s and Britannias as a result of falling demand, and that to justify the new orders the airline had to assume a doubling of the current growth rate to 14 per cent per annum.[30]

The growing burden of the VC10 order on BOAC's own increasingly parlous financial performance soon came to a head. With the ink on the April 1961 contract hardly dry, the Treasury (under Chancellor of the Exchequer Selwyn Lloyd) demanded cuts to the Super VC10 order. The Secretary of State for Air, Julian Amery (to become Minister of Aviation in July 1962), rejected this out of hand, and in October wrote to the Treasury:

"I would remind you that the VC10 project was closely considered by ministers in 1959 when Vickers [was] saying [it] would have to go out of the civil aircraft business altogether if this programme was not further supported. It was out of this situation that the Government decided it must continue with further support represented by the [June 1960] BOAC order for ten Super VC10s and additional support for development, and this was one of the considerations which led to the formation of BAC. To go back on all of this at the present stage would be quite unthinkable."

Amery continued:

"To continue the uncertainty at this stage would cause enormous difficulties with Vickers, with the inescapable implication that the VC10 order might be substantially reduced or even cancelled. A fundamental reassessment at this stage, with all the delay it would incur, the doubts that it would cast on the only big British jet in prospect and the uncertainty it would create in BOAC, would be a major calamity."[31]

To the Treasury it seemed as if the newly formed BAC was "not much better able to bear the setback of a cancelled order than Vickers alone would have been. But in view of the general policy considerations in relation to the aircraft industry, and of the fact as we understand it [that] BOAC [is] firmly committed to Vickers up to the figure of £151m (£3.1bn), we agree [that] we cannot press this point further".

The Treasury had accepted from the outset that while the aircraft would not be exported in numbers, and that it was not a productive investment for the Government, because of the importance of Vickers, and BAC's importance as perhaps the better of the two recently reorganised groups of manufacturers of civil aircraft, the view was taken in the Treasury that *"BOAC's interests must of necessity come second to those of the industry at this juncture".* [32]

In 1963 BOAC's deficit topped £80m (£1.5bn) with the prospect of further losses taking it to £90m (£1.7bn) by March 1964. The crisis forced Amery to appoint an outsider, John Corbett, to review BOAC's finances.[33] The Corporation's problems had been caused primarily (but by no means only) by the cost of its fleet planning. Some of the losses were attributed to bad

luck, such as the Comet disasters and the delays of the Britannia programme, but the financial burden of the VC10 programme was the largest single drain on BOAC's resources, and the latter should have simply walked away from the contract. The Corporation also contended that the VC10 fleet would cost around £7m (£133m) a year more to operate than a comparable fleet of 707s. The other part of the loss was down to bad management, some £15m (£286m) being lost in unsuccessful investment in associated companies.[34]

In November 1963 the Government requested the resignations of BOAC's senior management team of Sir Matthew Slattery and Sir Basil Smallpeice, and a new chairman, Sir Giles Guthrie, was asked to produce, "within a year, a plan for putting BOAC on its feet financially. This will involve a review of the organisation of the Corporation, of its route structure and of the composition of its aircraft fleet."[35] Guthrie would also receive a clarification of the "buy British" policy, which would define the circumstances and the compensation open to the Corporation if it was directed by the Minister of Aviation to act contrary to its own commercial interests in support of government policy.[36]

On appointment, Guthrie hinted at cancelling a large part of the VC10 order, at a cost of £20m (£380m) in cancellation charges. This, according to Treasury calculations, "would appear to be many times the cost in development

*The **Corporation** also contended that the **VC10 fleet** would cost around **£7m (£133m)** a year more to operate than a comparable fleet of 707s.*

BELOW: The VC10 prototype was rolled out of the Weybridge hangar on April 15, 1962, resplendent in its BOAC colour scheme of royal blue, grey and white, with gold detailing. Two months later it was ready to fly at last, after more than five years of development; it is seen here on June 29, 1962, being readied for its maiden flight. *BAE Systems via Brooklands Museum Trust*

ABOVE: The prototype undergoes engine trials at Weybridge with the help of a pair of bifurcated Cullum detuners in mid-June 1962. One of these detached during a full-power run of both engines on one side, blowing the unit 100ft (30m) down the taxiway.
BAE Systems via Brooklands Museum Trust

BELOW: Prototype G-ARTA lifts off from the Weybridge runway on **June 29, 1962.** *BAE Systems via Brooklands Museum Trust*

The **VC10** proved to be a very popular aircraft with passengers, attracting **ten per cent higher load factors** than the 707.

assistance which would have been required by the manufacturers of the VC10 [had a private venture not been insisted on when the aircraft was first ordered] to avoid the necessity for an inflated first order by BOAC".[37] Guthrie felt that BOAC had ordered 23 too many Super VC10s and wanted to cancel them and order seven more Boeings. Caught between its pledge to maintain Guthrie's freedom of action and responsibilities towards the aircraft industry (and with an election pending), the Government temporised. Eventually, the Government directed that BOAC should take 17 Super VC10s; the RAF would take three more (ultimately built as RAF Type 1106 hybrids), with the remainder "suspended without prejudice". BOAC also obtained a capital reconstruction.[38]

PROOF OF THE PUDDING

In the event, the VC10 proved to be a very popular aircraft with passengers, attracting ten per cent higher load factors than the 707.[39] It would also ultimately go on to give decades of stalwart service as a tanker/ transport for the RAF. But the commercial data are unyielding: a total of 12 Type 1101 VC10s and 17 Type 1151 Super VC10s were acquired by BOAC during 1964–69. After the last of the line, a Type 1154 Super VC10 for East African Airways, was delivered in February 1970, production was closed,

a mere 54 airframes having been built. In startling contrast, some 1,010 Boeing 707s and 556 Douglas DC-8s were sold to customers all over the world. Even the loss-making Convair 880 accrued 65 sales.

The VC10 as originally conceived was built to a narrowly-drawn specification; later attempts to broaden its appeal and improve its economics had only a marginal effect. Even the advantages of short-field performance from high-altitude airports were largely negated as many of the runways at those airports were lengthened to take the American jets.

So often seen as the villain in the post-war history of the British civil aircraft industry, BOAC found itself caught between the devil and the deep blue sea with the VC10. Statutory requirements to act in a commercial manner could be, and often were, compromised by constraints imposed by ideologically-driven government policies and/or appeals to patriotic duty to do the "right thing" by the domestic aircraft industry. This could be costly; the Corporation had overcome the aftermath of the Comet crisis as well as a difficult period with the Britannia. The 19-month delay in bringing the Britannia 102 into service had entailed a net loss to BOAC of some £3m (£67m). Delays in introducing the Britannia 312 series cost the airline at least £2m (£45m) in the financial year and every

ABOVE: Julian Amery, Secretary of State for Air during 1960–62 and Minister of Aviation from 1962 to 1964.

ABOVE: Rear Admiral Sir Matthew Slattery, BOAC Chairman during 1960–63, had previously held senior positions at Short Bros & Harland and Bristol.

ABOVE: Sir Giles Guthrie, who replaced Slattery in 1963.

ABOVE: BOAC's Conway-powered 707-436s entered regular service on June 6, 1960, with the inauguration of a thrice-weekly service from London to New York, the airline's Comet 4s being withdrawn from North Atlantic routes from October that year. The Corporation introduced the VC10 into service on African routes from April 1964. *TAH Archive*

month's delay thereafter added more than £500,000 (£11m) to its losses.[40]

In some cases, the quid pro quo was to demand aircraft "tailored" to its special requirements. This also applied to BEA, which seems to have been better able to drive harder bargains with both industry and ministers.[41] Sir Matthew Slattery tried and failed to get a clear mandate from Minister of Aviation Julian Amery. In Slattery's view, past chairmen had held "elastic" views on what were BOAC's best commercial interests.[42] In truth, as one authoritative review of post-war jet airliners observes, "neither Vickers nor BOAC seems to have shown much judgment of its commercial needs".[43]

The VC10 was the last of its breed; the last long-haul commercial aircraft to be built entirely in Britain. In the aftermath of a political requirement to operate the supersonic

Anglo-French BAC/Aérospatiale Concorde, BOAC (by then British Airways) would go on to win full independence of government direction over its aircraft procurement policy. Any remnants of the "buy British" policy would fade away completely with the privatisation of British Airways in 1987.

Ultimately, the British civil aircraft industry would survive and prosper as part of a European collective effort. But in the 1950s the Government adopted a pernicious and short-sighted doctrine, injurious to airline and manufacturer alike. The Corporation might have had the immediate advantage of tailoring designs to its requirements, but this meant nothing if operating the aeroplane cost it millions. For the manufacturer, tailoring carried the risk that other airlines would not buy the aircraft. In truth, the strategy was essentially conceived as a means for the Government to avoid directly supporting the civil aircraft industry. Instead, billions of pounds of taxpayers' money were wasted on an illusion; that the UK market could alone sustain increasingly complex and expensive aircraft programmes. ●

Acknowledgments
We would like to thank Abigail Wilson and Dick Curtis at Brooklands Museum (www.brooklandsmuseum.com) for their invaluable assistance with the preparation of this feature.

REFERENCES

1. See Keith Hayward, *The Blame Game – Vickers V.1000: The Ultimate Political Football?*, The Aviation Historian Issue 14
2. *Speedbird: The Complete History of BOAC*, Robin Higham, I.B. Tauris 2013, p210, and Keith Hayward, *Government and British Civil Aerospace*, Manchester University Press 1983, pp23–25
3. Sir Matthew Slattery, evidence to House of Commons Select Committee (HoCSC) on Nationalised Industries (1963–64), House of Commons Papers (HC) 42 Q 431; just sacked, Slattery was blamed for the huge deficit that BOAC had run up partly owing to its procurement policy
4. *A History of Aircraft Purchasing for the Air Corporations*, The National Archives (TNA) ref T319/141, 1963–64
5. BOAC evidence to HoCSC on Nationalised Industries (1963–64), HC 240 Q 431
6. Robin Higham, op cit, pp210–211; The Times, January 15, 1958. The costs of introducing the aircraft into service (proving), amounted to £10.7m p.a. (equivalent to £208m in 2017) in the early years, falling to £7.5m (£156m) as the aircraft became more established. TNA T319/141 op cit
7. Paper by Minister of Transport & Civil Aviation to Cabinet, September 13, 1956, part of Treasury document T319/141
8. ibid
9. While the VC10's aerodynamically clean wing did produce more lift, the choice of a rear-engined configuration added weight and reduced cabin length. Robin Higham, op cit
10. HC 240 op cit, paras 50–52 and Vickers evidence, Q 1547
11. Letter from Minister of Supply, May 6, 1957, to Chancellor of the Exchequer, TNA T319/141 op cit
12. ibid
13. Vickers and the Government also preferred to avoid a direct comparison with the American jets. Robin Higham, op cit, p212
14. *The Financial Problems of the British Overseas Airways Corporation*, Command Paper (5th series, 1956–86) passim, HMSO 1963; HC 42 (1963–64) Q 1542
15. Note of Cabinet Meeting July 27, 1959, TNA T319/141
16. Cited in Harold Evans, *Vickers Against the Odds, 1956–77*, Hodder & Stoughton 1978, p60
17. ibid pp58–59
18. Vickers papers, Box 445; held at the University of Cambridge Library
19. Note of Cabinet Meeting July 27,1959, op cit
20. See Keith Hayward, *Offers They Couldn't Refuse: Mergers in the British Aircraft Industry, 1957–62*, RAeS Journal of Aeronautical History, 2013
21. SCMS/165/1/1/2; Case for Maximum Aid for VC10 and VC11, November 11, 1959; Vickers Papers, op cit
22. Vickers papers, op cit
23. TNA AVIA 65/1084, Ministry of Aviation meeting with Vickers and English Electric, December 15, 1959
24. ibid, December 16, 1959. Also Cabinet Paper, note C.(59)185, December 16, 1959
25. Robin Higham, *Speedbird*, op cit, pp213–214
26. Treasury Minute January 21, 1960, T2251635
27. ibid
28. ibid
29. HC 240 (1963–64), op cit, para 240
30. T2251635, op cit
31. Letter to the Treasury, October 2, 1961, T2251635 op cit
32. ibid
33. Corbett's report, delivered in May 1963, was not published, but formed the basis of a White Paper published in November 1963; Command Paper, op cit
34. *Financial Problems of the British Overseas Airways Corporation*, memorandum by the Minister of Aviation, TNA AVIA 66/11, November 12, 1963
35. ibid
36. ibid
37. T2251635, op cit
38. Hayward, *Government and British Civil Aerospace*, op cit pp51–53
39. Robin Higham, *Speedbird*, op cit, pp213–214
40. Cabinet Minutes, October 14, 1957, TNA CAB/129/89/33
41. See Keith Hayward, *Trident: Britain's Fork in the Road*, The Aviation Historian Issue 16
42. HC 240, op cit, Appendix 19 and Q 1173
43. R. Miller and D. Sawers, *The Technical Development of Modern Aviation*, Praeger 1968, p201

BELOW: The scaled-down Super VC10 had a reduced fuselage stretch, from the originally intended 28ft to 13ft (3.9m), and no wingtip fuel tanks. The prototype, G-ASGA, made its first flight from Weybridge on May 7, 1964, and is seen here impressing visitors with its high-lift wing devices at the SBAC show at Farnborough the same year. *BAE Systems via Brooklands Museum Trust*

ABOVE: A magnificent publicity photograph of the third Trident 1, G-ARPC, which appeared alongside the first two examples at the SBAC show at Farnborough in September 1962, a mere two weeks after its first flight on August 25. Despite the innovative jetliner's sleek lines and excellent performance, its development suffered from political interference from the outset. *TAH Archive*

Trident: Britain's fork in the road?

Prof KEITH HAYWARD FRAeS turns his attention to the procurement of the Trident for BEA – a tragedy of errors which saw Britain hand the USA an uncatchable lead in the highly competitive jetliner market.

The 1955 cancellation of the Vickers V.1000 military transport and its airliner derivative, the VC7, is often viewed as the major failure of Britain's post-1945 civil aerospace policy. This is contestable.[1] But a clearer and far more damaging decision was the "tailoring" of the de Havilland 121, later to become the Trident, to a requirement set out by British European Airways (BEA). This lost the British aircraft industry an opportunity to forestall Boeing's successful entry into the medium-haul jet market with the three-engined 727, which would subsequently dominate the sector for a generation.

The most obvious villain in this sad story is BEA, whose shifting requirements undermined the Trident's wider commercial appeal; yet the airline's initial steadfast support for the D.H.121 was in some senses quite heroic, standing against Treasury and Ministry interference. Always in the background, however, were the effects of government policy, which forced reliance on a single domestic customer, and the underlying weakness of the UK aircraft industry, which forced it either to seek state aid or to follow the dictates of a dominant domestic customer.[2]

Led by Winston Churchill, the Conservative Government came to power in 1951 determined to end the policy of direct support for civil aircraft. Instead, projects would be funded by a mixture of private capital, buoyed by the anticipated profitability of the latest generation of aircraft, and launch orders from the nationalised airlines. In practice, problems affecting key programmes, notably the D.H.106 Comet and the subsequent government rescue of its manufacturer, de Havilland, forced a slower transition to the new regime. The government also wanted to improve the underlying strength of the aircraft industry by encouraging rationalisation through mergers, to be promoted by manipulating the award of public contracts.

From a legal standpoint the nationalised airlines – BEA and the British Overseas Airways Corporation (BOAC) – were free to choose their own equipment, but there was a strong expectation they would "buy British".

However, this could be costly; in addition to progress payments, the airlines would also carry the costs of "proving" airliners once in service, which could be very expensive, especially if the aircraft encountered problems that affected availability.[3]

By the mid-1950s BEA's business plan, centred around a fleet of turboprop-powered aircraft, was under pressure from competitors "rushing to jets", namely the French Sud Aviation Caravelle, the first short/medium-haul jetliner. Britain had no immediate answer, although de Havilland offered a Comet derivative. Concerned about the competition from jet operators, BEA rapidly adjusted its fleet-planning to include the Comet and a future new medium-range jet airliner.

LAUNCHING THE TRIDENT

At a press conference in April 1957 BEA's chair-man, Lord Douglas of Kirtleside, presented the airline's views on the future. In addition to six Comets as an interim jetliner, it wanted 24 advanced jets, with a preference for a 70-seat aircraft. Four companies had submitted designs to BEA's outline, these being: the Bristol Type 200; Avro (Hawker Siddeley Group) Type 740; Vickers VC11 (derived from the VC10); de Havilland 121.

The notion of buying the Caravelle, despite its British content – Rolls-Royce Avon engines and the nose and cockpit "borrowed" from the Comet – was dismissed out of hand. Development costs were estimated to be in the region of £20 million (equivalent to some £400 million today).[4]

The Ministry of Supply (MoS), the industry sponsor, wanted a speedy decision, "otherwise the thing will drag on indefinitely, with the risk of our losing the opportunity of repeating the 'killing' we made with the [Vickers] Viscount".[5] The Ministry was prepared to fund a prototype and a suitable engine, "in order to have adequate control over development".[6]

The Treasury, however, was less impressed. It was unprepared for the "bombshell" request for two types of aircraft and dismissed the "Caravelle bogey" as the usual MoS hankering after the old days of direct government funding.[7] At the end of August 1957,

ABOVE: An artist's impression of the Bristol 200, designed by project office staff at Filton to BEA's specification for a subsonic short-range jetliner. Similar in configuration to the D.H.121, with three rear-mounted engines and a high-T-tail, the unbuilt Bristol 200 had a span of 91ft (27.75m), and was to accommodate 79–99 passengers.
TAH Archive

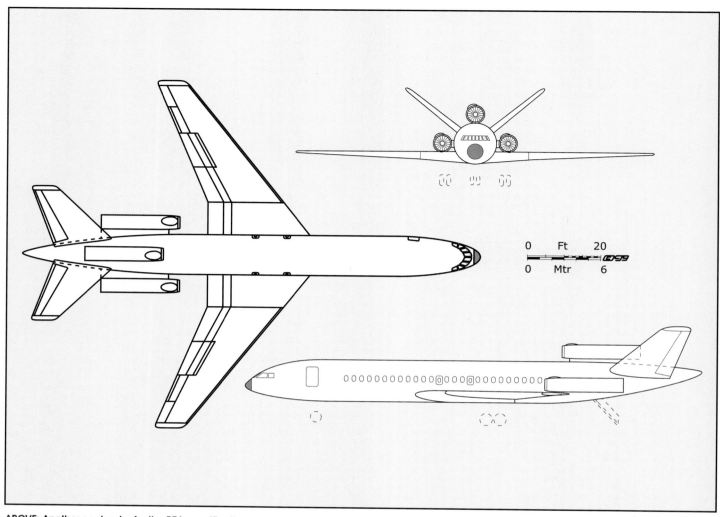

ABOVE: Another contender for the BEA specification was Avro, which proposed an unusual design in which the No 2 engine would sit atop the rear fuselage between the fins of the V-tail. Artwork by Chris Gibson. *CHRIS GIBSON © 2016*

under considerable pressure to approve funding so that the news could be announced at the SBAC show at Farnborough in September, the Treasury agreed to the purchase of Comet 4Bs for BEA, but not to the new jet or its engine.[8]

On September 4, 1957, BEA formally requested Treasury permission to acquire a new jet aircraft, namely the de Havilland 121.[9] The airline had wanted to stay with Vickers, but unfortunately the company "was not prepared to develop the type of aeroplane required". The same applied to the Bristol and HSG proposals and initially to de Havilland. However, having lost a substantial BOAC order to Vickers for the VC10, "de Havilland [has] accepted the views of the Corporation about the best type of aircraft to meet the requirement, and the company [has] now submitted proposals which are closely tailored to the BEA specification".[10]

The MoS was asked to order a prototype at

a cost of £2.5 million (£45.3 million today). The Treasury felt that the cost estimates of £1 million (£22.3 million) per aircraft was not unreasonable based on the Comet experience. However, "none of the reasons listed for preferring de Havilland as the manufacturer of the new aircraft touches on the cost of development or the ability of the manufacturer to bear this cost". Officials were puzzled by the rejection out of hand of Avro, which, as part of the Hawker Siddeley Group, "represents one of the wealthiest firms in the industry, and also one which has a dire need of a new project to keep it alive as an aircraft firm".[11]

A DEAL COMES TOGETHER

The Treasury felt that an initial order for 24 aircraft should be big enough for de Havilland to develop the new type as a private venture; officials saw no reason to buy a prototype, although they were attracted to the novel idea advanced by the

MoS that a proportion of the estimated development costs of the engine – £5 million (£112 million) – could be repaid by a levy on sales. "This is the first time the Ministry of Supply [has] proposed assistance for the development of an engine for a civil aircraft in this particular form, and whatever one may think of it, or of the whole question of government assistance to the aircraft industry, it is an improvement [at] any rate on the old-fashioned open-ended commitment of total or shared development costs".[12]

A more astringent official also noted that "this is probably none of our business, but I wonder how long the MoS is going to play shove-million with the taxpayers' money? A ray of hope appeared when BOAC and Vickers got together on the VC10 without looking for subsidies – why cannot BEA and de Havilland do likewise?"[13]

By November 1957 the bones of a deal were coming together. The MoS had moved away from directly funding a prototype, Rolls-Royce was prepared to risk £22 million (£492 million) on a new engine (with £5 million from public sources) and a launch order for 24 aircraft should be sufficient to cover costs.

The Treasury was well aware of the importance of the order to Rolls-Royce and

*The MoS was asked to order a **prototype** at a cost of **£2.5 million (£45.3 million** today). The Treasury felt that the cost estimates of **£1 million (£22.3 million) per aircraft** was not unreasonable based on the Comet experience.*

especially to de Havilland: "It is scarcely an exaggeration to say that de Havilland's future depends upon it". But, it added, the MoS "has drawn our attention to the fact that both firms will have to stretch [their] resources even with limited government help. They are aware that it is the policy of Her Majesty's Government [HMG] to withdraw from the financing of the aircraft industry as quickly as practicable. But if the axe is brought down too quickly the industry will collapse".[14]

Although BEA wanted the de Havilland design, a joint HSG/Bristol design was still in the race and increasingly favoured by the MoS and the Treasury on the grounds that the contract should be used to encourage rationalisation, and that de Havilland appeared to be financially the weaker contestant.[15] Treasury officials felt that "it would be desirable that the Government should seek to influence BEA, so far as possible, to place [its] order with Bristol rather than de Havilland".

The Treasury was hopeful that the Minister of Transport & Civil Aviation (MoTCA), Harold Watkinson, would "do his best to prod BEA in the direction of [an HSG/Bristol] consortium, because such unions are what the Government [is] trying to encourage in the British aircraft industry".[16] However, a closer examination of the financial position of the companies revealed that in some respects de Havilland was in a far better financial state than was initially evident: "I would pause before arguing that de Havilland does not compare on the grounds of financial strength". [17]

In December 1957 BEA reported that, having "tailored [its] design" to BEA requirements, de Havilland was now in the lead "by a fair margin". The specification was very tightly drawn; although de Havilland stated that it generally concurred with BEA, its management also stated that the terms were "more onerous than anything D.H. had previously undertaken".[18] But as de Havilland was already producing Comet 4Bs for the airline, and was in a desperate financial state following the earlier Comet disaster, it was keen to protect its position as BEA's preferred supplier. A formal decision was delayed while the company found financing for a private venture, but de Havilland refused to look for a group option until the D.H.121 contract was confirmed.[19]

THE MINISTERIAL DISPUTE
At this point the MoS and MoTCA began to diverge, belying their ostensible unity in public. If BEA had settled on the D.H.121 design, Aubrey Jones, the newly appointed – and harder-line – Minister of Supply thought otherwise. This difference of perspective set the scene for a brief but intense debate within the government, with BEA briefing heavily in support of the D.H.121.

Jones was forthright about the need to use the power of contract to push industry into stronger units, the better to compete with the Americans. As he explained: "To have pursued this policy through mere enthusiasm would have been profitless; to have resorted to compulsion would have been undesirable, and impossible without legislation; the only other course was to use the power of contract".[20]

The requirement of BEA for a short-haul jetliner was the first civil contract available for such "manipulation". A joint Cabinet memorandum by Harold Watkinson and Aubrey Jones dated January 23, 1958, states that "short of legislation, HMG has no effective method of bringing this policy to fruition other than the power of contract, though economic forces will also play their somewhat slow part. We have therefore been considering whether it is possible to combine the objectives of meeting the BEA requirement and at the same time laying the foundations for the rationalisation and redeployment of resources of the aircraft industry."[21]

The same month the Cabinet met to discuss the issue. Jones and Watkinson fought their respective corners for industry and airline; the Cabinet was unable to resolve the issue and decided to wait for further advice.[22] Jones felt that a grouping of HSG/Bristol "alone among British air-frame constructors would come within some distance of matching the strength of the present American competition". Hawker Siddeley was also part of a stronger diversified concern and had the most extensive research and development facilities in the country.[23] It was essential that these be put at the disposal of civil industry.

The joint HSG/Bristol design also had a wider market in mind and could meet a Pan American requirement for a larger aircraft. Unless HSG/Bristol got the nod, "we are only too likely to see continue... our post-war history of seeking the prizes that are obtainable in the field of civil aircraft but without an industrial organisation capable of realising them".[24]

This produced an immediate response from Harold Watkinson; Pan Am's requirement had no bearing on the issue and he had no power to force BEA to take the HSG/Bristol aircraft, "nor would I wish to". The British airline had a statutory requirement to act in its best interest and could see no reason why the de Havilland design would not go on to "wider commercial success".[25] On January 30, 1958, moving quickly to shore up its industrial position, de Havilland announced the formation of Airco, a group comprising the Fairey Aviation Co Ltd and Hunting Aircraft, to build the D.H.121.

The MoS was still not convinced that Airco's capitalisation of £100 million (£1.7 billion) would be enough. Watkinson was rather more confident. The Airco consortium appeared to have a solid financial and technical foundation and an order for 24 aircraft from BEA would enable de Havilland to finance

ABOVE: William Sholto Douglas, 1st Baron Douglas of Kirtleside, BEA's Chairman during 1949–64.

ABOVE: Peter Thorneycroft, who, as Chancellor of the Exchequer, held the government's purse strings from January 1957 to January 1958.

ABOVE: Harold Watkinson, Minister of Transport & Civil Aviation from December 1955 to October 1959.

ABOVE: An artist's impression of the D.H.121 as initially proposed to BEA in the spring of 1957, incorporating a straight-through intake for the No 2 engine and a low-set tailplane. By 1958 the design had been revised to include a T-tail and an S-shaped duct feeding air to the No 2 engine buried in the tail. *BAE Systems*

*Lord Douglas of Kirtleside was determined to have the **D.H.121**. It was exactly the **design** BEA had **specified,** and he was confident that de Havilland had the **resources.***

the new jetliner's development. The de Havilland group was also felt to be more experienced in the export business.[26]

On the other hand, Minister of Supply Jones felt that the government should not be rushed into a decision just because there was "public clamour for an announcement". He felt that the Airco offer was too vague and contained the future risk of "rescue operations of some magnitude".[27] The Hawker Siddeley Group had been hit hard by the 1957 Defence White Paper, and Jones feared that it might go "out of the aircraft business altogether".[28] The prospect of wider sales was also in Jones's mind: "It may well be that while BEA, in many ways a uniquely situated airline, inclines [its] preference one way, world demand may incline a different way. If this were to turn out to be so and we had prematurely opted for the aircraft of BEA choice, exports would prove to be limited and the promise of private venture would be nullified."[29]

Jones went further: "In the past it has been the practice to allow BEA to specify [its] requirements for a new aircraft without regard to the requirements of prospective foreign purchasers. The future prosperity of the British aircraft industry, however, [will] depend increasingly on its success in the export market. It [will] therefore be important to give greater weight to export prospects in determining the types of civil aircraft to be manufactured in this country. For this reason the present initiative of the HSG/Bristol consortium should be encouraged."[30]

The dispute did not go unnoticed by the press. Hawker Siddeley was forced into issuing a public statement, which read:

"Let there be an end to this ill-informed gossip that the product we are offering is technically inferior to that of our competitors, and that we are engaged in some form of plot with the connivance of Ministers of the Crown to force an inferior product on a reluctant customer".[31]

BEA GETS ITS AEROPLANE

Meanwhile, Lord Douglas of Kirtleside was determined to have the D.H.121. It was exactly the design BEA had specified, and he was confident that de Havilland had the resources to launch the programme on the back of the BEA order. Watkinson threw his weight powerfully behind the BEA position, stating categorically that he had "no power to require BEA to take the [HSG/Bristol] project against the Corporation's own wishes. Nor, if I had the power, would I wish to do so". He continued: "Whatever might go wrong with the project during development, whether delay in delivery or technical difficulty or misadventure of any kind whatever, would be attributed by BEA and by outside critics as my fault and that of the Government, [which] had forced the Corporation to take an aircraft not of its own choosing".[32]

Furthermore, he could not "refuse to allow BEA to place its order where it wants. I have gone as far as I can to help the Minister of Supply with his plans for the future of the aircraft industry. To go further would make me a party to the principle that, in connection with this order, which is being placed by the Corporation and not by the Government, BEA can, in a fashion which [it] believes to be contrary to [its] own best interests and to [its] statutory duty, be used as an instrument of Government policy for bringing about a reorganisation of the aircraft industry".[33]

Both groups of companies were offering their designs as private ventures and both were anxious to achieve overseas sales, and Watkinson could not see "on what grounds we can base a refusal to allow BEA to exercise its technical judgment".[34]

The UK clearly could not afford to see two aircraft going forward, as this would only increase the risk of financial failure and a "substantial risk that the Exchequer would have to rescue both of them before the end of the day". Politically, it was also desirable to avoid a public split with BEA, where there was a risk of wholesale resignations from the BEA board "if they did not get their way". There was no legal power to stop BEA from choosing the de Havilland product.[35] This broke Jones's resistance. On February 12, 1958, with little further debate, the Cabinet agreed to allow BEA to buy the D.H.121 – by now named Trident – subject to detailed negotiations.[36] Accordingly, that August, Airco was awarded a contract for 25 aircraft worth £574 million (£10 billion).

There is no evidence that de Havilland had any qualms about acceding to BEA's original specification. While the design team regarded some of the requirements as being rather onerous, the new aircraft's basic size was consistent with the company's views about wider market requirements. The initial airframe design could seat 111 passengers and the proposed Rolls-Royce RB.141 Medway low-bypass turbofan engine would provide plenty of "stretch" potential.[37]

Early in 1959, however, BEA began to express second thoughts about its requirement. The airline's commercial division predicted a sharp drop in demand, which would have led to over-capacity in its planned fleet of Trident and Vanguard airliners. As a result, BEA asked de Havilland to alter the Trident design to accommodate a maximum of 87 seats, with a less powerful engine, the RB.163 Spey. The airline paid de Havilland £200,000 (£3.5 million) for the change, but had, at a stroke, reduced the wider attractiveness of the aircraft and added six months to its development schedule. Objections from within the company were overruled by Aubrey Burke, de Havilland's Managing Director, who vetoed discussion with other airlines until the changes were made.[38]

The MoS was not happy with the changes, stating that "the aircraft is evidently tailored to meet the needs of BEA with a predominantly short-stage network. Other operators

BELOW: Aubrey Jones took over the reins of the Ministry of Supply from Reginald Maudling on January 16, 1957, and served as the last Minister of Supply until October 1959, when the ministry was abolished.

may well require longer stages, which would necessitate an increase in gross weight. BEA is unusual among large operators in having no stages longer than 1,400 miles [2,250km] and a preponderance of stages under 1,100 miles [1,770km]". Wider sales would depend on efficient operation over longer stage lengths, and "it is not known what steps the firm intends to take in developing the D.H.121's range capability, or the extent [to which it has] sought overseas requirements in this matter, but evidently this could be an important consideration affecting the type's sales prospects".

The airline disagreed, arguing that 70 per cent of the world's stage-lengths were less than 1,000 miles (1,610km) and that "operators would recognise the advantages of an aircraft specially tailored to short ranges".[39] Kirtleside was quick to defend the downsizing of the Trident, citing the fact that the Viscount had been optimised for the same sector lengths and had sold very well to other operators. The airline also claimed that de Havilland's own market research had been weak and denied responsibility for blighting the Trident's prospects.[40] Given that BEA was funding the programme, there was little that the MoS could do to affect the outcome.

OPPORTUNITY LOST

Inexorably, Aubrey Jones's gloomy forecasts were borne out by events. In 1959 Boeing launched its 727, designed from the outset for 130 passengers and with scope for further "stretch". The forecasts of BEA were soon proven to be over-pessimistic and the 727 ran away with the market, with more than 2,000 examples being sold, in contrast to the Trident's 115. To rub further salt into the wound, BEA would eventually express interest in acquiring a 189-seat version of the 727, a request that was turned down in favour of developments of the Trident.[41]

This was not to be the end of the Trident saga, however. As part of the rationalisation process which took place during 1959–62, which saw de Havilland absorbed into Hawker Siddeley Aviation (HSA), the newly formed consortium received retrospectively what was now described as "launch aid" for the Trident.[42] This did not come without some official doubts: "Critics are already beginning to say that it is ridiculous of us to put money into aircraft such as the D.H.121, which will be outdated by the time it comes into service".[43] But as Vickers was also to receive help for its proposed medium-range VC11 and the ailing VC10 programme, equity dictated that HSA should receive comparable backing.[44]

BELOW: With Air France ordering Caravelle short-haul jetliners in 1956, BEA had little choice but to order a fleet of six (upgraded to seven) de Havilland Comet 4Bs in April 1958. The stretched 99-passenger variant entered BEA service in November 1959, initially as a stopgap until the Trident could take over. This BEA Comet 4B is seen being loaded in July 1960. *BAE Systems*

In 1961 the Government was also approached for help in developing a larger version of the Trident, to be known as the Trident Two. This was largely motivated by HSA's growing financial problems and the Ministry of Aviation (evolved from the MoTCA and established in 1959) sympathetically supported the request. The Trident Two also had better sales prospects than the original Trident.[45] Hawker Siddeley Aviation believed that it could secure 140 sales out of a forecast world market of 300 aircraft and asked the Government for £7.5 million (£131 million) out of a total project cost of £27.5 million (£479 million).[46]

The Treasury was not impressed, stating: "This proposal is less than half-baked and it is highly doubtful whether any development

ABOVE: The first Trident, G-ARPA, made its maiden flight on January 9, 1962, in the hands of John Cunningham, before undertaking a thorough trials programme. "Papa Alpha" is seen here roaring away on one such test flight. A stellar performer in the air, the type acquired the nickname "groundgripper" owing to its reluctance to get airborne. *TAH Archive*

despairingly, another official asked: "Is it worth spending another £4.25 million [£74 million] in the hope of getting some of our money back?"[48]

It was soon apparent that these estimates were optimistic and that, in its eagerness to bail out HSA during 1960–61, the MoS had been somewhat economical with the truth. An August 1963 memo from the Treasury reveals the strength of its feeling about the MoS:

"Our main concern at the time was the financial soundness of the manufacturing company. It was, to say the least, very remiss of [the MoS] to present a proposition to us in this way. You may feel that it would be flogging a dead horse to complain about this now, but it is very relevant to the proposals which we shall get in due course to add [more] to the existing order."[49]

By January 1964 the Trident had secured only 44 sales, of which 33 were to BEA – and the Treasury was already writing off its investment.[50]

In 1965 the Treasury launched an official review of the history of the Trident, part of which stated that "BEA, for [which] the Trident was

The Trident *acquired the nickname* **"groundgripper"** *owing to its reluctance to get airborne.*

of the Trident can be called a promising project".[47] But by this time the Treasury appears to have given up the will to resist. "Unless we help HSA improve the aircraft to attract more customers, we can say farewell to our £5 million [£87 million]". Rather

BELOW: In October 1963 the fifth production Trident, G-ARPE, undertook the type's first overseas sales tour, which covered Japan, Hong Kong, Singapore, Pakistan and Syria. John Cunningham was at the controls for the tour, accompanied by BEA Captains A.S. Johnson and W.R. Mitchell. "Papa Echo" is seen here at Tokyo-Narita in Japan, where de Havilland was keen to garner orders from Japanese airline All Nippon. None materialised, unfortunately. Note the open No 2 engine access doors. *TAH Archive*

tailor-made, [has] changed [its] mind about the version [it] would need for future orders with bewildering rapidity. In terms of equity, however, the party that should really suffer is BEA, [which has] got everyone into this muddle".[51]

This was not to be. In 1967, instead of its preferred option – the British Aircraft Corporation's Two-Eleven, an entirely new design – BEA was compelled to take the even larger Trident Three as an interim

The **"tailoring"** of British airliner designs to the narrow interests of national airlines ended only with **British Airways' privatisation** in 1987.

LEFT: With its elegant, aerodynamically efficient contours and powerful Rolls-Royce Spey turbofan engines – as used in contemporary fighters such as the Blackburn Buccaneer and McDonnell Douglas F-4K Phantom – the Trident boasted superb performance in the cruise, often sustaining speeds of up to 600–610 m.p.h. (965–980km/h). *TAH Archive*

aircraft while an "airbus" was put into development.[52] This was something of a dog's dinner of a solution but was perhaps the natural outcome of the failure to launch an adequately-sized D.H.121 aimed at a world market.

The "tailoring" of British airliner designs to the narrow interests of a nationalised airline under pressure to "buy British" was a commercially deadly combination. The practice ended only with the privatisation of British Airways and the arrival of the multinational Airbus consortium, to the considerable benefit of both the national airline and aerospace industries. ●

BELOW: Flying the flag for Britain – tenth production Trident 1 G-ARPJ lifts its nose as it departs Hatfield. "Papa Juliet" was delivered to BEA in May 1964 and served with the airline until March 1975. *TAH Archive*

REFERENCES

1. See Keith Hayward, The Blame Game – Vickers V.1000: The Ultimate Political Football?, The Aviation Historian Issue 14, January 2016
2. This was an issue that would also affect the Vickers VC10
3. For a more detailed review of the "Buy British" policy see Keith Hayward, Government and British Civil Aerospace: A Case Study in Post-war Technology Policy, Manchester University Press, 1983, pp31–34
4. Minutes of Transport Aircraft Requirements Committee (TARC) meeting, April 2, 1957, The National Archives (TNA) reference AVIA 63/14
5. Ministry of Supply (MoS) memoranda to the Treasury, August 1 and August 7, 1957, TNA ref T 228/587
6. MoS memorandum to Treasury, August 15, 1957, ibid
7. Treasury memorandum, August 12, 1957, ibid
8. Treasury memorandum, August 29, 1957, ibid
9. BEA memo to the Treasury, September 4, 1957, ibid
10. ibid
11. Treasury note on the re-equipment programme, October 30, 1957, and Treasury memorandum November 6, 1957, ibid
12. This may well be the first formal manifestation of the Repayable Launch Aid (now Launch Investment) Scheme; ibid
13. Treasury memorandum November 4, 1957, ibid. Vickers had launched the VC10 on the back of a BOAC order; by 1959 the cost of development would have taken the former company close to bankruptcy
14. ibid
15. Treasury memoranda November 18, 1957, and January 3, 1958, ibid
16. Treasury letter to Sir Thomas Padmore, January 3, 1958, ibid; Padmore was chairing an internal inquiry into the state of the UK aircraft industry
17. Treasury letter to Sir Thomas Padmore, January 10, 1958, ibid
18. Flight, May 29,1959, p753
19. Minutes of TARC meeting, December 6, 1957, TNA ref AVIA 63/14; Hayward 1983, op cit, p29 and p33
20. Minister of Supply memorandum to Cabinet, February 4,1958, TNA T228/587. The MoD's OR.339 (TSR-2) contract would soon become an even more powerful "carrot"
21. TNA ref CAB 129/91/19
22. Aircraft for British European Airways, Joint Memorandum by the Minister of Transport & Civil Aviation and the Minister of Supply, January 23, 1958, TNA ref CAB 129/91/19
23. This is debatable, however. English Electric probably had the more modern facilities
24. Minister of Supply memorandum to Cabinet February 4, 1958, op cit
25. Minister of Transport & Civil Aviation memo to Cabinet, 4th February 4, 1958, ibid
26. TNA ref CAB/129/58
27. Letter from Minister of Supply to Chancellor Heathcote Amory, February 11, 1958, T228/587
28. TNA ref CAB 129/91/19
29. ibid
30. Memorandum by the Minister of Supply, January 24, 1958, TNA ref CAB/128/32
31. Flight, January 17, 1958, p69
32. British European Airways, memorandum by the Minister of Transport & Civil Aviation, January 31, 1958, TNA ref CAB/129/58
33. ibid
34. ibid
35. Treasury memorandum, February 11, 1958, T228/587
36. Cabinet minutes, February 12, 1958, ibid
37. Hayward 1983, op cit, p33
38. At BEA's suggestion, Boeing and de Havilland discussed the possibility of a joint project. Nothing came of this, but it did entail revealing key aspects of the Trident design. Hayward 1983, op cit, p34; based on 1981 interviews with a former senior de Havilland designer
39. TARC briefing on history of the Trident, May 1967, TNA ref AVIA 63/41
40. TARC minutes, September 16, 1959, TNA ref T225/1635; Hayward 1983, op cit, p34
41. Treasury memoranda, September 26, 1963, October 15, 1963 and January 2, 1964, TNA ref T225/2318
42. Now known as "repayable launch investment". The scheme was essentially the format proposed by the MoS for funding development of the Trident during 1956–57
43. Memoranda May 10, 18 and 20 and July 19, 1960, January 17 and 19 and February 13, 1961; AVIA 63/40
44. Although it was denied by Vickers, the larger VC11 was effectively a competitor to the Trident. Failing to win orders, the project was terminated in 1962
45. Note by the Ministry of Aviation, "Position of the Hawker Siddeley Aviation Group", November 29, 1961, TNA ref T225/2318
46. Letter from D.L. Havilland, Deputy Secretary, Ministry of Aviation, to A.D. Peck, Treasury, May 29, 1962, ibid
47. Treasury memorandum, December 4, 1961, ibid
48. Treasury memorandum, August 8, 1963, TNA T319/149
49. ibid
50. Treasury memoranda, September 26 and October 15, 1963 and January 2, 1964, TNA ref T225/2318
51. Treasury memorandum, June 21, 1965, T319/149
52. The airline was nevertheless "compensated" for the forced order; Hayward 1983, op cit, pp85–86

Trident

A close shave at Wellington

In 1959 a trio of Avro Vulcans of No 617 Sqn set off on a tour which was to set a new world circumnavigation record and fly the flag for the capabilities of the Cold War RAF. An important part of the trip was to make an impression at the opening of the new airport in the New Zealand capital, Wellington. An impression was certainly made – but not quite the one intended, as JONATHAN POTE relates.

BELOW: Still looking futuristic more than six decades after the type's first flight, three Vulcans of the first B.1 production batch formate in line astern in their distinctive all-over anti-nuclear-flash white markings. The Vulcan B.1 entered frontline RAF service with No 83 Sqn at Waddington in May 1957. *TAH Archive*

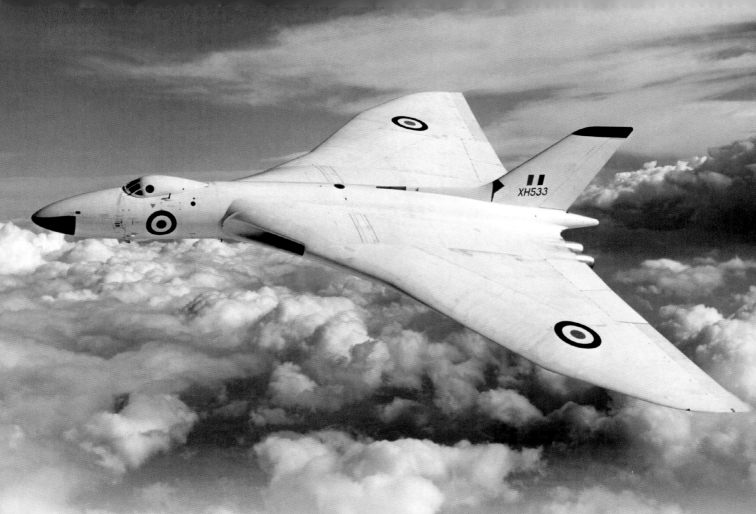

ABOVE: A magnificent Avro photograph of the first production Vulcan B.2, XH553, showing its supremely elegant delta form above the clouds. The B.2 introduced a modified wing with an extended and cambered leading edge, which improved handling and performance at altitude, and the more powerful Olympus Series 200 powerplant.
TAH Archive

Wellington, although the capital of New Zealand (and both the most southerly and most remote capital city in the world), is dwarfed by Auckland. A major reason for this is the former's cramped topography, set around a flooded volcanic depression open to the Cook Strait. The steep terrain (and the strong, turbulent winds of the Strait) meant that until the late 1950s there was no international airport. To rectify that, a hill of four million cubic yards surmounted by nearly 200 houses was levelled, clearing the northern approach while providing rock for the runway extension into the sea. The opening of Wellington International Airport on Sunday, October 25, 1959, was thus planned to be a memorable occasion. At last the capital would have something more than a small landing ground and passengers need no longer suffer the two-hour drive from Paraparaumu, itself only served by internal air services. The airport would be a huge economic boost to the city.

Memorable it was, but not in the way its organisers intended. Lockheed Lodestar ZK-BVE top-dressing the new runway was the least of the spectacles; when the day was over, a Royal New Zealand Air Force (RNZAF) Short Sunderland (NZ4113/"M") lay hurriedly beached at Hobsonville, near Auckland, awaiting major repairs after splitting its hull as it scraped the runway. It was not the only aircraft to strike the runway dangerously, as, at Ohakea, the RNZAF base

well north of Wellington, an Avro Vulcan lay slewed off the runway and would not fly again that year. Vulcan B.1 XH498 had nearly caused what would have been New Zealand's greatest ever loss of life. The navigator aboard XH498 that fateful day was Wg Cdr Bryn Lewis, who returned to New Zealand recently after more than 50 years to tell his story at Ohakea.

THINKING GLOBAL

In 1958 the Government of New Zealand requested the British Government to instruct the RAF to attend the opening of Wellington International Airport the following year. The RAF in turn saw a great opportunity to perform the Service's first world circumnavigation, gaining much operational knowledge and favourable publicity in the process. The task was given to No 1 Group, RAF Bomber Command, to organise, and No 617 Sqn – the famous "Dambusters" – was selected to undertake it. As the squadron's leading navigator, Bryn Lewis settled down to plan the epic flight for three Vulcans. Engineering support was to be provided by groundcrew flying in a Bristol Britannia of No 99 Sqn, XL638, *Sirius,* itself a new type in service. A de Havilland Comet C.2 and a Blackburn Beverley also joined the detachment.

The RAF station at Akrotiri on Cyprus was the obvious first nightstop, but then the route planning became difficult. The only available route in the late 1950s lay across Turkey and Persia to Karachi in Pakistan. Fine, except that this passed close to the Soviet border, and it was known that the Russians had an "evil twin" of the Turkish beacon at Van, intended deliberately to lure Western aircraft north into Soviet territory where they could be forced down for intelligence gathering. The Russian beacon, situated at Yerevan in Armenia, transmitted on the same frequency as the Turkish beacon at Van but with greater power and in 1958 lured a USAF Lockheed C-130A Hercules on an electronic eavesdropping mission across the border. The Hercules was shot down by Soviet MiG-17s.

In April 1959, just six months before the Vulcans' flight, Avro Super Trader G-AGRH, *Zephyr*, may have been similarly misled, as recounted by Roger Carvell in his feature *Ill Wind* in TAH2. The Super Trader crashed on Mount Süphan, a 13,000ft (4,000m)-high Turkish peak, while headed for the Soviet border. There followed an almighty rush by an RAF Mountain Rescue team from Cyprus to reach the wreckage, not primarily to recover the dozen bodies but because *Zephyr* was carrying highly secret missile components to the range at Woomera in Australia. These could not be allowed to fall into Soviet hands. A route via Aden and Gan in the Maldives would seem to have been far safer, but Bryn was not given reasons, just instructions.

On board with him in the lead aircraft, XH498, would be Air Vice-Marshal John Davis, Air Officer Commanding (AOC) No 1 Group. What a prize an intact (or even crashed) Vulcan and a very high-ranking officer, fully briefed on Nato war plans, would have been for the Soviets.

THE TOUR BEGINS
On October 14, 1959, four Vulcans of No 617 Sqn departed from the unit's base at Scampton between 1150hr and 1250hr. They were XH498, commanded by Sqn Ldr A.A.

Smailes; XH499 (Sqn Ldr D.B. Hamley); XH502 (Flt Lt L.G. Lunn) and XH483 (Flt Lt R.S. Trigg). The latter was not part of the antipodean adventure but was taking part in a *Profiteer* detachment to Malaya, in which aircraft from UK-based units were sent to reinforce local units for *Firedog* operations against communist terrorists. The big delta bombers flew singly, 20min apart, the last aircraft in the trail indeed seeing a pair of MiG-17s lurking in the distance across the Soviet/Turkish border.

Arrival in Karachi was not without incident. All pilots were ordered by the squadron commander to deploy braking parachutes on landing so as to reduce the demands on the brakes in the hot climate. Nevertheless, 10min after parking at Karachi, the wheelbrakes of XH483 caught fire as a result of a hydraulic leak. Fortunately, a crew member was able to insist that dry powder was used by the emergency vehicles; foam could have caused the ceramic brakes to explode, rupturing the wing tanks and causing a conflagration of all three aircraft. (The crippled aircraft was repaired and flew on to Butterworth in Malaya on October 19.)

The three remaining Vulcans departed Karachi for Butterworth on October 17, before heading on to Darwin, Australia, a place of which Bryn does not have fond memories – "wooden huts on stilts, 90°F temperature and 100 per cent humidity" – but, on October 19, flying at 45,000ft (13,700m), they easily broke the Darwin–Ohakea record. Few aircraft (and no jets) had ever flown the route.

SHOWING THE FLAG
In the days leading up to the Wellington ceremony the three Vulcans – XH498, XH499 and XH502 – "showed the flag" as widely as possible the length and breadth of New Zealand. Bryn's aircraft flew down the Southern Alps and over Aoraki/Mt Cook before descending to display at 500ft (150m) over Invercargill at the very southern tip of South Island before flying up the east coast at low level. The other Vulcans covered the west coast of South Island and much of the North Island, being seen by many people.

As well as the RAF presence at Wellington, the USAF contributed two Hercules and a Boeing KB-50 refuelling a North American F-100 Super Sabre, a McDonnell F-101 Voodoo and a Douglas B-66 Destroyer, while the Royal Australian Air Force sent several English Electric Canberras.

For the Wellington ceremony, the plan was for a "V" of three Vulcans to sweep majestically across the city, and for one to land. Sadly the weather had other ideas, and under low cloud just XH498 left Ohakea (although all three were seen over the city on practice days). The mighty jet completed two touch-and-goes before lining up for a landing on the 5,250ft (1,600m) runway, notorious for the turbulence on its final approach. Bryn was unstrapped and out of his seat. In the case of a repeat of the Karachi incident, he was to exit the cockpit immediately the aircraft halted,

In the days leading up to the Wellington ceremony the three Vulcans – XH498, XH499 and XH502 – "showed the flag" as widely as possible the length and breadth of New Zealand.

ABOVE: Vulcan B.1 XH498 was one of 20 built in the second production batch, delivered between January 1958 and April 1959, and was one of the three sent on No 617 Sqn's circumnavigation tour in 1959. It was also the one that came to grief during the Wellington Airport opening ceremony.
Alan Todd Collection via Lee Howard

holding a powder fire-extinguisher to attack the first brake unit to burst into flames. Instead of the normal sound and feel of a positive landing, however, there was a very loud impact and the aircraft veered to port.

As with all Vulcan crew, Bryn was well aware of the Heathrow tragedy three years earlier. On October 1, 1956, Vulcan XA897, returning from Operation *Tasman* (a visit to New Zealand and Australia with Air Chief Marshal Harry Broadhurst, AOC-in-C RAF Bomber Command on board), had attempted to land at Heathrow in very bad weather. The aircraft was too low on approach and impacted a cabbage patch half a mile short of the runway. The undercarriage was forced up into the wings, severing the control runs and rupturing the fuel tanks. The massive delta was now an unguided ballistic missile. The pilot, Sqn Ldr "Podge" Howard, ejected, and while the Air Chief Marshal bravely tried to control the stricken aircraft, his choice was stark. He could not save the others as they had no ejection seats; he could either die with them or save himself alone. He ejected late, the other five (there were two supernumerary persons aboard – a crew chief and an Avro representative) dying in the inferno.

CRUNCH!

In fact XH498 had struck the lip of Wellington's Runway 34 with both main undercarriage bogies. The port unit was forced back 45°, allowing the wingtip to drag on the runway. The damaged bogie also ruptured fuel lines within the undercarriage bay, fuel streaming out but mercifully not igniting ("or we would have beaten Concorde to it" as Bryn observes wryly).

In reply to a tense query from the pilot, Tony Smailes, air traffic control urgently replied "Go around, go around". Fortunately the four Bristol Olympus turbojets responded rapidly. As Bryn struggled to put his

WING COMMANDER BRYN LEWIS

As a teenager Bryn Lewis became a civilian meteorological observer attached to the RAF during the Second World War, and was thus debarred from call-up. In late 1942, however, the RAF began recruiting its own Met observers and Bryn was among the first of only 180 men ever awarded the "M" brevet of Meteorological Air Observers. He flew with No 521 Sqn from Bircham Newton and Docking in Norfolk in obsolescent Handley Page Hampdens and later in Lockheed Hudsons and Venturas. Moving to No 519 Sqn (Hudsons and Venturas), based at RAF Wick in northern Scotland, Bryn flew on *Recipe* sorties that headed north beyond the Arctic circle to sample the polar front at both low and high altitude.

He then transferred to No 518 Sqn, flying Handley Page Halifaxes out of Tiree in the Hebrides in 1945 (when the accompanying photograph was taken). These aircraft ranged as far out into the Atlantic as fuel allowed (700 nautical miles – 1,300km – with minimal reserves) and a change of wind direction could leave them in mortal danger. The Halifaxes flew fully armed with depth charges to be able to attack U-boats sighted by chance but Bryn never saw the human enemy in his 800hr Coastal Command tour. He met a more dangerous foe, the weather, daily. On June 3, 1944, it was the meteorological observations of 518 Sqn that predicted the storm of June 5, and the improvement expected on June 6. Meteorologist Gp Capt Stagg recommended to Gen Eisenhower that Operation *Overlord* – the D-Day landings – be delayed by 24hr, thus changing almost certain failure into hard-won success and defining the course of history.

After the war, in a twist that only the RAF could manage, Bryn was commissioned as an accounting officer, but was promptly retrained as a navigator. He was posted to RAF Kinloss and the Coastal Command Avro Lancasters of No 120 Sqn, soon seeing the Avro Shackleton into service. In one interlude he was back on the Halifax again, flying Met.6s out of Gibraltar with No 202 (Meteorological) Sqn, which had been formed with the renumbering of 518 Sqn after the war. Post-war Met observers had unique terms of service; being already fully trained for their role, they joined as aircrew for two years, with an option for two further years' service, being guaranteed continued employment with the Meteorological Service as civilians thereafter. Again the mysterious ways of the RAF decreed that as an experienced "low-and-slow" maritime navigator, Bryn should be sent to the high-and-fast V-bomber force, despite needing a year's retraining in English Electric Canberras, during which the now Sqn Ldr Bryn Lewis was deputy officer-commanding No 12 Sqn. Finally inducted into the Vulcan force, he was made navigator leader of 617 Sqn – the famous "Dambusters". **JP**

parachute back on and get strapped into his seat, he was relieved to see that the aircraft was responding to control inputs. The aircraft was not mortally wounded, but clearly badly damaged. Most significantly, the Vulcan was extremely low on fuel, partly because the sortie had been undertaken with comparatively little fuel to ease the landing at Wellington, but also because of the leaks caused by the impact, which showered the crowd with kerosene, leaving a pungent smell in its wake, and because the undercarriage could not be retracted or fuel cross-fed to the unaffected starboard engines.

The Vulcan headed for RNZAF Ohakea and its longer runway, 80 miles (130km) away. The crew of the Transport Command Comet, witnessing the near-disaster from the VIP stand, scrambled in an attempt to give the Vulcan an airborne inspection and damage report, but were unable to catch up. The Comet crew ignored a request by Wg Cdr Bower (OC 617 Sqn) to wait for him, but he passed an order for the Vulcan rear crew to bale out. This seemed perfectly sensible, as the pilots could then attempt a landing knowing that if things went awry, they could eject without leaving their compatriots to die. However, the undercarriage could not be retracted and thus the men would strike the nose leg as they exited the hatch into the slipstream under the cockpit.

ABOVE: Air Vice-Marshal John Davis, AOC No 1 Group, is greeted beside XH498 on arrival at RNZAF Ohakea on October 19, 1959. Note the two-star pennant and 617 Sqn badge on the fuselage of the Vulcan. Also part of the retinue was AOC-in-C Transport Command Sir Denis Barnett, who travelled in the Comet. *via author*

BELOW: With airbrakes deployed, a Vulcan engine testbed comes in to land at Filton. Big, noisy and hard to ignore, the big delta-winged V-bomber became synonymous with Britain's ability to project power during the Cold War era. *Philip Jarrett Collection*

For the **Wellington ceremony,** the plan was for a **"V" of three Vulcans** to sweep majestically across the city, and for **one** to land.

ABOVE: Vulcan XH498 just about to clip the bank on final approach for its landing at Wellington Airport on October 25, 1959. Just visible on the bank beyond and to the left of the buses, beneath the Vulcan's port mainwheel bogie, is Peter Boyd, who had positioned himself to get some dramatic photographs to die for – very nearly literally. *via author*

LEFT: Seconds after impact with the bank at the end of the runway, XH498's undercarriage has buckled and snapped at the knuckle joint, forcing the mainwheel unit into the wing and rupturing the fuel tank. The port wingtip dragged the ground and was also damaged. The pilot, Tony Smailes, had no option but to open the throttles wide and hope for the best. *via author*

Smailes respected their decision to stay, and, on finals into Runway 27 at Ohakea, jettisoned the cockpit canopy. This was standard procedure before firing the ejection seats but could be done as a separate operation, converting the aircraft to a "cabriolet" configuration – with a 140kt breeze on finals.

The touchdown at Ohakea, fuel virtually exhausted, was perfect. As the wings lost lift, the damaged wingtip touched and XH498 gently slewed to port on to the grass. All five occupants left via the open cockpit roof, running down the port wing. There was no fire. There were no recriminations from the AOC, who ordered the crew to fly the display at Ohakea's open day "to get back in the saddle". Thus the next day, in Vulcan

ABOVE: The Vulcans of No 617 Sqn, including XH498 and XH502, at the SBAC Display at Farnborough in September 1960. On each display day a four-aircraft V-Force scramble kickstarted the show, the Vulcans performing on the Tuesday and Saturday, Valiants and Victors doing the honours on the other days. *Alan Todd Collection via Lee Howard*

XH502, they swept low in salute over their stricken mount.

A NARROW ESCAPE

Amazingly, viewed from today's culture of health and safety, Peter Boyd was crouched on the runway lip at Wellington, taking photographs of the mighty bomber's approach. After the first two touch-and-goes he moved slightly to his left to get a perfect head-on view for the next approach. The main bogies impacted on either side of him, the powering-up Olympus engines showering him with gravel, the noise indescribable. Bill Howell, "Marshal One", driving a Vauxhall Zephyr, was immediately

sent by air traffic control with an RAF engineering officer to the impact point. They noted that the port bogie had impacted 18in (46cm) below the lip (the starboard bogie just clipped the edge) and left a score-mark visible for years afterwards along the runway. Debris they collected included parts of the Maxaret brakes and wingtip navigation lights.

The Vulcan was categorised as Cat 4A and declared ROS (repairable on site) at Ohakea on January 4, 1960, and was allocated to Avro at Woodford, the paperwork being backdated to

December 22, 1959. A team from Woodford was sent out to Ohakea, and repairs to XH498 had been completed by June 21, 1960, when the big V-bomber made a flight over Auckland, Wairoa and Wellington in the hands of Flt Lt C.R. Bell. It landed back at Scampton on June 24, having returned via a westabout route.

Had Smailes lost control at Wellington and not been able to get back into the air, the Vulcan would have veered to port towards the dragging wing-tip and collided with the static display (which included the Comet, Britannia, Beverley, an RNZAF Handley Page Hastings, RAAF Canberras ▶

Peter Boyd was crouched on the runway lip at Wellington, taking **photographs** of the mighty bomber's approach. After the first two touch-and-goes he moved slightly to his left to get a **perfect head-on view** for the next approach.

BELOW: Wrong place at the right time? – one of Peter Boyd's remarkable photographs of XH498 coming in over the buses at the runway threshold, taken from the bank the massive bomber would hit moments later. Having moved his position slightly for the final touchdown, Peter avoided being hit by the mainwheels by a matter of inches. *Peter Boyd via author*

ABOVE: The stricken Vulcan roars away, streaming fuel and with the port mainwheel skewed 45° aft. In all the excitement, Smailes had forgotten to retract the airbrakes, which could have caused further problems... *Lee Howard Collection*

RIGHT: The crew evacuate XH498 through the cockpit and down the port wing moments after the aircraft had stopped at Ohakea. The fire crews are on hand and the hoses from the fire truck are already being run out.

The touchdown at **Ohakea,** fuel virtually exhausted, was perfect. As the wings lost lift, the damaged wingtip touched and **XH498** gently slewed to port on to the grass. All **five occupants** left via the open **cockpit** roof.

BELOW: Thankfully further problems did not materialise, Smailes skilfully manhandling the aircraft to the RNZAF base at Ohakea, where it landed safely but ran off the runway, leaving a sizeable gouge in the grass in its wake. *via author*

and two USAF Hercules), then the crowd. The resulting carnage does not bear thinking about.

On October 31, 1959, the two remaining Vulcans headed on via night stops at Fiji and Christmas Island (then an RAF base) to Honolulu, Hawaii, where a somewhat "naughty" cargo of New Zealand salmon was smuggled from the bomb bay to a freezer overnight. The same happened at Travis Air Force Base near San Francisco the next day after a transit in which the Vulcans reached 55,000ft to clear cumulonimbus cloud. On November 7, as Bryn's aircraft, XH502, climbed out from Offutt Air Force Base, near Omaha, Nebraska, for the next leg to Goose Bay, Labrador, the crew heard XH499 declare a "Mayday" and request an immediate return. As the undercarriage had retracted, the nosewheel doors had operated out of sequence and fouled the bogie. Unsure of the situation and unwilling to continue, the crew elected to land back at Offutt as soon as possible. Repairs were made and XH499 returned to the UK, via Goose Bay, on November 19, landing back at Scampton on November 20 after a weather diversion to Lossiemouth. The incident had left just one Vulcan to complete the circumnavigation to plan.

AROUND THE WORLD IN 50 HOURS

The sole successful Vulcan, XH502, pressed on to Goose Bay after hearing XH499's "Mayday", and finally landed at Scampton on November 8, having flown 28,251 miles (45,465km) in 50 flying hours at an average speed of 565 m.p.h. (909km/h). Crossing the Atlantic, Bryn had been able to guide the Vulcan into the jetstream, giving an impressive ground speed of 720 m.p.h. (1,160km/h), or Mach 0.945, the Vulcan normally flying at Mach 0.84 or thereabouts. The crossing was made in a remarkable 2hr 49min 30sec, smashing the record. Avro was appreciative of the crew's efforts – but not overly so; each member received a

ABOVE: The damaged port mainwheel unit after landing at Ohakea. The broken rod is visible, although the tyres appear to have survived the incident. The kiwi symbol was applied to the insides of both mainwheel doors on arrival in New Zealand. Vulcan XH498 was converted to B.1A configuration in 1962 with the addition of electronic countermeasures equipment and remained in service until October 1967, when it was given maintenance serial 7993M at Finningley and used – appropriately – as a crew escape trainer.

copper tie pin with a Vulcan motif. The AOC, however, was presented with a silver model of a Vulcan by Avro's John Gray; rank has its privileges.

Much was learnt by the RAF as a result of the antipodean adventure, in particular that the "V-Force" did not yet have effective global reach. The Middle East had to be avoided if possible, so a route across the Indian Ocean via Gan in the Maldives was used until the British armed forces withdrew east of Suez. Now if the RAF wishes to reach the Far East or Australasia in times of tension, the route is via the USA. •

This revised and updated article was published in its original form in the April 2013 issue of *New Zealand Aviation News* (www.aviationnews.co.nz). We would like to thank Robert Owen, No 617 Sqn's official historian, for his invaluable help with the preparation of this feature.

BELOW: It was left to XH502 to complete the circumnavigation tour, which concluded when the Vulcan landed back at Scampton on November 2, 1959. Later that year it participated in the four-aircraft scramble display at Farnborough, where it is seen here. *Alan Todd Collection via Lee Howard*

WORLD CONGRESS OF FLIGHT
LAS VEGAS

Viva Las Vegas!

In April 1959 the brand new Las Vegas Convention Center became the futuristic epicentre of the ambitious first World Congress of Flight, in which the Western world's leading lights in aviation and spaceflight came together to exchange ideas and enjoy a week of spectacular demonstrations of state-of-the-art aeronautical hardware, as NICK STROUD explains.

TOP: Many of the more impressive displays of airpower demonstrated at the Indian Springs Armament Range during the week of the Congress were performed by F-100s, the type being the USAF's primary front-line fighter-bomber. This example, F-100D 55-2795, is seen at Nellis and later went on to serve with the Turkish Air Force. *TAH Archive*

ABOVE: The World Congress of Flight was by no means only about the military uses of aeronautical technology. Civil aviation was also well-represented, with America's most modern airliners on show, including Boeing 707 N7506A, named *Flagship District of Columbia* in American Airlines service, which had first flown in January 1959. *TAH Archive*

A t Las Vegas, a milestone in aviation history; the world's first Congress of Flight, sponsored by the Air Force Association, brings together the full cycle of flight; man in air and man in space ..." Thus the rich, American baritone of the anonymous *US Air Force News* announcer prefaces a vintage newsreel report on the ambitious World Congress of Flight, held in the famous gambling and leisure hotspot of Las Vegas, Nevada, nestled deep in the Mojave Desert, in April 1959. The idea was, to quote the promotional blurb of the time, "to bring together all elements of flight – designers, producers, operators, administrators and users – to unite them in a common cause; the advancement of aeronautics and astronautics – the twin sciences of flight".

As a projection of contemporary American air power it was unparalleled, with a week of dramatic (and by all accounts, ear-splitting) displays of civil and military hardware keeping the attendees thrilled, even if it turned out to be not quite the international affair the organisers had envisioned. Of the 77 nations invited to participate, only around half accepted, and their contributions were ultimately fairly meagre. Nevertheless, as a spectacle, it was the West's aviation event of the year, with formation aerobatic displays from homegrown and international teams cleaving the gin-clear cerulean canopy, state-of-the-art fighters trailing crimson blooms of napalm along the tumbleweed-strewn desert floor and nuclear-capable bombers tearing the sky asunder as they demolished the sound barrier on max-speed low-level runs past the makeshift grandstands at Indian Springs, 45 miles (70km) west of Vegas. Intended to

LEFT: Cutting edge meets God of fire – a North American F-100 Super Sabre of the USAF's Thunderbirds formation aerobatic display team and Avro Vulcan XH502 of the RAF's No 617 Sqn sit in the blistering heat on the ramp at Nellis Air Force Base, Nevada, during the World Congress of Flight at Las Vegas in April 1959. *TAH Archive*

be a "brains trust" for the great and good in aviation and spaceflight, where ideas could be put forward and discussed, the first World Congress of Flight (WCF) looked set to become America's equivalent of Europe's vital gatherings of industry at Farnborough and Paris.

A BRIGHT IDEA

The force behind the WCF, the Air Force Association (AFA), was formed in 1946 as a civilian independent non-profit organisation with the declared aim of "perpetuating the fellowship of former members of the Air Force and providing a national organisation which will help to educate its own members and the public at large in the proper development of airpower". The idea had grown from discussions between Gen H.H. "Hap" Arnold, C-in-C of the US Army Air Forces during the Second World War, and Maj-Gen Fred Anderson, Commanding General of the Eighth Air Force, based in the UK during the war. Both keen advocates of air power and its advancement, the pair appointed Maj-Gen Edward P. "Ted" Curtis, Great War fighter ace and Chief of Staff of the USA's Strategic Air Forces in the European Theatre of Operations during the Second World War, as the AFA's founding Chairman. The new organisation was formally established on February 4, 1946. Its objectives were

translated into action by means of annual conventions and symposia, and, significantly, lobbying for the establishment of an autonomous United States Air Force (USAF), independent of the US Army, which came into being in September 1947.

The AFA continued its work through the 1950s, organising pageants and educational programmes, as well as becoming a powerful lobbyist on behalf of American industrial and military preparedness. By 1958, with the Soviet Union's startling October 1957 launch into orbit of Sputnik I having stunned the USA into a crash catch-up programme, the subject of space was very much on the AFA's agenda. Accordingly, the Association set about educating the American public on the new capabilities and implications of aerospace power and its impact on modern society, and it was as part of this programme that the concept of a World (for which read Western world) Congress of Flight was first mooted.

The idea was to provide the infrastructure for a major exposition run in co-operation with the international aerospace community, including diplomats, industry executives, military leaders, scientists and policy-makers, against a backdrop of cutting-edge aerospace technology, such as missiles, spacecraft and state-of-the-art military and civil aircraft.

Billed as "The World's Greatest Air-Space Show", the WCF was announced in late 1958, ▶

BELOW: It wasn't just aviation either; General Motors displayed its space-age car, the Firebird III, the concept for which had been influenced by jet fighter design. *TAH Archive*

RIGHT: The main exhibition hall in the Las Vegas Convention Center contained stands advertising the wares of numerous companies, including those of Northrop... *TAH Archive*

ABOVE: ...and Lockheed. *TAH Archive*

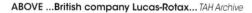

ABOVE ...British company Lucas-Rotax... *TAH Archive*

Aviation Week reporting that three major gatherings – a "Jet Age Conference", "Space Age Symposium" and "Missile Management Meeting" – would form the backbone of the week-long event to be held during April 12–19, 1959. By January that year it had been announced that some 88 companies had ordered space to exhibit at the outdoor and indoor display areas, including Rolls-Royce and the Hawker Siddeley Group from the UK and the *Société Nouvelle des Aéronautiques* (now GIFAS) from France, although of these only the British engine manufacturer ultimately attended.

THE SIX-MILLION DOLLAR VENUE

With numerous American aviation organisations signing up to support the venture, including the Air Transport Association, National Business Aircraft Association, Aero Medical Association, Flight Safety Foundation, Federal Aviation Agency and US Department of Education

and others, plus the worldwide *Fédération Aéronautique Internationale*, a venue capable of accommodating the diverse needs of such a large conclave had to be found – no mean task.

Founded as a city in 1905, Las Vegas had seen exponential growth since the legalisation of gambling in the city in 1931, which happened to coincide with the beginning of the construction of the nearby Hoover Dam, both of these factors insulating the city to some degree from the effects of the Great Depression.

By the late 1950s it had become obvious that the city's success as a gambling (and divorce) destination had reached a peak, and although "Sin City", as it was known, enjoyed lucrative holiday seasons, occupancy rates in hotels dropped through the floor in the slow tourist months. A new string to the city's gilded bow was required, and, with the surrounding desert offering plenty of space in which to develop, the city began exploring its potential as an attractive

conference venue, offering a convenient marriage between the business community and the recreation industry.

The result was the construction of the $6m Las Vegas Convention Center, one block east of the Las Vegas Strip on the site of the defunct Las Vegas Park Speedway horse- and automobile-racing track. Funds would be raised by the imposition of a room tax on nearby hotels, which would stand to gain from the proximity of the new conference venue. Designed by Adrian Wilson & Associates (with Harry Whitney as Consulting Architect), the 6,300-seat Convention Center represented a very 1950s idea of the future, its gleaming silver-domed rotunda giving the impression of a recently-landed flying saucer.

Next to the attention-grabbing centrepiece was a conventional exhibition hall of some 90,000ft^2 (8,400m^2), beyond which was another 2,000,000ft^2 (185,805m^2) of outdoor exhibition area. With McCarran Field, Las Vegas's civil airport, a mere five miles (8km) to the south, the USAF's Nellis base eight miles (13km) to the north-east, plus the Sky Haven general aviation airfield (now North Las Vegas Airport) three miles (5km) to the north-west, the new Convention Center offered the perfect spot to hold the AFA's inaugural World Congress of Flight.

The civil aircraft on show would be based at McCarran, the military hardware at Nellis and dramatic demonstrations of the latter could be undertaken at the USAF Armaments Range at Indian Springs. The exhibition area beside the Convention Center would house various static exhibits, including several missiles, a mock-up of the futuristic North American X-15 and various vehicles and equipment displays. In charge of the whole shooting match was Ted Curtis, the AFA's founding Chairman, who had subsequently served as President Eisenhower's Special Assistant for Aviation Activities and was then on the board of Eastman-Kodak.

Thus the stage was set for the most ambitious aviation event held in the USA up to that time, during which, according to the promo, "symposia and conferences will explore flight in terms of international security and human welfare". It would "analyse the social, economic, political and moral problems which accompany the progress of flight". Furthermore, the project was "dedicated to the belief that greater world knowledge of aircraft, missiles and spacecraft – in realistic perspective – will help bring the world closer to permanent peace". Despite the stirring rhetoric about bringing the world together through aviation and spaceflight, neither the Soviet Union nor the People's Republic of China was invited. Obviously.

START THE WEEK
By the end of March 1959 the Convention Center was on schedule for completion for the opening of the WCF, its maiden conference, and plans for the week's activities were well advanced. A preview for the press would be held on Sunday April 12, with the keynote Jet Age, Missile Management and Space Age conferences arranged for Monday April 13, Thursday April 16 and Friday April 17 respectively, with some 87 smaller specialist group meetings and conferences to be held by 47 different companies or organisations between the main events.

Flying demonstrations by the civil aircraft at McCarran would be performed on the Monday after the first Jet Age conference,

ABOVE: One of the more unusual general aviation exhibits at McCarran was McKinnon G-21C Goose N150M, converted by Angus "Mac" McKinnon to be powered by four 340 h.p. Lycoming flat-six air-cooled supercharged piston engines in place of the original Grumman amphibian's pair of 450 h.p. Pratt & Whitney Wasp Junior radials. *TAH Archive*

with a full day of military demonstrations on Wednesday April 15 (to coincide with the NATO tenth anniversary celebrations). The following Saturday and Sunday would be public days, with free access to the exhibition halls and McCarran Field for the flying displays. In typical 1950s American style, the organisers were determined to make the event bigger and better than its European counterparts. As American magazine *Flying* remarked in its March 1959 issue:

"Both Farnborough and the Paris show are excellent displays, but nowhere has it been possible to bring together all elements of flight on a worldwide basis to study, to discuss, to see demonstrated the full range of equipment which constitute the tools with which we must work to help build progress and security for all". Except the Russians and Chinese, of course.

Another interesting point in *Flying's* preview was its view that "to foreign observers, one of the most fascinating

features of the Congress will be general aviation – an element of flight which to date is almost exclusively a major development in the USA" – a statement that may have raised an eyebrow or two on the board of Auster or Jodel. The article continues: "Remember, there are more privately owned aircraft in the state of California alone than all the rest of the world, outside the USA, put together" – a thought-provoking statistic if true.

On Sunday April 12 the international press was allowed its first glimpse of the exhibits at the Convention Center, as the final touches were being added to the sprawling site. *Flight's* Kenneth Owen, who was there on a tour of the USA's missile sites, commented that "the last few dollars of the six million were being spent as the final pieces of lush carpeting were tacked in place at the entrance to the vast circular auditorium". It soon became

In typical 1950s American style, the organisers were determined to make the event bigger and better than its European counterparts.

BELOW: Representing the new generation of turboprop airliners at McCarran Field, along with a Lockheed Electra and a Fairchild-built Fokker F-27, was Convair 440 N440EL (formerly PP-AQE with VARIG), converted by Canadair in early 1959 to carry a pair of Napier Elands, to become a 540. *TAH Archive*

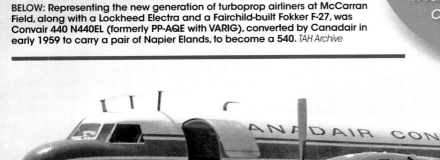

apparent that international exhibitors were thin on the ground, with only Rolls-Royce, Napier and Lucas-Rotax from the UK, Canadair from Canada and Dassault from France taking stand space in the main exhibition hall, although after the event it was claimed that officials from 47 countries had attended the WCF.

In the static aircraft and missile park behind the exhibition centre, a collection of rocket-powered missiles spiked the desert air. The largest, a Convair Atlas intercontinental ballistic missile (ICBM), had a door cut into its lower skin, which visitors were invited to enter. According to Kenneth Owen, the "loudspeakers vibrated with enthusiasm", a faceless voice announcing that "You are invited to be among the first people to enter a ballistic missile. We think you will find it interesting..." Indeed he did, taking a look around the display of colour photographs presented within the missile's interior. Alongside stood a composite of rejected parts forming a replica Douglas Thor-Able, the intermediate-range ballistic missile (IRBM) then being tested by RAF personnel up the California coast at Vandenburg AFB.

Also in the static park was a Martin TM-76 (MGM-13) Mace tactical cruise missile, Boeing CIM-10 BOMARC surface-to-air missile (SAM) and a Northrop SM-62 Snark surface-to-surface cruise missile. There were also models of a Discoverer

satellite and the Project Mercury capsule, plus the aforementioned wooden mock-up of the X-15. In the shadow of all this high-tech hardware stood examples of advanced technology from a bygone age in the shape of a Sopwith Camel, replica Blériot monoplane and Pfalz D XII biplane, accompanied by Frank Tallman and Nelson Lomis of Tallman Aviation, dressed as members of the Royal Flying Corps and *Fliegertruppe* respectively.

Using the showground beyond the static exhibition area were the numerous light aircraft and helicopters attending the show, the latter using the disused horse-racing track behind the Convention Center for spirited displays, the most notable by a Hiller UH-12. Other whirlybirds present were US Army and civilian examples of the insectoid Hughes 269A, and a Sud-Ouest SO 1221 Djinn and rocket-armed Sud SA.313 Alouette II flying the flag for France. The gliding and sailplane community was also well represented, with demonstrations at the horse-track under the ægis of the Soaring Society of America, which had invited the World Soaring Champion, Ernst-Günter Haase, from Germany.

THE FUTURE OF AIR TRAVEL
With the various symposia and conferences under way in the Convention Center, the afternoon of Monday April 12 saw a short flying display by the civil aircraft at McCarran Field, where a line-up of the USAF's "Century Series" of fighters – North American F-100

Super Sabre, McDonnell F-101 Voodoo, Convair F-102 Delta Dagger, Lockheed F-104 Starfighter, Republic F-105 Thunderchief and Convair F-106 Delta Dart – was also put on view to the public.

The commercial aircraft gathering included the very latest jetliners, among them Boeing 707 N7506A in American Airlines markings, the fourth production Douglas DC-8 and the third production Convair CV-880. The new generation of turboprops was also on hand in the form of a Lockheed Electra, Fairchild-built Fokker F-27 and a Canadair Napier Eland-engined Convair 540. Painted in the standard V-Force all-white anti-flash scheme, the Avro Vulcans of the RAF's No 617 Sqn turned heads alongside the jetliners, the British nuclear bombers (and a Transport Command de Havilland Comet 2) representing the only visiting air force flying its own national aircraft in its own national markings.

The 707 was the first to take off, departing McCarran 20min before the flying display was scheduled to start; it did not display and did not return, rather disappointingly. The DC-8 made a noisy departure from the longest runway and flew a single pass over the field, but also did not return. The CV-880 offered more value, making a short take-off from the shorter runway, followed by a series of low-level flypasts with varying percentages of power applied.

Up next was the Electra, which, according to British weekly magazine *The Aeroplane's*

LEFT: Based at Flabob, California, renowned film aviation specialist Frank Tallman brought a small collection of antique aircraft for display in the static exhibition area, including 1918-vintage Pfalz D XII N43C, which was later acquired by the Champlin Fighter Museum in Arizona; it is currently on display at the Museum of Flight in Seattle. *TAH Archive*

BELOW: "The World's First Manned Space Airplane", says the sign beside the full-size wooden mock-up of the North American X-15, although the type had yet to make a non-captive flight, either as a glider or under its own power. *TAH Archive*

photographer, Charles A. Sims, "performed like an accomplished and well proven airliner", Sims ruminating that "this made me think we had missed a wonderful chance to enhance British prestige. Surely it would have been worthwhile to send a Comet 4 or a Britannia to a gathering of this importance. Imagine the effect on the assembly if it had been announced that either or both of these aircraft had left London the day before on regular schedule and with a full load of fare-paying passengers, and would be back in London again the day after with another full payload, when most of the aircraft on show at McCarran were just experimental prototypes!"

Although the Vulcans did not display on the Monday, the RAF put up an excellent demonstration of British flying élan in the No 216 Sqn Comet 2, in which Flt Lt W. Somers performed a short take-off, a series of low passes with elegant turns and an impeccable landing, earning considerable applause from the spectators. Other display items included a JATO-equipped Dakota and the prototype McKinnon four-engined G-21C Goose amphibian.

The following day saw the turn of the general aviation attendees to display their wares at the horse-track behind the Convention Center, the latter playing host to the second day of the Jet Age Conference, during which Dr Edward Teller, father of the H-Bomb, announced that scientists would probably be able to confirm Einstein's theory of relativity by means of nuclear explosions high in the atmosphere – which seemed to be Teller's solution to most things.

SHOCK AND AWE

The centrepiece of the WCF was the demonstration of airpower scheduled to take place at the Indian Springs Armament Range on Wednesday April 15, in celebration of the tenth anniversary of the formation of the North Atlantic Treaty Organisation

ABOVE: The latest missile technology was put on display in the exhibition area behind the Convention Center and included the jet-propelled Northrop Snark surface-to-surface cruise missile (nearest camera) and the already largely-obsolete Boeing CIM-10 BOMARC rocket-boosted ramjet-propelled surface-to-air missile (standing vertically on mobile platform). *TAH Archive*

(NATO) on April 4, 1949. A number of crude but adequate stands were erected at a site in the shadow of the Rocky Mountain foothills, although these provided scant shelter from the merciless sun in the cauldron of the bleached desert basin.

The aircraft scheduled to take part were pre-positioned at Nellis, from where they operated on a time-over-target timing of ±5sec throughout the day, Charles Sims noting that the apron at Nellis held some 400 fighting aircraft at one point. The demonstration was made up largely of American types making full use of the elbow room afforded by the remote desert location, although there were contributions from the Italian Air Force's Diavoli Rossi (Red Devils) F-84F formation aerobatic team and the Chinese Nationalist (Taiwanese) Air Force's F-86-equipped Thunder Tigers, invited by dint of the 1955 Sino-American Mutual Defense Treaty.

The Royal Netherlands Air Force also weighed in with a performance from its Dash Four formation aerobatic quartet of borrowed USAF Republic F-84Fs

(as were those of the Italian team), despite having suffered a mid-air collision during rehearsals the previous Thursday. Thankfully there were no fatalities, one pilot ejecting, the other bringing his damaged Thunderstreak back for a landing at Nellis.

For more than two and a half hours the audience was treated – or subjected – to a remarkable articulation of airpower of every kind, from touch-and-goes on the scrubby desert floor by a Lockheed C-130 Hercules to a Mach-busting low-level run from a Convair B-58 Hustler, the shockwaves all but bowling over the front row of spectators. Scorching full-throttle runs at 50ft (15m) a mere 150ft (45m) from the crowdline were made by a Voodoo, Delta Dagger, Starfighter and Thunderchief in quick succession, an experience described by Charles Sims as "pretty shattering". A Douglas RB-66 Destroyer came hurtling through throwing out photo-flashes by the dozen, illuminating the desert sky in spite of the dazzling midday sun.

Other remarkable demonstrations with live ammunition followed, including the release of a sequence of Falcon missiles from an F-106, a napalm drop by four Super Sabres, another example of ▶

> In the static park was a **Martin TM-76 (MGM-13)** Mace tactical cruise missile, **Boeing CIM-10 BOMARC** surface-to-air missile (SAM) and a **Northrop SM-62 Snark** surface-to-surface cruise missile.

BELOW: The Convair Atlas ICBM (left) and Douglas Thor-Able IRBM are raised from a horizontal to a vertical position in the missile park, as the public address system announces: "There they are – the Free World's two major missiles..." *TAH Archive*

which released a salvo of high-velocity aerial rockets (HVARs) at a target on the scrubland below. One of the more extraordinary display items saw an F-100 release a target missile, then despatch a Sidewinder air-to-air missile to destroy it a matter of moments later.

A demonstration of the low-altitude bombing system (LABS) devised for the delivery of a nuclear weapon, in which the strike aircraft climbs vertically and releases its load "over the shoulder" at the top of the climb before pulling on to its back to exit the way it had come, was performed by another F-100, although it seems that this sequence may have been undertaken by an F-105 during the rehearsal on the Sunday.

The heavier hardware was equally impressive, with displays by various bombers and transport aircraft keeping the spectators' hands to their ears, including a demonstration of air-to-air refuelling in which a Boeing B-52 connected with a KC-135 Stratotanker for a flypast, and very low-level high-speed passes by three-aircraft formations of B-52s and B-47s. Arguably the USAF's *pièce de résistance* of the afternoon, however, was the simulation of a high-altitude nuclear strike by a B-52, in which the Stratofortress's bomb doors opened to reveal

a single sinister nuclear bomb practice round, which, fitted with a barometric fuze, exploded at a predetermined height after a long freefall.

Being on home ground, the USAF and US Navy formation aerobatic teams, the Thunderbirds and Blue Angels respectively, were not about to allow their foreign counterparts to steal the show and provided a characteristically vigorous aerial ballet for the tens of thousands of spectators who had made the drive out to the remote location.

With such an awe-inspiring spectacle having been provided by the home nation, the Vulcans of the RAF had a great deal to live up to. Charles Sims described No 617 Sqn's moment in the sun:

"Air Vice-Marshal G.A. Walker and his crews put up a most impressive display. After a series of fast and slow runs, they introduced a novel finish which deservedly won a spontaneous burst of applause. The formation opened up after a low-level flypast of the spectator stands to emphasise the size of the four-engined V-bombers, and then went straightaway into a near-vertical climb. Within seconds they were visible only as tiny white triangles in the deep blue sky. The effect was remarkable."

A RIVAL TO PARIS AND FARNBOROUGH?

The reaction to the WCF from the press and public alike was almost unanimously positive, the only negative comments lamenting the lack of international participation, although *Flight's* Kenneth Owen offered a typically British perspective on the rather more hubristic elements of the event:

"Whether the Congress will succeed in helping to bring the world closer to permanent peace by having people step inside an ICBM, by simulating the explosion of a nuclear bomb, and by its other and more obviously worthwhile activities, remains to be seen".

Gill Robb Wilson, the highly-respected Editor and Publisher of American magazine *Flying*, stated in his op-ed piece of July 1959 that the WCF should become a regular event, remarking: "It would seem to this writer that the World Congress of Flight, staged perhaps every third year on this side of the Atlantic in alternate staging with Britain's Farnborough and the Paris Air Show in Europe, might well serve not only American aeronautics and astronautics but the entire free world." *Life* magazine devoted five pages to coverage of the WCF, and an hour-long live telecast of

BELOW: A USAF Air Policeman makes the most of what little shade can be found on the Nellis ramp beneath one of the three 617 Sqn Vulcan B.1s sent to represent Britain's nuclear capability. Vulcan XH498, seen here in the background, suffered a major mishap in New Zealand six months later. *TAH Archive*

ABOVE: Using nine temporarily repainted North American F-86F Sabres borrowed from second-line USAF units, the Chinese Nationalist (Taiwanese) Air Force's Thunder Tigers formation aerobatic team performed impressively at the Congress, particularly in view of the fact that most of its members had an average of a mere 20hr on type. *TAH Archive*

ABOVE: The USAF's own four-engined delta-winged nuclear-capable bomber, the Convair B-58 Hustler, was a very different proposition from the RAF's Vulcan, being capable of Mach 2 as against the Vulcan's high-subsonic maximum speed, although the Vulcan was far easier to handle. This is the second prototype XB-58, 55-0661. *TAH Archive*

LEFT: The air demonstration element of the World Congress was largely a USAF affair, but the US Navy was represented by its formation aerobatic display team, the Blue Angels, which was in its second year of operations with the Grumman F11F Tiger supersonic carrier fighter. Blue Angel No 5 is seen here on the ramp at Nellis. *TAH Archive*

the airpower demonstration was broadcast across the entire NBC network, reportedly reaching some 20 million people.

A prospective date of September 13–19, 1962, for the second World Congress of Flight was announced in early 1961, with Las Vegas once again to serve as the epicentre of the event's activities. However, as the USA's free-spending, optimistic 1950s turned the corner into the more uncertain 1960s, in which the temperature of the Cold War increasingly fell towards freezing point, and the perception grew that the hardware on show at Las Vegas in 1959 may actually be called into action, the possibility of a repeat performance began to seem less likely.

With John F. Kennedy's election to the Presidency in January 1961, followed a few months later by the disastrous Bay of Pigs dèbâcle and a steady deterioration in relations with the Soviet Union, the prospect dimmed even further. By the autumn of 1962 Kennedy was on a collision course with his opposite number in the Kremlin, Khrushchev, which would culminate in the Cuban Missile Crisis of October 1962.

Far from practising for another expensive but highly enjoyable aeronautical shindig in Las Vegas, the military forces

of the USA were by then preparing their considerable air assets for the real thing. Despite its earnest ambitions to be a force for peace and human advancement, the first World Congress of Flight would prove to be the last. ●

BELOW: "Anything you can do..." The three visiting Vulcans of No 617 Sqn make a low-level pass with the bomb-bay doors open at Indian Springs. Leading the Vulcan team was Air Vice-Marshal G.A. "Gus" Walker, Air Officer Commanding No 1 Group. The same three Vulcans, XH498, XH499 and XH502, undertook the RAF's first world circumnavigation during October–November 1959, although '498 and '499 both suffered mishaps along the way. *TAH Archive*

*The formation opened up after a **low-level flypast** of the spectator stands to emphasise the size of the **four-engined V-bombers**, and then went straightaway into a **near-vertical climb**.*

Here come the Vixettes. When is a Sea Vixen not a Sea Vixen?

At the 1962 Royal Tournament at London's Earls Court Exhibition Centre, visitors were treated to a display of four state-of-the-art de Havilland Sea Vixens being prepared for launch from the deck of a Royal Navy carrier. On closer inspection, however, all was not quite what it seemed, as naval aviation historian MATTHEW WILLIS reveals...

TOURNAMENT 1962

The audience of Britain's annual Royal Tournament in July 1962 was treated to a spectacular sight; a remarkably accurate re-enactment of *HMS Hermes* launching a squadron of the Fleet Air Arm's most modern all-weather interceptor, the de Havilland Sea Vixen FAW.1. The thrilled spectators would have seen armourers fitting de Havilland Firestreak missiles to the wing-mounted weapon pylons, fuel hoses connected, the engines started using a turbine starter and the crew climbing aboard, all while maintainers and armourers swarmed around the aircraft. The attention to detail was astonishing. As the crew fastened their harnesses, a maintainer pulled the locking pin from the ejection seat and handed it to the pilot. The aircraft taxied to the catapult bridle at the gestures of the batsman, their wings unfolding as they did so.

Fortunately for those who weren't able to be at Earl's Court on that day, the Rank Organisation filmed a special demonstration of that year's setpieces at RNAS Lee-on-Solent for its *Look at Life* series. The results are undoubtedly impressive, and show a great deal of effort to get things right. In fact, there was only one thing giving away the fact

that this was not the real thing. The usually imposing Sea Vixens had apparently shrunk in the wash to around half their normal size. These all-weather fighters were in fact another type entirely, ingeniously disguised.

POCKET VIXENS

The exhibition centre at Earl's Court (the locality and its Underground station have an apostrophe but the exhibition centre, curiously, did not) could not accommodate aircraft of the size and weight of the Sea Vixen, and even if it could it would been highly challenging to use them in a demonstration. There were older and smaller aircraft available in abundance, but naturally the Royal Navy wanted to show its cutting-edge hardware at the British Forces' showcase event.

The Aircraft Holding Unit at Abbotsinch

in Scotland was at the time host to a large number of de Havilland Sea Venoms awaiting disposal. A few of these had been borrowed by the engineers of No 12 Hangar to create weird and wonderful spoof aircraft for the station's air days, briefly fooling audiences into thinking they were seeing new naval prototypes. It was understandable, therefore, for the station to be asked if it was possible to convert some of the surplus Sea Venoms into the likeness of a more modern type.

The engineers duly set about their task with enthusiasm, turning four of the aircraft into highly convincing miniature Sea Vixens, which they christened "Vixettes". The Sea Venoms gained an extended pointed nose, apparently formed from wood and canvas, a new rear fuselage giving the impression of twin jets, much more highly-swept wings, an offset cockpit (complete with

RIGHT: **Either the world's smallest Sea Vixen or the world's biggest deck crew – the Royal Tournament "Vixette" display was filmed at Lee-on-Solent for the Rank Organisation's *Look at Life* series.**

ABOVE: With no easy reference points by which to judge its size, Vixette "XJ602/247" is easily mistaken for the real thing, and is seen here at Lee-on-Solent in August 1963 with its outer wing panels removed. The real XJ602 was delivered to the Fleet Air Arm in October 1960 and was retired after an eventful career in late 1973. *Mike Stroud*

ABOVE: In one piece and bearing a pair of dummy Firestreak missiles on its starboard wing, Vixette "XJ603/246" provides an unusual sight for passers-by behind the fence at a Royal Navy base. There appears to be very little information regarding the true identities of the Sea Venoms. *author's collection*

radar operator's "coalhole") and deeper tailbooms with swept fins. The pocket Vixens were capable of moving under their own power, could accommodate two crew members (presumably in somewhat confined conditions) and had electrically-operated folding wings.

Two of the Vixettes appeared in the Rank film, named *Flight Deck*, one painted with the identity of a real Sea Vixen – XJ602/"247" – and one marked as XJ601/"241", both with the fin code "H". David Watkins's book *Venom: de Havilland Venom and Sea Venom – The Complete History* (The History Press, 2003), from which much of the above information was gleaned, and a photograph in the author's collection, reveal that a third aircraft was given the identity XJ603/"246", with the same fin code. The fourth, as we can see courtesy of our leading photograph, became XJ604/"245".

A ONE-OFF OCCASION

For the Royal Tournament, the Navy asked for volunteers to act as the deck crew for the demonstration. Bill Gibson, a stoker who served aboard carriers *HMS Ark Royal, Victorious* and *Hermes* during a career which spanned more than 20 years, broke the longstanding Royal Navy tradition of never volunteering for anything, in order to take part. He and his fellow volunteers assembled at Lee-on-Solent for rehearsals, where they encountered the Vixettes.

"There were all sorts of trades there", Bill recalls. "They gave us all new roles for the Tournament. Captain J.D. Treacher was in charge – he later became an Admiral. We had a practice to get the timings right". This was important as the Vixettes did not move as conventional naval aircraft did. "They put a big electric motor in them," Bill reveals, "so they could move about. It worked on the concrete at Lee-on-Solent but when they got to the tournament, the surface was too soft and they couldn't move.

"In the end, they fixed the aircraft to a big rope and had a load of squaddies behind the scenes, pulling them about. When it got to the catapult, they pulled like mad and the aircraft shot forward. The lights were lowered, and the rope was dark, so you couldn't see it that well, and it all looked quite convincing."

After the Royal Tournament the assembled crew members went back to their regular roles, and it appears that the Vixettes were never used again in a live demonstration. At least two became gate guardians at Royal Navy bases, including "XJ601", which was photographed at Lee-on-Solent minus its outer wings, and "XJ603" at an unknown location. ●

ABOVE: Minus its outer wing panels, Vixette "XJ601/241" is seen here with at least one Firestreak on its port inner wing section (but not on the starboard side) in its position as a gate guardian at RNAS Lee-on-Solent. The station was designated *HMS Ariel* during 1959–65, after which it reverted to *HMS Daedalus* again. Curiously, serial XJ601 was never allocated to a real Sea Vixen, or indeed any aircraft. *author's collection*

BELOW: The genuine article – a pair of early production Sea Vixens take off in formation, the nearest, XJ490, carrying four Firestreaks on its underwing hardpoints, the furthest toting a pair of auxiliary fuel tanks. The Sea Vixen entered operational service with No 892 Sqn in July 1959, the Sea Venom leaving front-line service in 1960. *TAH Archive*

"It was a Jaguar D-Type on steroids. It was the Rolling Stones in surround-sound after 8 gallons of LSD"

In December 1967 journalist and keen aviation enthusiast JEFFREY WATSON secured the ride of a lifetime when he persuaded the men from the Ministry that he needed a flight in a two-seat version of the brutishly beautiful English Electric Lightning. The training for the supersonic sortie – including a ride on the dreaded ejection trainer – was tough; then came the ballistic trajectory to 40,000ft in a double-barrelled shotgun...

As a journalist back in the 1960s I was careful to cultivate a friend at the Ministry of Defence, who could get me rides in some very nice aeroplanes. I had a long list, which included the Hawker Hunter, Hawker Siddeley Harrier, McDonnell Douglas F-4 Phantom and English Electric Lightning. The latter I thought was a "big ask". This was the RAF's front-line interceptor – a missile with a man in it – which could do twice the speed of sound in level flight. It was a ferocious-looking beast; a big aeroplane with its two Rolls-Royce Avon engines mounted not side-by-side but one on top of the other. It looked for all the world like a double-barrelled shotgun.

At the same time that the Lightning was in squadron service, work on Concorde was progressing at Filton. Airline passengers would soon be flying at twice the speed of sound and military pilots were doing it already. Of course, Concorde passengers would be sitting in air-conditioned luxury sipping champagne. But the angle of my prospective story was – what was it like to fly at twice the speed of sound?

THE RIGHT STUFF

The only other journalist I knew who had ever been in the Lightning was Mac, a friend of mine. I phoned him. "Going in the Lightning? Lucky sod!", he said with a rather strange laugh. "Let me give you a word of advice. For God's sake get your teeth fixed". I was about to ask him why when he said he had to go, gave another strange laugh and hung up.

My flight was approved in the winter of 1967. I was told to report to the RAF Aeromedical Training Centre at North Luffenham in Rutland, to see whether I was made of "The Right Stuff". Most of it was fairly routine; blood pressure, lungs, heart-rate etc. Medical types put me in a cubicle with headphones on and played me high- and low-pitched sounds. If you heard the sound you pressed a button, which was supposed to establish how fast your reaction times were. I was also told that I had to see the dentist, who was not very impressed and decided that I had to have two fillings right there and then.

Later, Mac called me on the telephone. "Did you get your teeth fixed?" I said I had. He told me a story which was enough to give anyone the willies. The Lightning had an astonishing climb rate, even by today's standards. It could reach 30,000ft (9,100m) in 1min. During take-off the reheat was engaged on both engines

and a long orange flame roared out from the exhaust. The aircraft literally stood on its tail and went up vertically like a rocket. Mac, it had transpired, had some dodgy dental work, with two loose fillings. As the aircraft streaked into the stratosphere the change in pressure caused two fillings to blow clean out of his bottom jaw. This was made even worse by the fact that he was being violently airsick. So for the duration of his flight he sat there with a mouth full of amalgam and vomit.

I raised the matter with the RAF dentist. To him it was a familiar story. The British are not known for dental hygiene. In the bleak days of food-rationing after the war, children supplemented their diet with gobstoppers and similar cheap confectionery. Small wonder, then, that young people were sometimes fitted with false teeth in their twenties. The RAF dentist told me that exploding fillings were a common phenomenon in the RAF and potentially extremely dangerous. With the rapid change in pressure, a piece of amalgam could blow from the bottom jaw and lodge in the roof of the mouth, exerting pressure on the brain and even causing un-consciousness. There was good evidence that a number of unexplained accidents involving fighter aircraft had been caused by a rogue piece of amalgam. As a result, some British pilots had their teeth capped, like the Americans.

There were two more hurdles to overcome before the flight. One was to ride the

ejection-seat trainer. This looked like a piece of railway track angled into the sky with a rocket-powered seat attached to its base. When you pulled the handle or D-ring between your legs it would accelerate you from 0 to 60 m.p.h. (100km/h) in 1/20th of a second. Used incorrectly, it was a very good way of breaking your neck. You were carefully strapped in and then an explosive charge like a big brass shotgun cartridge was placed in a chamber behind your head. The safety pins were removed and waved in front of your face.

"I am now removing the safety pins, sir. The seat is now live..." said the sergeant with a malevolent smirk. It was the way he said "sir". But then all non-commissioned officers were sadists, and they always had it in for civilians – especially journalists. I was told to fix my eyes on the horizon and keep my chin up. Should one be looking down when the seat fired there was a good chance you would dislodge a few vertebrae. The waiting was the worst bit.

You place your right hand over the wrist of your left and grasp the handle firmly. On the command "Eject", you pull it briskly towards you and – boom! In a fraction of a second you have travelled to the top of the rails and your further progress appears to have been stopped by a ratchet mechanism. There is a puff of smoke, a whiff of cordite and it's all over.

RIGHT: "The waiting was the worst bit" – a trainee steels himself for a very brief but very fast ride on the ejection-seat trainer at West Malling in the early 1960s. The Lightning T.5 was fitted with a pair of state-of-the-art Martin-Baker Mk 2 4BSB ejection seats. To date, some 332 lives have been saved by the use of the company's Mk 2 seat. *TAH Archive*

LEFT: Production of a two-seat training version of the Lightning was put in hand in 1956, the T.4 prototype, XL628 (seen here up from the SBAC show at Farnborough in 1959) making its first flight on May 6, 1959. Based on the single-seat F.1A, the T.4 retained the "witch's hat" fin; the later T.5 variant, as experienced by the author, was fitted with a cropped squared-off fin. *TAH Archive*

ABOVE: With the crew in full flying gear, space was at something of a premium in the two-seat Lightnings. The prototype T.5 made its maiden flight on March 29, 1962. Production of the T.5 commenced in 1964 and deliveries of the variant to No 226 Operational Conversion Unit at Coltishall began in April 1965. *Philip Jarrett Collection*

"GETTING A LITTLE ODD..."

After this, the decompression chamber was easy. Six of us were made to sit in what looks like a small submarine with windows. We were all kitted out in flying helmets and oxygen masks. The engineers then simulated a rapid de-compression and the chamber filled with fog. This is what would happen if the pressurisation failed on the aircraft – in other words, if the canopy was holed. The aeromedical boys observed us carefully.

At one point in the process we were starved of oxygen, at which point people started getting a little odd. Like scuba divers, we were suffering from nitrogen narcosis. When this happens there is a tendency to laugh and behave irrationally. Unfortunately you are not aware that you are making a prat of yourself.

We were given a notepad and told to write our names on it. When the oxygen was restored I found that I had written meaningless scribble. Later they showed us a film of pilots behaving oddly under the effects of hypoxia.

I was told that if I should catch a cold or have any obstruction in my ears or nasal passages I would not be allowed to fly. If the aircraft had a rapid

decompression at 40,000ft (12,200m) we would have to descend very quickly. Without oxygen at that height we would be dead in 5sec.

THE FRIGHTENING

The Lightning. Some people called it the Frightening. Nobody who has flown in a Lightning is ever the same again. Many British aircraft were elegant – not this one. In no sense was the Lightning beautiful. It looked like the Angel of Death. It was designed to chase away the Soviets in their lumbering bombers. It was ballsy and functional.

Pilots were excited by the Lightning, a far more powerful machine than the Hunter. It was very fast with a snappy rate of roll owing to its short wingspan. A Lightning had no great trouble performing a dash to 60,000ft (18,300m) and some may have unofficially reached 78,000ft (23,800m), at which point it was no doubt as aerodynamic as a brick. The Lightning could climb like a rocket but ran out of juice very rapidly. It was a Jaguar D-Type on steroids. It was The Rolling Stones in surround-sound after eight gallons of LSD.

I was told to report to RAF Binbrook in Lincolnshire, home to No 5 Sqn, which carried a maple leaf on the fins of its aircraft, on December 14, 1967. It was cold and wet and the days were short. Another potential hazard was the prospect of ejecting from the aircraft and coming down in the North Sea. In winter the sea temperature is such that you would die of exposure in about 3min. So in addition to a g-suit and flying overalls, I had to wear a cold-water immersion suit – a large rubber affair which sealed around the neck. Thus, trussed like a chicken, it was

time to be strapped into Lightning T.5 XS451. Strapping-in was a complicated business. There was a full harness and leg restraints, the latter attaching to the bottoms of your legs. If an ejection had to be made, the straps would automatically pull the feet back hard into the seat, in theory ensuring you didn't leave them behind in the aircraft.

The strapping-in went on forever. The strapper had to retrieve the harness and make sure it was tight. By the time it was all finished I was so restricted for movement that it was difficult to turn my head and look back along the wing.

My pilot was Sqn Ldr Bernard "Bunny" St Aubyn, a serious, quietly-spoken chap who had previously flown Hunters and Supermarine Swifts at Jever in West Germany. "We can get anywhere in Western Europe in the Lightning in about half an hour – but we won't necessarily get back", he informed me, as he swirled his finger to the groundcrew. The isopropyl-nitrate monopropellant (Avpin) engine-starting equipment in the spine of the aircraft kicked in and the Avon engines spooled up. Avpin is a nasty, toxic substance that can burn without oxygen. I was glad it was nowhere near me.

There was enough isopropyl-nitrate for six starts. It was injected into the engine and ignited, which was enough to turn the engine over. The Avpin system was famously troublesome, but more reliable than ground-start systems, which might be hard to come by if Lightnings had to operate from remote airfields.

AWAY WE GO!

We carefully taxied out, the Lightning being something of a handful on the ground. The high-pressure

tyres could be skittish if the runway was wet, and the enormous fin was prone to weathercocking, meaning you could be blown off the runway by a Lincolnshire gale.

The take-off was sensational. Once we were lined up on the runway the two engines were brought up to full power and the brakes released. Bernard put the throttle through the gate and both afterburners lit up. A 25ft flame streaked from the rear of the aeroplane. It was like being kicked in the backside by a middle-aged camel with PMS. We went from zero to 100kt in 4sec; at 160kt we were airborne and climbing almost vertically.

The acceleration was breathtaking. We went supersonic in the climb, leaving a sonic boom somewhere over Skegness, and reached 30,000ft (9,150m) in a little more than a minute. In the aircraft you appear to be lying on your back with your legs stuck out as if they were in birthing stirrups. At this point a number of my amalgam fillings detached.

The Lightning was a thirsty beast; it leaked, dripped and smelt of fuel, and although it started the day with a full tank of fuel it very quickly started emptying. The pilot was obsessed with how much juice he had and how far it would get him. Even flying subsonically the endurance of the Lightning was only an hour, hence the need to top up with juice from Handley Page Victor tankers patrolling the North Sea. It was called "bootlegging" and it could extend the endurance from 1hr to 3hr.

Soviet aircraft, such as the impressive Tupolev Tu-95 *Bear*, also patrolled the North Sea and frequently made incursions into British airspace. The Lightnings acted as policemen; they would be scrambled to intercept the bombers and chase them away but by the time they reached them the big Russian bombers had usually steered themselves back into international airspace. ▶

> A **25ft flame** streaked from the rear of the aeroplane. It was like being kicked in the backside by a **middle-aged camel with PMS**. We went from **zero to 100kt in 4sec**.

ABOVE: The author (right) and Sqn Ldr St Aubyn at RAF Binbrook. St Aubyn ejected from Supermarine Swift FR.5 XD928 in April 1959 while serving with No 2 Sqn at Jever. "I was in the sea for about half an hour", he explained. "It was cold, wet and rather unpleasant". *Kenneth Green via author*

LEFT: A line-up of No 5 Sqn Lightnings at a typically rainy Binbrook, with the author's mount, T.5 XS451, nearest the camera. The unit received its first Lightnings in October 1965, having previously operated all-weather Gloster Javelins in West Germany from 1960. *Philip Jarrett Collection*

We were hoping to find a Bear but it was not to be. Bernard told me that this happened several times a week. So much so that Lightning pilots often recognised the same Russian crew members. They waved to each other and on one occasion the observer in the rear gun position of the Bear held up a *Playboy* centrefold for the titillation of the Lightning pilot.

A mere 10min after tucking up the wheels, cruising at slightly less than the speed of sound, we were 100 miles away from home. It made you proud to be British. In those days the Yanks had nothing like it. Although we were flying in a two-seat trainer, the Lightning was designed as a single-seat interceptor, which resulted in a very high workload for the pilot. As soon as we levelled off Bernard was constantly talking to the ground radar station to plan our sortie. Today's air superiority fighters would have two people to do the job – a pilot plus a navigator/weapons-systems operator.

On the upper starboard side of the instrument panel was a small radar scope surrounded by rubber. Looking down it revealed a luminescent orange screen with a small blip on it advancing towards us at what seemed to be a terrific speed. The ground radar controller's voice came through the headphones: "One bogey, port side, four miles, well clear". "Its probably a Yank out of Upper Heyford", said Bernard. By this time we had flown nearly to the coast of Norway, so we turned around and headed homeward.

Guided on to our target by the ever-closing blip on the radar we crept up on a McDonnell F-101 Voodoo up from the USAF base at Upper Heyford in Oxfordshire. We must have been at something like the speed of sound. I looked out over the starboard side of the instrument panel. "We'll have visual soon. On your side", explained Bernard.

There he was! A big aeroplane with swept wings going quite slowly. We crept up from below and behind and pounced on him. I had a fleeting glimpse of a big white star on the wing, then he was gone. He hadn't seen us coming but he would probably see the flame from our afterburner as we departed.

HOMEWARD BOUND

It was time to go home – we were almost out of gas. The weather was still appalling and we undertook a ground-controlled approach back into Binbrook, which was like having a wet sock pulled over your head while you were looking for your contact lenses. I couldn't see a thing and I felt sick. I knew enough not to throw up into the oxygen mask, so noting we were below 10,000ft (3,050m), I took it off. Bernard suggested that, if necessary, I should use one of my rather spiffy thin-leather gloves, which must have cost a fortune. As it happened the nausea passed and I had nothing to chuck anyway, having had no dinner the night before and not so much as a glass of water for breakfast.

Once again the ground-controller's voice crackled through the headphones: "You are 100 miles from touchdown". Almost in the same breath: "You are 70 miles from touchdown". How fast were we still going? The mainwheels hit the ground with an enormous bang and the drogue parachute yanked us to a halt. We had been doing close to 200 m.p.h. (320km/h) when we touched down on Binbrook's wet concrete.

The Lightning was supposed to be Britain's last manned fighter aircraft. Its forerunner, the experimental P.1A, first flew in 1954 and variants of the type were still in service 30 years later. But even in old age it could still see off newer fighters like the Phantom and Dassault Mirage.

Late in the Lightning's service life a relatively inexperienced USAF pilot in an F-16 tried to take on an RAF pilot in a Lightning F.3, and found that the "old dog" repeatedly frustrated his missile attacks. The American pilot blindly kept at it and was later asked what he was trying to accomplish. He replied: "I was trying to get alongside, open my canopy and club the son-of-a-bitch to death". ●

> *The mainwheels hit the ground with an **enormous bang** and the drogue parachute yanked us to a halt. We had been doing close to **200 m.p.h. (320km/h)** when we touched down on Binbrook's wet concrete.*

ABOVE: The T.5 prototype carrying a pair of Red Top missiles. The two-seat Lightnings were every bit as agile as their single-seat counterparts, the author describing a hard turn at supersonic speed, during which his body became four times its normal weight, thus: "Weighing 50-stone is like having an elephant sitting on your neck..." *Philip Jarrett Collection*

BELOW: Lightning T.5 XS451 – unusually, without the belly fuel tank – awaits clearance for take-off from Binbrook on October 29, 1970. The aircraft made its first flight on June 3, 1965 at Samlesbury and joined No 5 Sqn that November. It was retired from RAF service in 1976 and later continued its flying career in South Africa as ZU-BEX. Sadly, it was lost in a fatal accident at an airshow at Overberg Air Force Base on November 14, 2009. *Adrian M. Balch Collection*

Happiness is... vectored thrust

CHRIS FARARA examines the career of Hawker Siddeley's unique civil-registered two-seat Harrier demonstrator G-VTOL – a history with more than its fair share of ups and downs.

ABOVE: Hawker Siddeley Harrier Mk 52 demonstrator G-VTOL in the distinctive and stylish – although unfortunately rather short-lived – initial red, white and blue colour scheme designed by John Fozard, hovering at Dunsfold shortly after its first flight in September 1971. *Mike Stroud*

Hawker Siddeley Aviation (HSA) Kingston's two-seat Harrier Mk 52 demonstrator was a unique variant of the RAF's T.2 trainer, and undertook a great deal of invaluable work throughout its career, as will be detailed in this feature. We should, however, begin with a brief history of the development of the two-seat variant of the aircraft that would gain worldwide fame as the apogee of British aviation engineering and design excellence.

GENESIS OF THE TWO-SEATER

Early RAF Harrier experience following the type's entry into service in April 1969 had indicated that a two-seater was required for training and that such a machine would also have to be usable operationally with minimum performance penalty – and of course it would have to be as inexpensive as possible.

As a result, in 1965 an Air Staff Target (AST) was sent to HSA's Assistant Chief Designer (Projects), Ralph Hooper, creator of the P.1127/Harrier series, who produced a general arrangement (GA) drawing. Based on this GA, Jack Simmonds in the Design Office schemed a number of possible layouts. ▶

ABOVE: Although the Harrier was built entirely with function in mind and was arguably not the most beautiful of aircraft, John Fozard's initial colour scheme for G-VTOL accentuated the jet's unusual lines and even managed to create an impression of elegance. *TAH Archive*

A tandem cockpit was chosen to keep the fuselage shape forward of the intakes as similar as possible to that of the single-seater to avoid changing the airflow ahead of the short, and hence aerodynamically sensitive, intake ducts. To satisfy the Ministry of Defence's requirement that the instructor's view from the rear cockpit be as good as that from the front, the rear seat was raised. Also, to minimise nose length and centre of gravity (c.g.) forward movement, the cabin-conditioning equipment was repackaged and housed in the rear seat fairing, allowing the cockpit to be moved aft between the intake ducts.

A formal HSA Project Study for this, HS.1174, to satisfy Air Staff Requirement (ASR) 386, was in the process of being prepared when legendary designer Sir Sydney Camm died in March 1966, making the two-seat Harrier the last Kingston-created aircraft to which his design experience was applied, albeit more by way of criticism and approval than direct contribution.

The two-seat design solution was ingenious and combined minimum change with reasonable appearance – always important to Camm and necessary to gain his approval. The standard Harrier front fuselage was "cut off" aft of the cockpit and moved forward, leaving enough space to insert a plug containing the raised second cockpit. New side-hinged canopies covered each cockpit. To balance the aircraft a "sting" extension, carrying detachable ballast weights, was added to the tail. To restore directional stability, which was degraded by the extra forward side area, the fin was moved aft and mounted on a stub fin to increase its area, and a larger ventral fin was fitted. Apart from duplicated controls and systems for the second pilot, almost everything else was unchanged. In time of war the second seat and detachable tail ballast could be removed,

*The **first flight** of the new variant, made from Dunsfold by Chief Test Pilot Hugh Merewether on **April 22, 1969** showed that its **handling qualities** were very similar to those of the **single-seater.***

reducing the weight penalty over the single-seater to only 800lb (363kg). The weapon load capability of the two-seater was the same as the single-seat Harrier GR.1.

TWO'S UP

The first flight of the new variant, made from Dunsfold by Chief Test Pilot Hugh Merewether on April 22, 1969, showed that its handling qualities were very similar to those of the single-seater, although directional stability at high angles of attack was inadequate. This was explored and many fixes were tried, including the placing of vortex generators near the canopy and revised upper intake lip contours, as disturbed airflow from that region was understood to be the cause. However, more fin area was the solution and a taller broader-chord fin was designed under Deputy Chief Engineer John Fozard's

BELOW: G-VTOL is prepared for another flight at Dunsfold. Two-seat Harriers intended for use only in the training role, essentially non-RAF operators, retained the broader-chord fin as seen here, the RAF retrofitting its two-seaters with a smaller fin for better ground-attack performance. *TAH Archive*

ABOVE: In September 1971 a reception was held at Dunsfold for the directors and executives of the suppliers which had contributed to the building of G-VTOL. This group photograph shows the guests and their Hawker hosts, notable among the latter being Purchasing Manager Ambrose Barber, third from right in the top row in front of the tailplane, to the right of which is Commercial Manager Colin Chandler. The guests included representatives of Rolls-Royce, Dowty Rotol, Flight Refuelling, GEC Marconi, Hymatic, Vickers Sperry Rand, Smiths Industries, Triplex, Normalair, SARMA (UK) and Fireproof Tanks Ltd among others. *Ambrose Barber via author*

supervision. This was initially adopted for the RAF but it degraded the aircraft's ground-attack weapon-aiming characteristics and generated excessively high fin loads in rolling pull-outs. As the RAF intended an operational, as well as training, role for the two-seater, its aircraft were later retrofitted with a smaller fin. The large fin was retained on export two-seaters, however, where the operators intended only a training role for their aircraft.

The smaller fin of the RAF's two-seaters was a slightly taller version of that fitted to the Harrier GR.3 variant in order to accommodate the latter's RWR (radar warning receiver) aerial. It was eventually standardised on all RAF and Royal Navy single- and two-seat Harriers.

A CIVIL JUMP-JET

The building of a Harrier two-seat demonstrator to attract export orders, designated the Mk 52, was put in hand by HSA at Kingston. Allocated civil registration G-VTOL (for Vertical Take-Off and Landing) – one of the first off-sequence personalised UK registrations – it was to be funded entirely by HSA. Subcontractors which supplied parts for Harrier production were persuaded by Kingston's Purchasing Manager, Ambrose Barber, to provide equipment free of charge. This was vital as the Hawker Siddeley Board had decreed that there would be no demonstrator unless all the suppliers agreed to back it in this way. Changes from the RAF T.2/4 included the fitting of Magnavox ARC 164 UHF

and 657R VHF radios, a Collins VHF 20 alternative radio, a Collins 51 RV1 VOR, a Collins DF206 ADF and a Cossor 2720 ATC (air traffic control) transponder. Also fitted were a digital JPT (jet pipe temperature) indicator for clarity, a PRL (pressure ratio limiter) on/off switch to mute its operation at high-altitude airfields to prevent surprise thrust reductions, and a rear cockpit water-injection on/off switch so the company pilot could override any incorrect front cockpit selections. The tail ballast was fixed as the aircraft was to have no operational role. Clearance was extended to permit operations at sea-level air temperatures from -26°C to +45°C. The aircraft was fitted with the large fin throughout its career to retain good handling qualities at high angles of attack.

The new demonstrator was the 12th two-seater and made its first flight (1hr 10min) in the hands of Chief Test Pilot Duncan Simpson on September 16, 1971, to become the world's first jet V/STOL aircraft with a civil Certificate of Airworthiness. This Special Category document, No A.11640, permitted "testing the aircraft; exhibiting the special flight capabilities of the aircraft, demonstration to potential customers and demonstration in flight to properly briefed passengers at the direction of the Commander of the aircraft".

Equipped with airline-standard communications and navigation equipment 'VTOL was ready to fly the airways of the world. It was a striking sight in its patriotic red, white and blue livery designed by John Fozard. The primary purpose of the aircraft ▶

ABOVE: Dr John W. Fozard joined Sydney Camm's design team at Kingston in 1950, becoming Chief Designer (Harrier) in 1964 and Deputy Chief Engineer three years later. *TAH Archive*

ABOVE: Test pilot Duncan Simpson greets a foreign naval officer with Ralph Hooper, HSA Executive Director and Chief Engineer, at Dunsfold in 1972. *TAH Archive*

ABOVE: Taken sometime during the three-week period G-VTOL was flown in its first colour scheme, this photograph captures the aircraft making a turn over the western perimeter track at Dunsfold. Within a matter of days it would run off the runway during a test flight and be repainted in a desert camouflage scheme for its upcoming promotional tour. *TAH Archive*

BELOW: The manufacture of G-VTOL depended on the goodwill of numerous firms, including Rolls-Royce, which loaned and provided technical support for a total of six Pegasus 11/Mk 103 engines throughout G-VTOL's career. *Mike Stroud*

> The new **demonstrator** nearly came to a premature end when it **overran** the 7,000ft (2,100m) **Dunsfold runway** on Flight 12, just three weeks after its first flight.

was to enable potential customers' pilots and influential officials to experience Harrier flight at first hand under the guidance of a company pilot, and so demonstrate the many outstanding and unique qualities of the type. It would also show that an ordinary suitably experienced pilot could fly it.

EARLY DRAMAS

The new demonstrator nearly came to a premature end when it overran the 7,000ft (2,100m) Dunsfold runway on Flight 12, just three weeks after its first flight. The last part of this test flight, before a Middle East and India sales tour, was to measure the end speed on a simulated 550ft (168m) flight deck representing the Indian Navy (IN) carrier Vikrant by means of a short

take-off (STO) hop. The aircraft hopped into the air at the end of the "deck" but the power was reduced too slowly and the touchdown was late and fast. The use of nozzle braking (nozzles forward, full power) was then necessary, but as this might cause foreign object ingestion damage to the engine the pilot, Tony Hawkes, chose to rely on wheel brakes with nozzles forward but without full power. The aircraft ran off the end of the runway on to the grass overshoot, which, unfortunately, was very slippery and hard owing to a prolonged dry spell, and provided little retardation. The aircraft continued down a steep slope into trees, suffering extensive damage.

The aircraft was ready again by May 1972, repainted in desert camouflage, and set off in June, with Tony Hawkes and John Farley, on the delayed sales tour, managed by Kingston marketing executive Johnnie Johnson assisted by his colleague Robbie Roberts. Salesmen and a five-man Dunsfold maintenance team travelled in a Hawker Siddeley 748. Sales promotion stops were made at Tehran in Iran and Kuwait before setting off for Bombay and Cochin in India, hampered by the monsoon weather activity.

From the Cochin base the aircraft was flown aboard the carrier *INS Vikrant* by John Farley. In two days he flew 17 sorties from the ship plus two return trips from Cochin to the *Vikrant*. The first day's operations were to establish handling and performance data relevant to the ship and local conditions (a Dunsfold flight test team led by Eric Crabbe had flown out) and the second day was devoted to flying Indian Navy pilots. Next, interrupted by the heavy monsoon rains, G-VTOL left Cochin, with an IN officer aboard, for Goa and thence to Delhi, demonstrating a low-level mission as requested by the IN. In Delhi there was more IN and Indian Air Force pilot familiarisations with Hawkes ▶

THE VIEW FROM THE BACK SEAT
BY MIKE CRADDOCK

TAH Archive

The date was September 16, 1971, and it was to be G-VTOL's first flight. The aircraft positively gleamed in the sun at Dunsfold, magnificent in its unusual red, white and blue colour scheme. All the system checks and engine runs had been completed and it was time to get some pictures for publicity. On the ground the company photographer was present with senior managers, technicians and fire crews; in the air the photo-support aircraft was ready. Duncan Simpson would fly the aircraft and I would be the observer in the back seat. We strapped in, started up and took off and, after a few checks, climbed to the rendezvous point for the photographs. At the agreed time a company Hawker Siddeley 125 appeared beside us, and we could see the photographers watching us through their lenses. Duncan arranged suitable manoeuvres with the 125 pilot, so we banked and turned around the 125, got some spectacular close-ups (as seen in the accompanying colour photograph) and, when all were satisfied, broke off and returned to Dunsfold; a successful flight with some great pictures obtained.

INTO THE WOODS
A few weeks later I was called to another sortie in G-VTOL and this time Tony Hawkes was to be the pilot. Tony was meticulous and could fit tests into flights in rapid succession so I knew it would be a busy afternoon! We did a short take-off (STO) and then performed navigation and radio checks before landing at Thorney Island. We returned to Dunsfold for a vertical take-off, hover and short landing. We then commenced another STO but a few seconds after lift-off returned suddenly to the ground (subsequently Tony explained that he had belatedly decided that the fuel remaining was too marginal for another full circuit). By then we were doing about 120kt (138 m.p.h.– 222km/h) and it became clear that we were too far down the runway to stop in the remaining distance. Tony was using wheel brakes and had the nozzles in the braking position, but our rate of deceleration was unsatisfactory. Shortly we reached the end of the concrete and ran on to the grass overshoot. Wheel braking became ineffective and we were aware that we were closing fast on a wood at the end of the grass and were unlikely to stop before reaching it. "Cover up!" said Tony at the last moment as we plunged down a slope into the woodland.

I braced myself and amidst a flurry of thrashing branches and flying leaves we came to a sudden halt pointing downhill (as seen in the accompanying black-and-white photograph).

Chris Farara Collection

Fortunately there was no fire, Tony turned off the main systems and we started to unstrap. My canopy opened but Tony's jammed owing to fuselage distortion and he was forced to use the miniature detonating cord to shatter the canopy so that he could climb out. His shoulders were peppered with debris as a result and he needed treatment for this afterwards. By the time we were out the fire truck and an ancient ambulance had arrived at the scene with several worried people, including Duncan and various managers. A decision was made that we needed medical checks and should both go in the ambulance to Surrey County Hospital. There followed a fast 20min journey, with the bell ringing continuously, to the casualty department where we both had to stand in the waiting area in full flying suits and harnesses, carrying our helmets. We had a few funny looks and it was certainly an unusual event for the doctors! We were discharged that evening and only Tony had to suffer further treatment for the blast effect on his shoulders.

That was the last time I flew in G-VTOL and I subsequently left Dunsfold and took up a different career, but I am regularly reunited with it at Brooklands Museum.

and Dunsfold test pilot Andy Jones, who had replaced Farley in the team.

From Delhi G-VTOL flew via Bombay and Masirah to Abu Dhabi, one of the Emirates on the Persian Gulf. A demonstration to the Ruler and Minister of Defence had been organised to take place at a semi-prepared strip near Al Ain. During a hover in front of the assembled VIPs a cloud of dust engulfed the aircraft and, instead of climbing away, Hawkes, with no visual cues, reversed into the cloud, lost height and hit the ground with a thud, breaking an outrigger and the noseleg ...end of tour. The machine was flown back to Dunsfold in a Canadair CL-44 Guppy to be repaired, and John Farley returned to the Middle East and demonstrated a GR.1 to show that there was nothing fundamentally wrong with the aircraft. Harriers were never sold in that region but the Indian Navy did eventually became an important customer for the Sea Harrier. Previously it had operated Hawker Sea Hawks and eventually would acquire Hawk trainers, another Kingston type. Difficulties in obtaining liquid oxygen

during the tour led to the later substitution of a gaseous system.

STEADY WORK

The two-seat demonstrator flew again in February 1973, performed a great deal of pilot familiarisation work, demonstrated at Dartmouth, Yeovilton, Wildenrath and Staverton, and made the first of many appearances at the Paris Air Salon before being air-freighted to Rio where it was assembled and air tested in preparation for an extensive tour of South America. The tour was managed by John Parker, Kingston's South American regional marketing executive, and flown by John Farley and another Dunsfold test pilot, Don Riches. The tour ran from September 12 until October 19 and consisted of 62 flights of demonstrations, pilot familiarisations and carrier operations. The route started in Brazil at Galeão (Rio) and moved on to San Jose (São Paulo), Santa Cruz and San Pedro before returning to Galeão; then on to Asunçion in Paraguay, Cochabamba in Bolivia, Lima in Peru and on to Ecuador to visit Guayaquil and Quito

before returning to Peru to visit Las Palmas and conclude the tour at Lima, where the aircraft was broken down for return to Dunsfold in a CL-44 Guppy. The São Paulo Air Show was attended and the Brazilian Navy carrier, *Minas Gerais,* was visited from Santa Cruz. In spite of generating great technical interest in the Harrier, the tour resulted in no orders. Spectacular publicity photographs were obtained, however, including G-VTOL flying past the Corcovado statue of Christ at Rio and hovering in front of the enormous airship hangar at Santa Cruz.

G-VTOL GOES TO SEA AGAIN

Next, in November, a wf French naval aviators was familiarised in preparation for trials on the French Navy carrier *Foch*, with John Farley at the controls again. Later that month G-VTOL flew from *HMS Bulwark*. In January 1974 it was off to Algeria, in May it was sent to Italy and in September the aircraft attended the SBAC Display at Farnborough where the BBC's Raymond Baxter memorably broadcasted from the back seat during a Farley demonstration.

LEFT: Following its mishap at Dunsfold in October 1971 G-VTOL was repaired and made ready for a sales tour of the Middle East and India, for which it was painted in a new desert camouflage colour scheme with pale blue undersurfaces. It is seen here hovering during tests at Dunsfold before setting off on the first leg of the tour. *TAH Archive*

BELOW: Crunch! Groundcrew take precautionary measures after G-VTOL comes to grief during a demonstration in Abu Dhabi on July 16, 1972. Damage was confined to the starboard wingtip and outrigger, the noseleg and a twisted nose. *TAH Archive*

The tour ran from September 12 until October 19 and consisted of **62 flights** of demonstrations, pilot familiarisations and carrier operations. The route started in **Brazil at Galeão (Rio).**

Throughout G-VTOL's flying career UK demonstrations and pilot familiarisations were interspersed with more exciting overseas and development work. In 1975 the aircraft flew from *HMS Engadine, HMS Bulwark* and *HMS Fearless*, attended the Paris Air Salon and trained McDonnell-Douglas test pilots Charlie Plummer and Bill Lowe in the art of jet V/STOL flying.

BELOW: Flying down to Rio – G-VTOL pays a visit to the 125ft (38m)-high Cristo *Redentor* statue on the peak of Corcovado mountain in Rio de Janeiro, Brazil, during the 1973 South American sales tour. *TAH Archive*

ABOVE: Managed by John Parker (furthest left) the 1973 South American sales tour took in Brazil, Paraguay, Bolivia, Peru (which had acquired Hunters in the mid-1950s) and Ecuador. *TAH Archive*

ABOVE: Also on hand was John Glasscock, HSA Kingston General Manager (centre photograph, in suit) *TAH Archive*

ABOVE: The flying was undertaken by John Farley (in flying overalls) and Don Riches. Although impressed with the Harrier, none of the nations on the tour acquired it. *TAH Archive*

1976 was a year of UK-based "demos and famils" with a smoke system which was ultimately deemed unsuccessful, as the smoke hid the aircraft. In 1977 'VTOL flew from *HMS Hermes* on Harrier service release trials and helped celebrate the launching of *HMS Invincible*, the Sea Harrier's future home,

with a display over Barrow-in-Furness. It also demonstrated from the Australian carrier HMAS Melbourne.

That October the aircraft participated in ski-jump trials then in progress at the Royal Aircraft Establishment at Bedford, with the ramp set at 9°. In 1978 the angle

was increased through 15–17½° and that September the first public ski-jump demonstrations were flown at the SBAC Air Display at Farnborough on a ramp constructed by the Royal Engineers from Fairey Engineering medium girder bridge components. This proved to be the highlight ▶

BELOW: The hardworking G-VTOL aboard *HMS Hermes* during service release trials in February 1977. Trials at sea gathered pace during 1977–78 in preparation for the introduction of the Sea Harrier, the first of which, XZ450, first flew in August 1978. *TAH Archive*

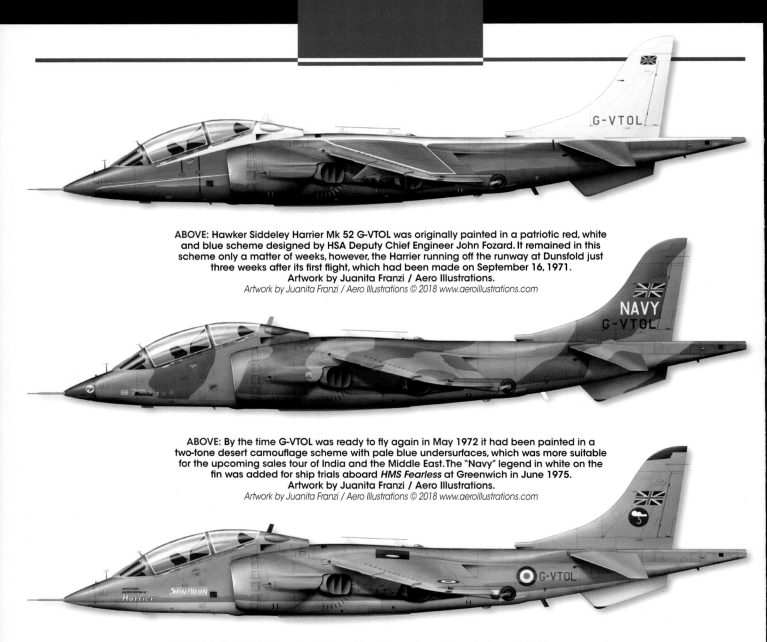

ABOVE: Hawker Siddeley Harrier Mk 52 G-VTOL was originally painted in a patriotic red, white and blue scheme designed by HSA Deputy Chief Engineer John Fozard. It remained in this scheme only a matter of weeks, however, the Harrier running off the runway at Dunsfold just three weeks after its first flight, which had been made on September 16, 1971.
Artwork by Juanita Franzi / Aero Illustrations.
Artwork by Juanita Franzi / Aero Illustrations © 2018 www.aeroillustrations.com

ABOVE: By the time G-VTOL was ready to fly again in May 1972 it had been painted in a two-tone desert camouflage scheme with pale blue undersurfaces, which was more suitable for the upcoming sales tour of India and the Middle East. The "Navy" legend in white on the fin was added for ship trials aboard *HMS Fearless* at Greenwich in June 1975.
Artwork by Juanita Franzi / Aero Illustrations.
Artwork by Juanita Franzi / Aero Illustrations © 2018 www.aeroillustrations.com

ABOVE: In 1979 G-VTOL underwent another change in markings, being painted in a grey and white semi-naval scheme which matched that of its demonstrator stablemate BAe Hawk ZA101/G-HAWK. When G-VTOL was selected for trials with the Skyhook system in 1985, the Skyhook legend and badge were applied to the forward fuselage and fin respectively.
Artwork by Juanita Franzi / Aero Illustrations.
Juanita Franzi / Aero Illustrations © 2018 www.aeroillustrations.com

of the show. For these trials extra nozzle-lever STO stop positions at 20° and 35° were fitted as were stronger main and nose undercarriage legs. In November there were more Controller Aircraft (CA) Release trials aboard *HMS Hermes* as the latter had been fitted with a 12½° ski-jump. In 1979 Bedford ski-jump trials were completed with the ramp set to what seemed an impossibly large exit angle of 20°, but the Harrier still flew easily and effortlessly away. The Royal Engineers erected their medium girder bridge ski-jump at Le Bourget for the Paris Air Salon in June and 'VTOL stole the show again. For marketing reasons the desert camouflage was replaced by a grey-and-white scheme which matched Hawk demonstrator G-HAWK/ ZA101, and the military serial ZA250 was added. The year finished with another visit to *HMS Hermes*.

SKYHOOK AND RETIREMENT

1980 was a quiet year for G-VTOL, with servicing being undertaken by HSA at Holme-on-Spalding Moor, but the aircraft did appear at the SBAC Display at Farnborough that September. It was also evaluated by the Brazilian Air Force. During 1981–82 the aircraft was flown by Indonesian, Chilean, Japanese and Indian pilots and during 1982–83 large numbers of Indian Navy pilots were fully trained flying from Dunsfold, RNAS Yeovilton and *HMS Hermes* in preparation for India's receipt of Sea Harriers. This was contracted work helping G-VTOL to pay its way. Swiss Air Force pilots flew it in 1984 and there was much chase-flying for various Harrier and Hawk development and production programmes.

In 1985 G-VTOL became an integral part of the development of the "Skyhook" concept invented by Dunsfold Chief Test Pilot Heinz

Frick for small ship operations. A Harrier hovering alongside would dock with a ship-mounted space-stabilised crane, then be swung aboard for rearming and refuelling. The replenished aircraft was then ready to be swung overboard and released into the hover for transition into its mission. It fell to G-VTOL to prove that a Harrier could be positioned accurately enough for safe and repeatable capture by the crane. Sadly this brilliant idea was not pursued by the Ministry of Defence or British Aerospace (BAe – of which HSA had become a part in April 1977), although much design and test work had been performed by Diggy Mottram's project team at BAe Kingston, by Dowty Boulton Paul (on the crane) and British Robotic Systems (on the capture system), which proved the feasibility of the concept.

In 1985 BAe was privatised and G-VTOL was used for a "photo opportunity" publicity

ABOVE: With roundel applied on the aft fuselage, G-VTOL points towards the ski-jump erected at Farnborough by the Royal Engineers. The aircraft would later also have military serial ZA250 applied, to allow the carriage of trials weapons, which was not permitted on civil aircraft. *TAH Archive*

stunt, in which it hovered with the company's share price painted underneath. As hoped for by the management, the photographs were published in all the national daily newspapers, gaining wide publicity for the share issue.

The long and valuable career of G-VTOL was brought to a close on February 19, 1986, after a decade and a half of service which had accumulated some 1,389 flights and 721hr 33min of flying time. Pilots and officials from 19 countries had flown in the faithful G-VTOL, an aircraft that had done much to develop V/STOL operations on land and at sea.

Proposals for further uses of G-VTOL included adaptive camouflage trials, "Harrier 3" large-span wing development flying, Skyhook system development and avionic systems trials as well as continuing chase and pilot training tasks. With this work G-VTOL would still have been flying in the early 1990s. However,

the aforementioned projects were not funded by BAe and so this historic aircraft was retired. It now resides at Brooklands Museum near Weybridge in Surrey, where an enthusiastic band of volunteers, including old Hawker hands, keep it in pristine condition with "live" systems. ●

THE "SKI JUMP"

The "Ski Jump", an upward-curving ramp fitted to the bow end of an aircraft carrier's deck, was proposed by Lt-Cdr Doug Taylor of the Royal Navy in 1973. It was in fact an ancient and familiar notion – that of increasing the time of flight of a projected body by imparting an initial upward momentum. Taylor perceived that, given an aircraft having enough thrust to accelerate in an initial upward trajectory, the increased time of flight would enable the vehicle to be launched at a lower speed and with a poorer lift-to-weight ratio. Airspeed would build throughout the part-ballistic trajectory until the aircraft was able to fly under its own power. As a result, deck runs could be much reduced and fuel and weapon loads increased. In addition there was a safety benefit as the aircraft always left the deck end in an upward trajectory, giving the pilot more time to eject in an emergency.

Taylor's studies were given qualified support by HSA engineers at Kingston, with performance engineer Trevor Jordan and structural dynamics engineer Doug Thorby refining Taylor's ideas until, in mid-1974, HSA effectively espoused the concept. The active support of a few far-sighted men in the Ministry of Defence and Royal Navy led to small study contracts for HSA at Kingston, which by late 1975, was publicly championing the concept. An adjustable test ramp was built at RAE Bedford and the idea would ultimately be applied to RN carriers.

BELOW: G-VTOL leaps into the air from the variable-angle ski-jump at the Royal Aircraft Establishment at Bedford. The multi-hydraulic-jacked structure at Bedford was an ingenious piece of engineering, capable of rotating 20,000lb (9,000kg) of Harrier moving at speeds of up to 100kt (185km/h); its total cost was reported to be less than £250,000. *TAH Archive*

The Stefan KarWOWski factor

To the jaded UK airshow visitor in 1980, the arrival on the scene of a scarlet Hunter flown to the very edges of its flight envelope by a prodigiously gifted pilot determined to wring the last drop of performance from the sleek jet was a revelation. With the help of Stefan Karwowski's friends and former colleagues, PAUL FIDDIAN profiles a high-octane life in aviation.

Scintillating in its presentation, the debut of Spencer Flack's striking scarlet Hawker Hunter F.51, G-HUNT, was a compelling highlight of 1980's Biggin Hill International Air Fair that May. Significant in launching on to the UK airshow circuit its first privately-owned jet fighter, it was a textbook example of the exhilarating flying style brought to the display scene by the late Stefan Karwowski. In the dashing Hunter lay the perfect mount for Stefan's exuberant airshow routines but, during a lifetime cut tragically short, many other types also found their way into his logbook, notably the Grumman Bearcat and Folland Gnat.

Staged in five successive British summers' skies, Karwowski's virtuoso displays were the product of an intensely varied flying career, assimilated from a multitude of experiences, including service with four air arms. Among many British enthusiasts, these displays still provoke a deep sense of awe today, and many of that era's foremost airshow performers recall Stefan's defining characteristics and the weighty contribution he made to a vibrant period in UK airshow history. Such contemporaries include Stephen Grey – then just starting to establish what would become The Fighter Collection – and Adrian Gjertsen, at that time spearheading, alongside Stefan, the first generation of classic-jet display pilots.

IN THE BLOOD

Stefan Witold Karwowski arrived in the world on June 4, 1945. He was born into a family with an already-solid aviation heritage; his Polish father, Włodzimierz Eugeniusz Karwowski, had flown with France's *Armée de l'Air* and the RAF during the Second World War, latterly as a flight commander, while Pamela, his English mother, had been a Women's Auxiliary Air Force (WAAF) cipher-operator.

Stefan's earliest years were spent in Middlesex but in February 1948 the Karwowskis moved to New Zealand, ultimately settling in Whangarei, the country's northernmost city. In leaving the UK, Stefan's father left behind his flying career and took up farming. For Stefan, no such path lay ahead. A keen athlete, he may have become a professional sportsman – but it was in aviation that he would find his true calling.

According to the memoirs he would later write, Stefan became interested in the concept of flight when aged six and shortly afterwards experienced it first-hand in a New Zealand National Airways Corporation de Havilland D.H.89B Dominie. He joined the local Air Training Corps squadron, built and flew large-scale models and then, aged 18, applied to join the Royal New Zealand Air Force (RNZAF). In November 1963 this first application was rejected on account of his medical examination results, these revealing both a "periodic rapid pulse rate" and "sensitivity to light". The following month an RNZAF medical consultant reassessed the report and suggested that this decision be overturned. Consequently, on January 7, 1964, Stefan joined the RNZAF. On July 26 the same year, however, after 10½hr spent flying North American Harvards at Wigram, his RNZAF career ended when he won an RAF jet-flying scholarship and promptly moved back to the UK.

During his six months with the RNZAF Stefan had impressed his superiors, eliciting from them deep praise in his End of Course Report:

"Karwowski grasped principles and techniques quickly and thoroughly; after an initial demonstration of each exercise, little prompting was necessary", the report stated.

"By the end [of the course] he was flying smoothly, confidently and accurately and was making rapid progress towards solo standard in the circuit. His general air sense is outstanding and he was criticising and correcting his own flying largely unaided". ▶

LEFT: Stefan Karwowski in the seat of Hunter G-HUNT during his relatively short but extremely memorable tenure as its chief pilot during 1980–82.

ABOVE: Stefan brings the scarlet-painted G-HUNT in to land after another typically spine-cracking display at RNAS Yeovilton's Air Day in August 1980.

ABOVE: The original incarnation of the four-aircraft Carling Red Caps aerobatic team in 1974. From left to right: Bill Loverseed (team leader); Mike O'Hanlon (right wing and Stefan's room-mate); Karwowski (left wing); Debbie Gary (slot and first woman pilot of a full-time professional aerobatic team) and team manager/ferry pilot/commentator Nick Daniel. *Debbie Gary Collection*

ABOVE: Stefan in the cockpit of his Carling Pitts S-2A. *Debbie Gary Collection*

*The **Carling Red Caps** team lasted just long enough to complete the **1974 season**, flying more than **70 displays**, all much appreciated by **Canadian spectators**.*

INTO THE RAF

Stefan's rise through the RAF's ranks was no less rapid. Honing his craft on Hunting Jet Provosts and Gnats, he became especially proficient in both solo and formation aerobatics, and by July 1966 had acquired the rank of Flying Officer. Soon after, he was posted to No 208 Sqn, at that time stationed at Muharraq in Bahrain. For 2½ years he flew Hunter FGA.9s on penetrating ground-attack sorties over the local terrain.

Stefan's next posting reunited him with the docile but solid Jet Provost, this time in an instructing role, before a second overseas deployment prospect presented itself. This, his most exciting assignment yet, saw him spend three years in No 140 "Osprey" Sqn of the Singapore Air Defence Command (Republic of Singapore Air Force from 1975). In a role that neatly stitched together several elements of Stefan's already extensive flying career, he taught No 140 Sqn's pilots the art of aerobatics. In 1973 he helped establish the air arm's first aerobatic team – Osprey Red – with Hunters.

From Singapore, Stefan moved to Canada in 1974, having transferred to the RAF Reserves. It was in Canada that Karwowski met up with Michael "Manx" Kelly, who, in 1970, had founded the Rothmans Aerobatic Team, the world's first full-time civilian display unit. In a bid to replicate the team's success in Europe, Kelly established an equivalent Canadian team – the Carling Red Caps – with a fleet of Pitts S-2As as used by the Rothmans team since 1973. To the already-multinational line-up of British pilot Bill Loverseed (initially team leader before Manx took his place), Mike O'Hanlon (Canadian) and Debbie Gary (American), Stefan's addition proved a popular move. As Debbie explained to the author, "the girls loved his New Zealand accent and were often nice to me just to get a chance to meet him! I thought we were an awesome team, always thinking up and trying new manœuvres and combinations and trying to be the best out there. We were all evenly matched in skills and drive and had a wonderful time flying together."

Humour was another vital part of the team's *ésprit de corps*, Debbie explaining that "Stefan was the object of many of my pranks and he made fun of me whenever he could", as was Stefan's sense of visual flair. "We all had assigned duties, so Stef was in charge of our team clothes. He was the only one of us with any sense of style; he designed our red leather team jackets and picked out the things we wore."

The Carling Red Caps team lasted just long enough to complete the 1974 season, flying more than 70 displays, all much appreciated by Canadian spectators. However, despite the team's popularity, Stefan appeared to tire of it. Debbie recalls one particular late season rehearsal that he missed, a strong indication that "he was restless and maybe ready to move on." The team, she adds, was temporarily "the perfect vehicle for him, but I think at the end Stef was just ready for more freedom and stimulation. Being on a team means minding the boss and conforming to the team rules – and Stef was no conformist. He was fickle, easily bored, loved variety and was always looking for the next challenge and thrill."

His formation team days over, he was soon to find that next challenge. Following his stint with the Carling team, Stefan rejected the prospect of a commercial aviation position in New Zealand and returned to operational military flying on Hunters and Sepecat Jaguar GR.1s (from 1974). In 1975 another RAF secondment saw Stefan posted to the Sultan of Oman's Air Force (Royal Air Force of Oman from 1990), then operating Hunters and BAC Strikemasters. Surveyed from typically low altitude, the blurred rush of Oman's desert stretches streaked below Stefan throughout much of 1975. On one occasion he experienced engine failure, and on another a surface-to-air missile strike shattered his jet's windscreen. As a result he was awarded the Sultan's Gold Cross, which he later received special permission to wear on his RAF uniform.

CIVVY STREET

In January 1976 Stefan's service career drew to a close and he retired with the rank of Flight Lieutenant. New adventures loomed. Back in the UK Stefan's pursuit of aviation took a somewhat less-high-octane turn with his leasing-out of Airmore International's pre-flown Beechcraft King Airs at Elstree. But it was at the Hertford-shire airfield that Stefan's career would be reignited when, on March 20, 1980, he took Spencer Flack's Hunter F.51, G-HUNT, aloft for its first post-restoration flight.

For the next 18 months Karwowski was the Hunter's principal display pilot, his thrilling performances showcasing his impeccable sense of choreography and flair in the low-level arena, effortlessly blending the flying skills he had amalgamated in Singapore, Canada and Oman. Following its Biggin Hill Air Fair debut, the scarlet Hunter quickly became a highly desirable airshow asset and, to cope with the demand, the services of a second pilot, Adrian Gjertsen, were quickly secured. Adrian refers to Stefan as "a naturally very talented pilot, who displayed aeroplanes close to their limits – and what I imagine was close to his limits, too". He recalls:

"Stefan's displays were always extraordinary and great to watch. The manœuvres he used were pretty much what you'd see in a lot of displays, but one of the things that was always exciting was the height at which Stefan finished them – probably the lowest and fastest I've ever seen any aeroplane flown".

In August 1981 Flack suffered engine failure in his Hawker Sea Fury FB.11, G-FURY, near RAF Waddington and had to make a forced landing, during which the aircraft was destroyed. The following month Flack decided to sell off G-HUNT and his Supermarine Spitfire FR.XIV G-FIRE, both having been regularly flown by Stefan. The Hunter's new owner was the late Mike Carlton, who went on to establish the Hunter One organisation and take the UK's classic-jet movement to a new level. There ended Stefan's association with G-HUNT as, according to Adrian, he and Carlton simply didn't get on:

"I'd say he had a habit of falling out with the people who owned the aeroplanes. He and Mike didn't see eye-to-eye on quite a number of things, so Stefan never actually flew the aeroplane for him".

"FLY LIKE A HOOLIGAN..."

Undeterred, Stefan moved on to pastures new, and into the employment of Stephen Grey, who, by early 1982, had started to build his warbird collection at Geneva

around North American P-51D 44-73149, *Candyman/Moose*, which he had acquired in May 1980. The 1982 Biggin Hill Air Fair was the UK launchpad for Grey's newly-obtained Grumman F8F-2P Bearcat N700HL, and Stefan's dazzling performance in the pugnacious yet supremely agile little naval fighter certainly drew attention to the arrival of a new kid on the block.

Remarkably, Stefan had spent very little time in the Bearcat before its public debut and only stepped in when Grey, who was due to fly it, became unavailable. "In front of a big crowd, it was his first display on type and it was absolutely stunning", recalls Adrian Gjertsen.

Stephen Grey remembers his former employee's exceptional piloting abilities – and the impact such high-energy routines had on the aircraft he flew: "There's no doubt that he shook up the airshow scene doing what he did. Stef was an exceptional pilot and an exceptional person but he always wanted to get the best out of an aeroplane. After a few flights with us, we had to educate him to give a little more respect to the kind of

engineering that was around in the 1940s, rather than the 1960s and 1970s.

"Stef definitely had something to prove but I don't know what it was. I think it was just natural in him: you're in a machine, you put the pedal to the floor and you make sure it stays on the track. That's one way of going about it and no doubt, if we'd been at war with dispensable machinery, I would have very much liked to have Stef alongside me and not on the other side!

"He was a nice person to be with; extremely intelligent and a very professional pilot. We had our ups and downs but always in a positive sense. Sometimes he just wouldn't listen – exceptional people can be like that! If he'd taken the opportunity to be a bit more knowledgeable about the aeroplanes and a little more respectful, I think he'd have been a better man."

Stephen suggests that Stefan's flying style was probably better suited to the Hunter and the Gnat, types a generation or two on from the Bearcat, with higher airframe limits and aerodynamic features simply not present in World War Two-era technology. ▶

ABOVE: The dynamic duo – G-HUNT and Flack's Spitfire FR.XIV G-FIRE perform a scorching high-speed run at the Biggin Hill Air Fair in May 1981. In its obituary, *Flight International* described Karwowski as having "a responsible attitude to display flying [which] was exciting but never reckless". *Mike Stroud / TAH Archive*

BELOW: Adrian Gjertsen at the controls of G-HUNT during the Hunter's display at RAF Valley on August 15, 1981. Built at Kingston as an F.51, G-HUNT originally served as E-418 with the Royal Danish Air Force from June 1956 until 1975. Spencer Flack acquired it minus its powerplant in 1978, obtaining an Avon engine from an Air Training Corps unit in Balham. *Stephen Wolf via Adrian Balch*

"He was a wonderful jet warbird pilot", he explains. "An exceptional Gnat driver and, of course, the Gnat could handle the throttle being all the way up.

"He was also a brilliant Hunter pilot; he could fly it like nobody I'd seen before. I'd flown a Hunter or two and thought I knew my way around them but he was extremely experienced and I think was able to advance his knowledge of them – and how you could fly them like a hooligan – as a result of being in Oman."

A TRAGIC END TO A FINE CAREER

On July 31, 1982, G-GNAT made its public debut at RNAS Yeovilton's Air Day, with Stefan delivering another outstanding performance. Two months later a very soggy West Malling hosted the inaugural Great Warbirds Air Display, at which Stefan, this time in the Bearcat, dazzled yet again. Future editions of this show would include an award that bore his name, presented to the best individual warbird display pilot.

In 1984, as the UK warbird movement gathered pace, the first Fighter Meet was inaugurated at North Weald. Stefan's G-GNAT solo won great acclaim, not least from the aviation press, which, while accustomed to his flying style, nonetheless singled out his sparkling routine as a particularly special moment. This was one of Stefan's last UK displays as, by the following spring, he was back in New Zealand.

On April 25, 1985, he took off in Pitts S-1E ZK-ECO for a flight that would ultimately end in the worst possible way. Stefan was extremely familiar with the Pitts, having flown it extensively with the Carling Red Caps. Stephen Grey recalls: "I flew a Pitts with Stef once and his view was that it was an easy aeroplane; you could spin for as long as you like and you could stop it immediately, which is almost true.

"However, it is also a very small aeroplane, making small changes quite dramatic. I think that's what might have caught him in the end."

Started at an estimated 3,000ft (900m) altitude, Stefan's spinning manoeuvre ultimately proved unrecoverable as, at a site close to Wanaka, the aircraft met the ground. He initially survived the crash, but died two days later in hospital in Christchurch. Tributes flowed in, and a missing-man formation was flown for Stefan at that year's Great Warbirds Air Display.

So, what is this extraordinary aviator's legacy? Both G-HUNT and G-GNAT have long since been sold abroad, and only two airshow performers flown by Stefan still grace the UK's skies: the Bearcat and P-51D *Candyman/Moose*, the latter having been acquired by the Old Flying Machine Company in 1991 and now painted in new colours as *Ferocious Frankie*. Further afield, the Royal Singapore Air Force's modern-day Black Knights team exists as the polished successor to the team Stefan helped to establish.

In terms of display style, Stefan's uninhibited solo flying techniques are almost impossible to replicate in the 21st Century, such are the rigorous (albeit essential) restrictions placed on UK display flying since the advent of the CAA's CAP 403 regulations in the late 1980s. Pushing both his and his mounts' capabilities to their limits, Stefan could spear about the sky virtually unhampered in somewhat less

BELOW: By the summer of 1982 Stefan had found a new outlet for his audacious displays in the form of Stephen Grey's potent Grumman F8F Bearcat, in which he is seen here in June of that year. In an interview with the *Sunday Telegraph* in July 1981, Karwowski explained that "a modern warbird is a highly stressed aeroplane, put together without any fat ... comparing it with a civilian aircraft is like comparing a taxi with a racing car". *Mike Hooks*

Two months later a very soggy **West Malling** hosted the inaugural **Great Warbirds Air Display**, at which **Stefan**, this time in the **Bearcat**, dazzled yet again.

ABOVE: Stefan loved to fly high-performance vintage warbirds like the Bearcat, but placed high demands on them, a fact not always appreciated by their owners. *Michael O'Leary*

restricted times. In the wake of the tragic Hunter crash at Shoreham in 2015, the CAA's classic-jet display limitations and total Hunter ban have seen an even tighter regulatory backdrop prevail.

"I sometimes wonder whether he would have found display flying these days as exhilarating as he did back then", concludes Adrian Gjertsen. "He liked the freedom to do what he wanted with the aeroplane... you wouldn't be able to do that these days. That doesn't mean the displays would be any less entertaining but, certainly, today's rules and regulations would not permit him to fly an aeroplane to those limits anymore. I'm sure he'd still be flying now, though."

Stefan would surely have enjoyed the state of today's classic-jet scene, its array of types much expanded from those first few types present at the movement's genesis. It is also worth remembering that, much like the machinery he displayed, Stefan was, in Stephen Grey's words, "a fish out of water". Neither was truly intended for the environment in which they found themselves: Bearcats and Hunters had been developed as fighting machines, and Stefan had been trained to bring the best out of them in a military context. Nevertheless, even if only for a short period, the combination of this remarkably gifted pilot and these potent aircraft set the benchmark for display flying for years to come. ●

LEFT: The famous BBC presenter Raymond Baxter described Stefan, seen here at Elstree, as "a virtuoso in his field; he was to aerobatic flying what Yehudi Menuhin is to music..." *P. Boyden via author*

Falklands confidential

When Argentina invaded the Falkland Islands in April 1982, the British government was determined to fight. But what position would the USA, Britain's long-standing ally, take? Using documents recently declassified by the UK's National Archives, BEN DUNNELL reveals some of the intriguing plans mooted in the corridors of power during the conflict.

"Terry, we need Ark Royal." So wrote Admiral Isaac Campbell "Ike" Kidd, then SACLANT (Supreme Allied Commander of the Atlantic Fleet), to Britain's First Sea Lord, Admiral Sir Terence Lewin, in February 1978. His concern? That the impending retirement of *HMS Ark Royal* (R09), the last of the Royal Navy's "flat-top" aircraft carriers, would leave in Nato's maritime capability a significant, possibly a crucial, gap. "By the end of 1978," said Kidd, "we sailors will be faced with a requirement/resources problem that keeps me awake at night... I ask that the most serious consideration be given to my request that *Ark Royal* should continue beyond 1978 for as long as possible in the active Fleet."

It did not come to pass. Kidd would just have to live with his sleeplessness, while the Royal Navy waited for a return to the fixed-wing carrier-borne combat aircraft game. With the Cold War still central to defence planning, it would be a nervous few years. And when the call to arms came, unexpectedly in the South Atlantic instead of the North, still Britain's carrier gap had not entirely been filled. This situation gave rise to a decidedly odd proposal, one brought to the fore through declassification in December 2012 under the 30-year rule of UK government papers relating to the Falklands War. Far from the USA urging Britain to keep a carrier, now it was offering the loan of one.

AMERICA AND THE FALKLANDS

The familiar narrative regarding American attitudes to the South Atlantic conflict has it that the USA was, shall we say, not as ill-disposed towards the Argentinian aggressor as Britain would have liked. Of course, this ignores the fact that never before or since has a relationship between British Prime Minister and American President been as close as that between Margaret Thatcher and Ronald Reagan. It also neglects to consider what actually happened, a story told – at least in part – through the papers now to be found in The National Archives.

THE AMERICAN PERSPECTIVE

A degree of context is required here. The USA's position towards the Falklands conflict was more complex than is often credited. After all, it was dealing with a situation involving both one of its longest-standing allies and another country on the American continent. In public there was a need to maintain a stance calculated not further to inflame the crisis caused by Argentina's invasion of a British sovereign territory. In private, things were rather different. Take the reaction to an entirely inaccurate report on ABC television news on April 6, 1982, four days after the Argentinian landings, that a USAF Lockheed SR-71A reconnaissance aircraft had performed intelligence-gathering sorties over the Falklands ten days before the invasion, and done so at Britain's request. More than that, the item stated, the Blackbird missions were ongoing.

In a telegram, the then British Ambassador to Washington, Sir Nicholas Henderson, reported to the Foreign Office: "Haig has just telephoned me about this story, telling me how mischievous it can be in the light of the present criticism in the UK". Haig, of course, was the American Secretary of State Alexander Haig, then undertaking a round of shuttle diplomacy between the warring parties. In a subsequent telegram Henderson told his superiors that Haig and the American Defense Secretary, Caspar Weinberger, "had a most useful talk today. They were determined to stop the talk about the USA being neutral. It was monstrous to put a long-standing ally on to the same level as Argentina. There were ways of helping without any publicity that he

BELOW: One of the plans proposed during the Falklands conflict was the use of the American aircraft carrier *USS Dwight D. Eisenhower* (CVN-69) for British aircraft operations should the need arise. British Aerospace Sea Harriers would ultimately see operations from the carrier, these No 800 Naval Air Squadron FRS.1s being seen aboard the Eisenhower during an exercise in October 1984.

would undertake. I had only to get into touch with him if there was anything we wanted him to do. It was nonsense to talk about neutrality when Britain was concerned, and Argentina had committed aggression".

There followed further discussion in London about how this offer might best be taken up. By the end of April 1982 a paper had been prepared by one of the Assistant Chiefs of the Defence Staff entitled "Operation *Corporate*: US Assistance", in which areas of potential help were identified. At its outset were laid down a number of assumptions, chief among which was the following: "The US would not be prepared to participate with the UK in operations against the Argentine [sic]". Furthermore, this section went on, "HMG [Her Majesty's Government] would not wish to embarrass the US Administration by requesting measures of support for which Congressional approval could not be achieved. Lend-Lease of ships and aircraft might fall into this category". The section listing those areas in which the USA could potentially assist begins: "The Lend-Lease of a US attack carrier for Harrier GR.3 operations would add significantly to the overall capability of the UK Task Force and to its sustainability, despite the practical difficulties involved. It would, however, have a high political profile and it might be prudent to exclude it from an initial UK approach". Rather, the document went on to outline areas in the fields of intelligence, communications, indirect operational support, logistic support and weapons, equipment and materiel supply. At all times, expectations were moderated: it was "probable", the document says, "that the US would be reluctant to offer air-to-air refuelling support for offensive air operations" in spite of how valuable this would have been, although a request for additional air transport, "especially [Lockheed] C-5As", was deemed more reasonable.

A MOBILE LANDING STRIP AT SEA?

None of this stopped the carrier idea from being discussed. In a special commemorative supplement paying tribute to former Prime Minister Margaret Thatcher upon her death in April 2013, *The Sunday Times* published an article by Robin (now Baron) Renwick, Head of Chancery at the British Embassy in Washington at the time of the Falklands War. In it he wrote: "Weinberger was so concerned about the critical gap in our military capabilities – the lack of a large aircraft carrier – that he appeared at the embassy one morning to suggest that we might lease one from the United States". In his diary memoir *Mandarin* (Weidenfeld & Nicolson, 1994), Sir Nicholas Henderson recalls this meeting as having occurred "when Weinberger took me aside at a party at the British Embassy". Whatever, the offer, described by the British diplomat as one "of spontaneous and practical generosity that must be unique in the annals of the Washington–London relationship", was reported back to the Foreign Office in the following telegram from Henderson dated May 3, 1982:

"In the few minutes I had with Weinberger while the Secretary of State was called away to talk to Haig he spoke to me of his eagerness to give us maximum support. He was really waiting to hear whether he could help by sending down a carrier. It would take 15 days for it to get to the South Atlantic. He had the [*USS Dwight D.*] *Eisenhower* marked for the task. ▶

> He was so **concerned** about our lack of a **large aircraft carrier** he suggested that we might **lease one** from the United States.

ABOVE: The British Prime Minister, Margaret Thatcher, addresses the nation in a press conference at Downing Street on June 9, 1982, the day after the bombing of the British landing ships *Sir Galahad* and *Sir Tristram* by Argentinian A-4 Skyhawks. Beside her is the American President, Ronald Reagan, who was committed to supporting the British cause.

ABOVE: Sir Nicholas "Nicko" Henderson, the British Ambassador to the USA at the time of the Falklands conflict, was a close personal friend of President Reagan and helped to foster the "special friendship" between Thatcher and Reagan.

ABOVE: Alexander Haig, the American Secretary of State during the Falklands War.

It was now just off Gibraltar. What he was thinking was that it might serve as a mobile runway for us. This would not mean that the US forces were going to be engaged against the Argentinians. I said that I supposed US reconnaissance 'planes could fly off the carrier and provide information for us. As regards our own landing requirements I was sure it could be of great importance to have, as it were, a mobile landing strip. How would he view the idea of [Blackburn] Buccaneers using the carrier, manned of course by the RAF? Weinberger seemed to have no trouble with the idea."

Well, maybe; but it seems likely that neither Henderson nor Weinberger was fully aware of the effort required to make such a thing possible. Even those ex-Fleet Air Arm Buccaneer pilots who had carried on flying the type with the RAF were by now far from carrier-current, to say nothing of their colleagues with no naval background. Clearly the idea was impractical. Robin Renwick notes as much, and an unidentified official's scrawled comment on Henderson's original telegram agrees, saying, "I think this is crazy, and so, oddly enough, does CNS to judge from his remarks this morning". CNS is a reference to the Chief of Naval Staff, a title held by the First Sea Lord, at that time Admiral Sir Henry Leach. Another handwritten note on the document concurs, adding that the Ministry of Defence's views on the proposal would not be sought. Indeed, it does not seem to be mentioned again in the relevant files. The idea of RAF Buccaneers flying from a US Navy aircraft carrier would remain a wild pipedream.

But this was far from the end of the story. While several of the key players in relation to these events – Henderson, Leach, Weinberger, Haig – are no longer with us, there are still many important retrospective insights to be gained. Admiral James A. Lyons Jr was Commander of the US Second Fleet, and became heavily involved in another proposal, this time relating to the potential use of an *Iwo Jima-class* amphibious assault ship by British

ABOVE: Haig and Thatcher during the latter's visit to the USA at the end of June 1982. Haig conducted shuttle diplomacy between Buenos Aires and London in the early stages of the conflict, but, by mid-April 1982, negotiations had broken down.

LEFT: Caspar Weinberger, the US Secretary of Defense during 1981–87.

The **idea** of RAF Buccaneers flying from a **US Navy aircraft carrier** would remain a wild **pipedream.**

ABOVE: Looking somewhat battle-scarred, *HMS Hermes* returns to Portsmouth on July 21, 1982, having been a vital asset during the conflict. Had the Hermes or Invincible been put out of action, Americans assets may have been called upon to maintain British carrier capability. *TAH Archive*

ABOVE: "*Mighty Ike*" – the nuclear-powered *USS Dwight D. Eisenhower* (CVN-69) is one of the ten Nimitz-class aircraft carriers built, all of which were still in service in 2019. Recently-declassified documents reveal that proposals to operate RAF Buccaneers from the Eisenhower were considered during the Falklands conflict. *US Navy*

helicopters and Harriers had either *HMS Hermes* or *HMS Invincible* been lost. In an interview in May 2013 he told the author: "The *Eisenhower* issue never, let's say, filtered down to the Commander of Second Fleet, which was my command at the time. But I knew about the *USS Iwo Jima* possibility. I was alerted to the possibility of making it available, and I made certain preparations in the event of that actually coming to pass. With the losses the British fleet was sustaining down there at the time,

LEFT: Hawker Siddeley Harrier GR.3 XZ963 aboard *HMS Hermes* during the conflict. This aircraft saw combat against Argentinian helicopters and ground positions before being lost as a result of small-arms fire on May 30, 1982. The pilot, Sqn Ldr Jerry Pook, ejected into the sea and was rescued by a Royal Navy Sea King. *TAH Archive*

I think Margaret Thatcher said that if you lost one more ship you would have thought about calling off the operation.

"The *Iwo Jima* was with me down in the Caribbean area where we were conducting exercises, so it was the most immediately available option: it was ready, it was at sea. We looked at certain crew members we would keep on the ship to help operate it: what we would need to ensure its good, continued operation."

As has been stated by both "Ace" Lyons and the then US Secretary of the Navy, John Lehman, these individuals would probably have been used on a "contract advisor" basis so as to avoid direct American military involvement in offensive operations. There does not, so far as the author can find, appear to be any reference to the *Iwo Jima* proposal in the declassified National Archives files, but perhaps this is not surprising when one considers Lehman's comments in a speech made in Portsmouth last year: "We would leave the State Department, except for Haig, out of it. As in most of the re-quests from the Brits at the time, it was an in-formal request on a 'what if' basis, Navy to Navy".

Of course, it never came to pass, so the issue of how American personnel would actually have been retained aboard the ship was not fully explored. As a Foreign Office

document outlining the USA's offer of a stores ship, the *USNS Sirius*, for Operation *Corporate* use makes clear, "this is principally a question for the Americans... our own attitude to this point should take fully into account the great operational advantages". In the event of the Royal Navy losing a carrier, such advantages would certainly have been conferred by the *Iwo Jima*-class vessel itself, that type of ship having already been qualified for operations by US Marine Corps AV-8A Harriers. It was, as Admiral Lyons says, "half-way there and ready to go". He also stresses that the practical difficulties inherent in the US Navy and Royal Navy coming together to employ the ship in the South Atlantic would have been minimised by the extent of previous joint operations.

"GIVE MAGGIE EVERYTHING SHE NEEDS…"

Undeniable, when one examines the archive papers, is the sincerity of Reagan's statement to Weinberger: "Give Maggie everything she needs". This had perhaps its most potent expression in the urgent supply of 100 (according to Lawrence Freedman's *Official History of the Falklands Campaign, Volume 2*; Renwick claims 105) AIM-9L Sidewinder air-to-air missiles

WOT, NO BUCCANEER? ALL DRESSED UP WITH NOWHERE TO GO...

Even if notions of RAF Buccaneer operations from the *Eisenhower* during the Falklands War were never likely to be followed up, the brutish strike aircraft could still have played a part in Operation *Corporate*. Towards the end of April 1982, No 12 Sqn at RAF Lossiemouth received word of potential involvement. "The last ten days of April was a busy and uncertain time for the squadron", its Operations Record Book (ORB) notes. "Certain preparations were made and cancelled for possible actions in connection with the crisis in the Falkland Islands."

The unit's commanding officer, Wg Cdr Yates (ex-Fleet Air Arm), added: "Many enquiries have been made by higher formations about possible 12 Sqn involvement as a result of the Falkland Island troubles. Investigations have been made in various depths on (a) Buccaneer maritime attacks from Ascension Island using AAR [air-to-air refuelling] support; (b) Buccaneer presence on Gibraltar during the period of tension; (c) Buccaneer presence on Falkland [sic] after the Islands have been retaken; (d) Buccaneers in the AAR role assisting the tanker force, which is heavily committed in the southern hemisphere. At the moment there is natural frustration that one of the country's main ship-attack system [sic] cannot be used in the naval scenario off Falkland Island [sic]."

It came to naught, despite No 12 Sqn being instructed on May 26, 1982, to prepare four aircraft, six aircrews and support personnel for deployment. "This is part of a plan to establish a garrison at Port Stanley should it be required once the Islands are again under British control", says the ORB. The garrison was required, but the Buccaneers were not, the presence of Harrier GR.3s and Phantom FGR.2s being deemed sufficient. **BD**

BELOW: Tough as nails and in a class of its own at low level, the Blackburn (later Hawker Siddeley) Buccaneer may well have proved an invaluable maritime strike asset during the Falklands War, but in the event it was not called upon to serve in the conflict. Here a pair of Buccaneer S.2Bs of No 237 Operational Conversion Unit are captured in the type's element – fast and low. *TAH Archive*

ABOVE: Admiral James A. Lyons Jr.

ABOVE: The American assault ship USS Iwo Jima (LPH-2) in 1979. It was in the Caribbean at the time of the Falklands conflict, and it was proposed that it could be sent to the South Atlantic and used for British Harrier and helicopter operations against the Argentinians – although the American crew would have to be "advisors" only. *US Navy*

for the Royal Navy's Sea Harrier force, the missiles supposedly drawn from USAF war stocks already present in Europe. Other procurements were similarly rapid, as the Pentagon, Freedman recounted, "managed to dispense with some 15 stages in the normal authorisation process."

That same willingness to assist Britain in its hour of South Atlantic need led to the carrier offer. One is left in little doubt from talking to Ace Lyons that Royal Navy use of the *Iwo Jima*-class carrier was considered a practical proposition by him, by Lehman and by others

involved. How it would have functioned in reality, we will never know. The Falklands War may well have been "a damn close-run thing" as Major-General Jeremy Moore famously said, but thankfully not quite so close-run as to result in the loss of a Royal Navy aircraft carrier. Britain never needed the *Iwo Jima* – but the knowledge that it was waiting in the wings, and backed at the highest level in Washington DC, must have been of some comfort to those few who knew. ●

LEFT A united front; kindred spirits Thatcher and Reagan.

BELOW: Sea Harrier FRS.1s XZ451 (nearest) and ZA176 both participated in Operation Corporate, the former using its AIM-9L Sidewinders, which it is seen carrying here, to shoot down several Argentinian aircraft, including a Canberra on May 1, 1982, and a Hercules on June 1. *TAH Archive*

Flying the Pucará: the Boscombe Down verdict

Argentina's IA-58 Pucará is one of the more unusual aircraft to have flown in British military markings during the post-war period, and the type's evaluation at Boscombe Down in the aftermath of the Falklands conflict offered fascinating insights into what had initially been a feared adversary. BEN DUNNELL talks to the team tasked with investigating the capabilities of this intriguing but ultimately disappointing war prize.

ZD485

ABOVE: FMA IA-58A Pucará ZD485, formerly A-515 with the *Fuerza Aérea Argentina*, with which it served during the Falklands conflict, up from Boscombe Down on June 17, 1983. The manœuvrable ground-attack aircraft retained its Argentinian camouflage but had RAF roundels and fin flashes applied for its A&AEE evaluation. *Adrian M. Balch Collection*

ABOVE: Pucará A-515 was the best airframe found on the Falklands after the ceasefire in June 1982, and is seen here being inspected at Stanley Airport by British forces including members of the Ministry of Defence's Technical Intelligence (Air) Department, sent over from London. Note that the serial number was not applied to the port side. *John Davis via author*

Evaluating enemy aircraft: something Britain did a lot of in World War Two of course, but not so much afterwards. One feels there might be much still to emerge regarding potential exploitation of Warsaw Pact types, but that is a subject for another day. The last time it happened with public knowledge was in 1983, when, in the aftermath of the Falklands conflict, a formerly feared weapon of the Fuerza Aérea Argentina (FAA – Argentinian Air Force) was put through its paces. The results, according to one of the test pilots who flew it, forced some-thing of a reassessment. The FMA IA-58 Pucará ("Fortress" in the native South American Quechuan language) wasn't nearly the threat it had initially been considered.

Why the Aeroplane & Armament Experimental Establishment (A&AEE – Aircraft & Armament Evaluation Establishment since 1992) at Boscombe Down came to fly an example of the Argentinian-built twin-turboprop ground-attack aircraft was, of course, related to the Falklands campaign. The opportunity presented by the capturing of an intact Pucará was deemed too good to miss, especially given the risk of further potential South Atlantic conflict. Finding a suitable airframe was another matter.

For many years the Technical Intelligence (Air) Department at the Ministry of Defence (MoD) had busied itself investigating the latest in Soviet military aircraft technology. In 1982 the Falklands conflict took its research down a different avenue. Wing Commander John Davis, whose RAF career had already seen him flying Canberras, graduating from the Empire Test Pilots' School and serving as deputy superintendent of the A&AEE, was at the time working in Technical Intelligence – specifically, he says, "looking at new Soviet aeroplanes. But with tension building up as far as the Falklands were concerned we then became responsible for technical information on the Argentinian Air Force. In fact we produced a lot of the visual aids that were used by the task force, and, in conjunction with our colleague branch at the MoD responsible for orders of battle, assessed what the intelligence was".

ACQUIRING AN AIRFRAME
The work that led to a Pucará flying in Britain began after the Falklands conflict ceasefire on June 14, 1982. "My boss told me to go down to the Falklands", says John,

"It was **bleak, it was snowy**. It was knee-deep in ammo, **exploded** or **unexploded**. The place was **absolutely filthy.**"

"and I took with me an armament specialist and a radar specialist. Our idea was to look at all the technical intelligence, look at as many of the crashed aeroplanes as possible to see what kit they had, look at all the ground side, look at the armament side – for example the Exocets that were on the island – and send home as much kit as we thought would be useful."

Getting there by RAF Hercules was itself an adventure. The small team from Technical Intelligence (Air) went down on only the second flight into Stanley after fighting had finished, the Governor of the Falkland Islands, Rex Hunt, having been on the first. "We did three lots of [air-to-air] refuelling on the way down", John recalls, "and there was no radar on the island, so we had three goes at getting our Hercules in. If not, we would have gone straight back to Ascension. One or two aeroplanes did that, with about a 24hr round trip. However, we got in". The scene that greeted them was hardly the most welcoming: "It was very bleak, it was snowy, it was the winter. And it was knee-deep in Argentinian ammunition, exploded or unexploded. The place was absolutely filthy. There were mines everywhere.

"When we initially arrived, we commandeered a helicopter to visit all the sites at which Pucarás and other Argentinian aeroplanes had been based, to glean what intelligence we could. Because we were still officially at war with Argentina, our bosses wanted an assessment of the aeroplane with regard to how we would be able to counter it. In that respect, one of the jobs we had to try and do was find out all the technical details. We went to every base, and we discovered between us that we could find no technical information at any of the sites at which Pucarás had been based [Stanley Airport plus grass strips at Goose Green and Pebble Island]. This surprised us. We looked carefully to see if things had been burned, shredded or otherwise, but we could find nothing. It transpired that the reason for this was that major servicing was done on the mainland – all they did on the Islands was, if you like, the first-line work; filling up with fuel and ammunition and flying."

The main cache of Pucarás was located at Stanley Airport, renamed Base Aérea Militar (BAM) Malvinas by the Argentinians. When the aircraft were found, Argentinian soldiers were found sleeping in some of the airframes, taking advantage of the space inside the fuselage. Indeed, it was possible to carry an engineer in there. It is said that some rather less pleasant remnants of these temporary living quarters were left behind, too...

"In looking at all of them, we found only one that was whole," says John Davis. "All the rest had been sabotaged by the SAS at some time beforehand. We commandeered this one, plus two 'Christmas tree' aeroplanes". The complete example was serialled A-515,

which still had underwing rocket pods fitted, while the airframes earmarked for spares use were A-533 and A-549.

RETURN TO AIRWORTHINESS

On July 10, 1982, exactly a month after the last Pucará mission of hostilities, RAF Chinook HC.1 ZA707 airlifted A-515 to the SS Atlantic Causeway conveyor ship, which took the airframe on a 15-day sea voyage from Port William to Devonport dockyard in Plymouth. There it arrived on July 27, soon to be moved by road to Boscombe Down, ready for a return to the skies.

Owing in part to the aforementioned lack of technical information, this was not the work of a moment. However, John Davis and his Technical Intelligence (Air) colleagues had much to offer. Several times in previous

BELOW: Royal Navy Sea Harrier pilot David Morgan strikes a pose at the Pucará graveyard at Stanley Airport. Morgan was an RAF Harrier pilot who was on an exchange programme to learn to fly the Sea Harrier when the Falklands conflict began. He later shot down four Argentinian aircraft and flew a Sea Harrier against the Pucará during its evaluation in the UK.
David Morgan via author

years FMA had exhibited the Pucará at the Farnborough and Paris airshows. From a Le Bourget visit had been brought back to the MoD what John calls "a fair drawer-full of technical information, which we gave to Boscombe Down. It certainly helped them; I wouldn't say it was the be-all and end-all, but it certainly assisted in getting the aeroplane serviceable."

"It needed a huge amount of restoration", adds Sqn Ldr Tony Banfield, then a test pilot on B Squadron of the A&AEE. The multi-engine expertise of Banfield – a former Vickers Valiant and Handley Page Victor captain, and a hugely experienced RAF instructor – would be brought to bear during the evaluation of the Pucará. First, though, came its return to airworthiness. "They brought it back as deck cargo", Tony recalls, "so it had got a lot of salt in it. The A&AEE trials engineers, and there were some very clever people there, virtually took it apart". Some of what they found said little for the levels of maintenance undertaken by the aircraft's original operator. It is reported that inspections at Boscombe Down showed the Martin-Baker ejection seats not to have been removed for servicing since the day they were installed. The drogue 'chutes had been rotted through by ultraviolet rays, rendering them unserviceable.

At least the Turboméca Astazou turboprop engines were well-known from use on the RAF's Scottish Aviation Jetstreams, but much else was not. "One of the big problems was getting tyres and wheels for it", says Tony Banfield.

*For the purposes of the **Boscombe trials,** the aircraft would be limited to a maximum speed of **350kt;** for inverted flight **160kt** was the limit, while **150kt** with the undercarriage down and **140kt** with flaps were other speed restrictions.*

Those on the "Christmas tree" airframes had been left too badly damaged. "Eventually I think it was Beagle Basset wheels that we used."

While that work was ongoing, Sqn Ldr Russell Peart of the A&AEE's A Squadron was – with, no doubt, substantial help from the manufacturer's information provided by Technical Intelligence (Air) – making his own preparations. In March 1983 he handwrote the Pucará's flight reference cards, which are today held by the RAF Museum. For the purposes of the Boscombe trials, the aircraft would

be limited to a maximum speed of 350kt; for inverted flight 160kt was the limit, while 150kt with the undercarriage down and 140kt with flaps were other speed restrictions.

A maximum of 3.5g was imposed for initial flights, later increased to 5g, while the aircraft's negative-g limit was -1.5. No more than 30sec of continual negative-g flight were to be made. Stall entry was to take place no lower than 10,000ft (3,050m), and stalls discontinued by 7,000ft (2,130m). Aerobatic manœuvres permitted were rolls, loops, stall turns and Immelmanns, spins being prohibited.

ABOVE: On April 28, 1983, Sqn Ldrs Russ Peart (front cockpit) and Tony Banfield took the Pucará for its first flight after its reassembly in the UK. Despite the ground-attack and counter-insurgency aircraft's reputation as an agile and effective performer at low level, the evaluation team found the type to be something of an under-achiever. *Russ Peart via RAF Museum Hendon*

BELOW: With its British military serial ZD485 applied and wearing RAF roundels and fin-flashes, the Pucará was demonstrated at the Empire Test Pilots' School open-day held at Boscombe Down on June 11, 1983. Eagle-eyed observers will notice that the nosewheel door carries the last two digits of its original Argentinian serial, A-515. *Peter R. March via author*

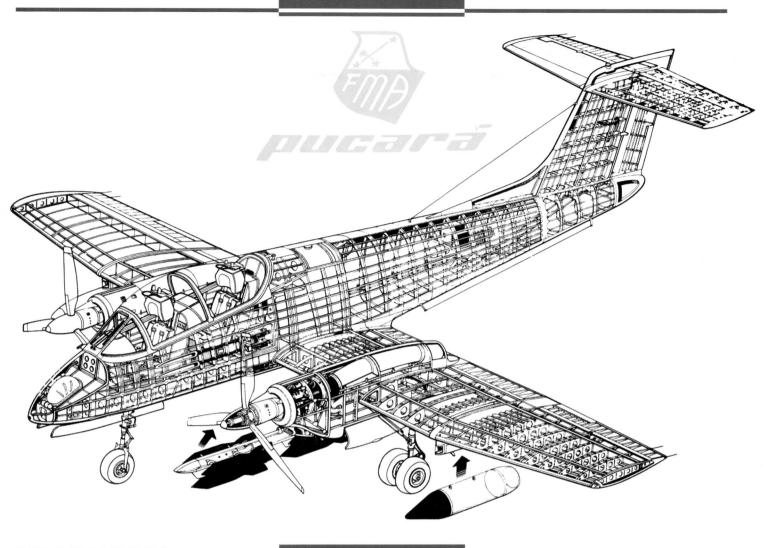

INTO RAF ROUNDELS

Pucará A-515 was allocated the British military serial ZD485, this being applied, along with RAF roundels, atop the basic Argentinian camouflage scheme in which it had been found at Stanley. Spares aircraft A-533 and A-549 were also given British serials, ZD487 and ZD486 respectively, although these were never worn by either airframe. They provided several parts for the restoration of A-515/ZD485, which progressed well enough in six months to allow taxying trials on February 22, 1983. The thought of an unfamiliar aircraft going on to the UK military register, being put through an extensive restoration and all but readied for flight in such a short space of time would probably give the airworthiness bureaucrats at today's risk-averse Military Aviation Authority convulsions. Those were very different times.

Russ Peart took the Pucará for its first test flight from Boscombe Down on April 28, 1983, with Tony Banfield in the back seat. Thus ensued the A&AEE's limited trials and handling assessment. Being a ground-attack expert, Peart led the way when it came to evaluating that aspect of the aircraft's performance, albeit without it being heavily laden, while Banfield examined its

survivability. To that end, Tony undertook his first sorties as the pilot of the Pucará on May 9, performing asymmetric engine work and relights. With that, he reports, "there was no problem at all", helped by the large, power-assisted rudder. But what was his view of how it would have fared in combat? "It wouldn't have stood a chance against a Rapier [surface-to-air missile]", Tony says. "The Pucará's reputation was fearsome, but it was never put to the test". Such can be deduced from its underwhelming record in the Falklands campaign, during which significant numbers were destroyed on the ground: three at Goose Green by Sea Harriers, and six at Pebble Island by the SAS.

Given the aircraft's other limitations, Tony Banfield believes the pilots of those wrecked machines were lucky to get taken out of the fight. "We did a lot of radar simulation work", he told the author, "and we discovered that the radar returns from those huge turboprop propellers, together with the sound that they made in warning of their approach, meant that against Rapiers it would have been like a pheasant shoot". This much was gleaned from numerous sorties in which the Argentinian aircraft's combat capabilities were put to the test, not least over the Larkhill ranges on Salisbury Plain; ▶

and, on June 23, 1983, simulated attacks against a Rapier battery.

"MORE OR LESS USELESS…"

In all, Tony flew 7hr 10min in the Pucará, 4hr 40min of that time as captain; it was an interesting diversion from the Hawker Siddeley Nimrod AEW.3 testing he was doing at the same time. "It was a fun aircraft to fly – a splendid aerobatic aircraft", he says of the IA-58. "If you were doing a stall-turn you could virtually do a cartwheel if you chopped the inboard engine, like Jan Zurakowski used to do in the Meteor. I could never get all the way round, though.

"In respect of carrying out its task, it was more or less useless. Although it was very heavily armed, and everyone feared it, when you put it in the dive the trim-change as speed increased was enormous. In order to hold it you had to trim, and you had to take your hand off the throttle to do that, so you couldn't do your radar-ranging and things like that. In addition, as speed increased the controls became heavier and heavier and heavier, and you virtually had to use two hands on the stick to move the ailerons, so actually aiming the thing was very difficult. It wasn't 'fit for purpose'."

Keeping an eye on the flight assessment of the Pucará, given that it was being

> "The size of the **radar contact** was actually **quite huge**, I suspect from the **big props.**"

conducted on behalf of Technical Intelligence (Air), was John Davis.

On June 10, 1983, he flew in the aircraft for a 40min trip with Russ Peart, focusing largely on take-offs and landings, and naturally took the stick himself. "Interesting aeroplane", says John. "Quite easy to fly, relatively good controls, but got very, very heavy as the speed increased – it was similar in that respect to an early-mark Canberra. But, generally speaking, quite pleasant, with lots of room in the cockpit. We did both hard and grass runway operations at Boscombe; it's very rugged."

Russ Peart was at the controls when the Pucará was put up against a variety of British military aircraft types for simulated combat trials. Records at the RAF Museum show that "1-v-1" combats with Westland Puma and Sea King helicopters took place on June 27–28, 1983, followed by fighter affiliation versus two McDonnell Douglas Phantoms on July 12. The results have yet to be made publicly available.

AIR-TO-AIR COMBAT TRIALS

Testimony from another sortie is on hand thanks to Lt-Cdr David Morgan DSC, the RAF Harrier GR.3 pilot (then a flight

lieutenant) who transferred on exchange to the Royal Navy's Sea Harrier FRS.1 force shortly before the Falklands conflict, and went on to score two helicopter and two A-4 Skyhawk kills. On July 18, 1983, in an engagement decidedly reminiscent of some conducted during the previous year's conflict but this time staged between Boscombe Down and Yeovilton, he flew his No 899 Naval Air Squadron Sea Harrier, XZ459, against the Argentinian aircraft.

"We got a call from Handling Squadron at Boscombe Down, asking if we could spare a Sea Harrier or two to come and do some work with the Pucará", David says. "Basically, we were looking at pick-up ranges, manœuvrability and what the missile would do against the turboprop engines in manœuvre; that sort of thing. We started with some intercepts to check the radar cross-section – off the top of my head, we were doing about 25–30-mile [40–50km] splits, and then coming in from various angles: 180° out, 150° out and so on, just recording the maximum pick-up ranges and the size of the radar contact, which was actually quite huge, I suspect from the big props. We were certainly getting very good pick-up ranges, way outside the normal fighter-size target."

Then came some air combat manœuvring. "It was set up so that the Pucará was evading and I was trying to take as many shots as I

Pucará A-515 (c/n 018) was delivered to the Fuerza Aérea Argentina by its manufacturer, Fabrica Militar de Aviones (FMA), during 1975. It was built as part of an export batch intended for, but not delivered to, Mauritania. Grupo 3 de Ataque, part of III Brigada Aérea, received the Pucará at Base Aérea Militar (BAM) Reconquista in the province of Santa Fé, and used it on operations against guerrilla groups in north-west Argentina. Further action was not long in coming.

In late May 1982 A-515 was deployed to Port Stanley in the Falkland Islands as part of post-invasion reinforcements and attrition replacements. It had been, says the RAF Museum, repainted "using Fiat car paint" in a largely tan-and-light-green scheme. Before leaving for "las Malvinas" it had performed armed-reconnaissance sorties over the Argentinian mainland coast as a deterrent to potential British special-forces attacks.

Now it would get to take on the British face-to-face.

Among the missions known to have been flown by A-515 is the final Pucará sortie of the war, a three-aircraft effort against British artillery positions and troops on East Falkland, specifically the northern side of Mount Kent and Murrell Ridge. Flown by Lt Morales, A-515 was hit by small-arms fire on June 10, 1982. Four days later, Argentinian forces surrendered.

All 24 Pucarás operated in the Falklands had either been destroyed or were now captured by the British. For A-515, it was the beginning of a new chapter. **BD**

The history of IA-58 Pucará A-515/ZD485 is covered in depth in a downloadable document by Andrew Simpson, which is available on the RAF Museum website at www.rafmuseum.org.uk.

could. Initially I did what every good fighter pilot should do – keep the energy up, keep the speed up and just make slashing attacks, get a missile lock and then break off, go high, reposition and drop in for another one. I was actually pursuing the attack further than I normally would have done, because you'd normally take the missile shot and then pull off straight away, but I was recording it in the HUD [head-up display] right through to when I estimated missile impact would be, to see how many angles the Pucará could get on me. It was quite a lot – they were getting about 150° out, so about 330° of turn by the time the missile would have hit, but it was staying locked the whole time, so there was no problem with that.

"Right at the end, when we were getting a little bit low on gas, I thought, 'OK, I'll do what I shouldn't do': drop the flaps, slow the aircraft right down and try and match the turn and get a guns kill. It became rapidly obvious that he was out-turning me

considerably, so I then slammed the nozzles aft and pulled the nose up to try and get out of the way. From what I remember, he said he might just have got a guns shot at me, because I couldn't get out of the way quick enough. It was a classic case: if you try and go slow with a low-wing loading aircraft, he's going to be biting your arse fairly quickly."

That flight was almost the last of the Pucará evaluation. Three days later, a performance assessment was carried out en route to RAF Greenham Common, where ZD485 appeared on static display at the following weekend's International Air Tattoo. It then flew back to Boscombe. About 25 flying hours had been expended on the trial, but the aircraft had been serviced on the basis of a 50-flying-hour programme, the original estimate made by Technical Intelligence (Air). "We had an aeroplane there, serviceable, and pilots who could fly it", says John Davis. "My thought was to offer it to the RAF so that, in the summer of 1983, it and a Harrier could fly around

all the RAF open days and 'At Home' days to show the Harrier and the Pucará side by side. This was rejected at a very high level by the Ministry of Defence, on the basis that they couldn't afford it. So, what we ended up doing was filling it up with every litre of fuel possible, planning a cross-country round every unit in the south of England, and dropping it off at Cosford."

FROM EVALUATION TO EXHIBITION

That took place on September 9, 1983. It became part of the then RAF Aerospace Museum collection, today Royal Air Force Museum Cosford, and remains there to this day. For a time it was joined by the incomplete airframe of Pucará A-528, which has since gone to the Norfolk & Suffolk Aviation Museum at Flixton. Of the two airframes used for spares, A-533 was scrapped after some years on display at

Continued on page 120

BELOW: The Pucará at the International Air Tattoo at RAF Greenham Common on July 23, 1983. Although the Argentinian machine flew in and out of the show, it remained in the static aircraft park for the duration of the weekend. *Mike Stroud*

PUCARÁ IN THE FALKLANDS: THE ARGENTINIAN PERSPECTIVE

In November 1982, five months after the end of the Falklands conflict, MICHAEL O'LEARY visited Argentina to conduct interviews with FAA veterans of the Malvinas Campaign, including two Pucará pilots of Grupo 3 de Ataque, part of III Brigada Aérea, based at BAM Reconquista in north-eastern Argentina at the time of the interviews.

Premier Teniente Juan Luis Micheloud

"May 21, 1982 – Mayor Juan Carlos Tomba [in Pucará serial A-511] and I were flying a two-aircraft sortie near San Carlos strait when suddenly we saw three [Sea] Harriers flying above us. Two came down to attack – we were very low at the time. Tomba and I broke left and right, hugging the earth, and both Harriers decided to come after me. I flew even lower and headed into a canyon. The two fighters tried to box me in but the terrain prevented them from hitting me, so they pitched up out of the fight and the third Harrier had a go. By this time both Tomba and I were flying around the terrain trying to give each other mutual support; it must have worked as the third Harrier couldn't hit me either.

"The other two Harriers attacked Tomba, making two passes at him. On the first pass Tomba could see the impact of the 30mm cannon on his port wing – the rounds were punching holes in the skin. Tomba saw the Harrier break away upwards and into a second pass. This time, when the Pucará was hit, the starboard wing was almost cut in half by the 30mm fire and Tomba ejected. He came down by parachute near Goose Green, which was in our hands, so he was rescued by our own people.

"We lost many Pucarás on the ground, and by the end of the war had only eight intact, with maybe only two of those really capable of flying combat sorties. One aircraft, flown by Teniente Miguel Angel Gimenez, was lost on May 28 to a missile, but we have no idea what happened. Regarding anti-aircraft fire, our worst threat was the [Shorts] Blowpipe [surface-to-air missile], because we couldn't see it, but it could see us owing to our heat signature, and we were very close to the troops firing them. Sometimes our aircraft would return to base heavily punctured but still in one piece. The Pucará turned out to be quite resilient. Since we had two engines, we often returned with one shot out. But the Blowpipe would always destroy enough of the controls to make the aircraft unflyable.

"We saw Harriers continually but we were always extremely low and in poor visibility at very high speed. We would only see them briefly and that was it. Mayor Tomba was the only pilot downed by Harriers. Personally I did not think it was difficult to see the Harriers because they were very dark against the sky. The Sea Harriers, with their grey paint, were more difficult to see than the RAF Harriers.

"We usually operated over our own anti-aircraft artillery in the Malvinas, which gave us a degree of defensive cover. We lost all 24 of our Pucarás in the Malvinas, five of these in aerial combat. They were lost to the following: Blowpipe – 3; Harrier – 1; MIA – 1; Take-off accident – 1.

CAPITÁN RICARDO A. GRÜNERT

"The dense concentration of automatic anti-aircraft fire was very hard for the Pucará to take, although it held together and got us home. We found that the electronic firing system also gave us problems, with poor micro-switches and the electrical system in general. The humidity was too high and the cold

BELOW: Pucará A-567 photographed by MICHAEL O'LEARY while up from BAM Reconquista in November 1982. This was one of 14 new Pucarás received by *Grupo 3 de Ataque* in 1982 as replacements for those lost in the Falklands conflict, and remained in service until 2002. The long-serving Pucará still operates with the FAA today. *Michael O'Leary*

weather was very hard on the aircraft. We didn't consider mounting Sidewinders on the Pucará because our unit had never really trained for air-to-air combat, which would have meant equipping the aircraft with radar. An anti-ship missile would have been fine.

"I would say that around 80 per cent of the operational Pucará flying during the conflict was from unprepared dirt or grass runways, and operating under very marginal weather conditions. These strips were about 450m long [1,475ft] by 450m wide. With the constant bombardment, rain and landing of troops, we were constantly on the go. The runway itself was around 450m long and about 6–7m [20–23ft] wide, but we could usually get in and out within 365m [1,200ft] fully loaded [1,360kg/3,000lb] with bombs and rockets.

"One of our major problems was the wheels sinking into soft ground. Goose Green was the only airfield where we could operate with no problems to speak of; there was good drainage so the water could run off. At times we could not take off and that helped the British. Also, our aircraft were all lined up and often could not leave – easy pickings for the Harriers.

"We often used the rockets of unserviceable aircraft as artillery. The 7.62mm [0.3in] machine-guns and 20mm cannon from our unserviceable aircraft were used against the Harriers that would come over the end of the runway – we are sure we hit one.

"We never attacked ships; the closest

we got to them was during reconnaissance missions. We made some attacks on artillery areas but we have no record of what, if any, damage, was caused. We fired rockets at about 1,500–2,000m [5,000–6,500ft]. This was at Mount Kent and we launched the rockets to hit the artillery over the hills. The Pucará turned out to have exceptional qualities for low-level flight in combat. We normally flew in the worst weather and under very low ceilings, when the Harriers could not fly – this gave us a much-needed extra margin for survival. I am sure the enemy felt the effects of this, and that this factor determined, to some degree, their ability to move against us.

"The Pucará was able to take a great deal of damage. Of the total of 44 days that we were in combat, we only lost two pilots despite being under continual bombardment. Practically all of the Pucarás were hit by small-arms fire in one way or another, but kept flying. One Pucará was hit in the canopy, aileron and tail, yet still flew the next mission. Another came in with hits all over the engines, one of which had its prop feathered. A rudder had a big hole in it, so we repaired it by hand and then sent the aircraft on its next mission.

"We had a sizeable store of parts, and we would strip the aircraft that could no longer fly of radio equipment, everything that we could use. We found the Pucará excellent against rotary-wing aircraft. Our four 7.62mm machine-guns and two 20mm cannon were very effective against the British helicopters."

> The runway itself was around **450m long** and about **6–7m [20–23ft] wide**, but we could usually get in and out within **365m [1,200ft]** *fully loaded* [1,360kg/3,000lb] with **bombs and rockets**.

BELOW: Although of poor quality, this is a unique photograph; it shows the ghostly image of the Pucará through the head-up display of David Morgan's Sea Harrier, XZ459 (itself a veteran of Operation *Corporate*, the Falklands campaign), during the comprehensive air combat trial undertaken on July 18, 1983.

Argentina's remaining 30 in-service examples are set to be updated, according to a November 2011 contract, with new Pratt & Whitney Canada PT6A-62 engines.

ABOVE: Despite British curiosity about the Falklands war prize, the Pucará made only two appearances at public airshows during its A&AEE evaluation; one was at RNAS Yeovilton on July 11, 1983, and the other was at the International Air Tattoo at Greenham Common two weeks later, where it is seen here making a pass on arrival. *Peter R. March via author*

Continued from page 118

Middle Wallop's Museum of Army Flying, only the nose being kept by the Boscombe Down Aviation Collection at Old Sarum, while A-549 may be seen at IWM Duxford. Visitors to Cosford will note that A-515 has been put back into its original camouflage scheme, as worn during pre-Falklands service. While authentic, it is, to some extent, a pity that no outward trace remains of its British military colours.

Now an ageing design but subject to upgrades, the Pucará remains in service with the air forces of Argentina and Uruguay. Despite occasional bouts of Argentinian sabre-rattling over the Falklands, it must be said that the capabilities of the Fuerza Aérea Argentina in terms of equipment have increased little since the 1982 conflict. Tony Banfield offers a postscript: "Russ Peart and I were at Farnborough [for the SBAC show] some years later – we were all friends with the Argentinians again, more or less, and they had a stand there. We started chatting to them, and of course told them we'd flown the Pucará. They were delighted to talk to us because they wanted to get the RAF test pilots' impressions, which we gave them".

Whether those faults have been acted upon, one can only speculate. The idea of turboprop-powered aircraft being used for counter-insurgency missions has enjoyed a new vogue in recent times, yet no direct successor to the Pucará appears in sight. Argentina's remaining 30 in-service examples are set to be updated, according to a November 2011 contract, with new Pratt & Whitney Canada PT6A-62 engines to replace the old Astazous, so it remains committed to the indigenous design. Uruguay, which has made its Pucarás compatible with the use of night-vision equipment, may do likewise.

Never has the RAF sought to acquire a similar type of aircraft, preferring such work to be done by fast jets. But the experience gained with the Pucará in 1983 was of technical value, and an interesting footnote in the A&AEE's history and the careers of those who got to fly it. ●

Acknowledgements
As well as those interviewed, the author would like to thank Denis J. Calvert and Santiago Rivas for their assistance. The Aviation Historian would like to thank Michael O'Leary and the RAF Museum's Peter Elliott.

FMA IA-58A PUCARÁ DATA

Dimensions

Span	47ft 6¾in	(14.5m)
Length	46ft 9in	(14.25m)
Height	17ft 7in	(5.36m)
Wing area	326.1ft²	(30.3m²)
Wing chord at root	7ft 4¼in	(2.24m)
Wing chord at tip	5ft 3in	(1.6m)
Wing aspect ratio	6.95:1	
Wheel track	13ft 9¼in	(4.2m)
Wheelbase	11ft 5in	(3.48m)

Weights

Empty, equipped	8,900lb	(4,037kg)
Maximum take-off	14,991lb	(6,800kg)
Maximum landing	12,800lb	(5,806kg)

Performance

Max level speed at 9,850ft (3,000m)	310 m.p.h.	(500km/h)
Cruise speed at 19,680ft (6,000m)	298 m.p.h.	(480km/h)
Stall speed with flaps and undercarriage down	89 m.p.h.	(143km/h)
Climb at sea level	3,540ft/min	(1,080m/min)
Service ceiling	33,000ft	(10,000m)
Range with max fuel at 16,400ft (5,000m)	1,890 miles	(3,042km)

ABOVE: The Pucará at the RAF Cosford Aerospace Museum (now RAF Museum Cosford), where it was delivered in September 1983. It retained its RAF roundels and fin flashes for some time, but was later repainted in its original Argentinian markings and pre-Falklands light camouflage. In 1995 it was allocated Maintenance Serial 9245M. *Andrew March via author*

BELOW: The Pucará continued to soldier on with the Argentinian and Uruguayan air forces, and there were plans to modernise those still on the former's inventory with 950 s.h.p. Pratt & Whitney Canada PT6A turboprops, to create the IA-58D "Super Pucará". The Sri Lankan Air Force also used the type in the nation's civil war during 1993–99. *Chris Lofting*

The fall of Damien. The ditching of Nimrod R.1 XW666

In May 1995 exemplary airmanship was demonstrated by the crew of one of the RAF's three specialised Hawker Siddeley Nimrod R.1 intelligence-gathering aircraft when it was forced to ditch in the Moray Firth during a routine air test. LEWIS GAYLARD interviewed the pilot of XW666, Flt Lt Art Stacey, who recalls the day's dramatic events.

The Nimrod was essentially an extensively modified military variant of the de Havilland Comet, the world's first jet airliner. Originally designed by de Havilland's successor, Hawker Siddeley, it subsequently had its development and maintenance undertaken by that company's own successor, British Aerospace (BAe).

Intended to replace the RAF's fleet of ageing Avro Shackletons, the Nimrod was designed to Air Staff Requirement (ASR) 381, issued in 1964. Introduced into RAF service in 1969, the Nimrod MR.1 and MR.2 were used extensively thereafter in the anti-submarine warfare (ASW) and maritime surveillance (MS) roles. A lesser-known variant was the Nimrod R.1, a dedicated signals intelligence-gathering (SIGINT) and surveillance platform. The R.1s were often referred to as "Radar Calibration Aircraft" to hide their true role, and it was not until the fall of the Berlin Wall and the end of the Cold War that the real purpose of these aircraft was officially acknowledged.

INTO SERVICE

The Nimrod R.1 was operated exclusively by No 51 Sqn at RAF Wyton, the unit having reformed from the renumbered No 192 Sqn on August 21, 1958, and having previously operated adapted English Electric Canberras and the Comet 2R until the Nimrod R.1 replaced them in 1974.

Three Nimrod R.1s (originally designated HS.801Rs) were ordered in 1969, with development costs of an estimated £2.38m and projected production costs of £11.5m. The first R.1, XW664, was delivered as an empty airframe to Wyton in July 1971 but it took a further two years to equip the highly secret aircraft with its highly specialised electronic equipment.

Externally the R.1 differed very little from its ASW and MS counterparts, the only recognisable difference being the absence of the latter's distinctive magnetic anomaly detector (MAD) boom, used to find submarines. Internally, however, the R.1 was vastly different from the MR.1/MR.2, and received a number of substantial upgrades throughout its service life. From 1980 the three R.1s – XW664, XW665 and XW666 – received upgrades to their surveillance equipment, including the installation of an ECKO 290 weather-radar suite to replace the antiquated ASV.21 ASW radar system and the addition of a Delco AN/ASN-119 *Carousel IVA* inertial navigation system (INS) to replace their long-range navigation (LORAN) suites. Wingtip-mounted pods, similar in appearance to the electronic support measures (ESM) equipment fitted to the MR.2, were also fitted to the aircraft.

Although official information about the R.1's participation remains scarce even today, the variant was sent to war when XW664 was posted "down south" during the Falklands conflict in 1982. Although not part of the main task force, it did provide valuable intelligence to the surface commanders. The big "mystery" surrounding the R.1's semi-covert operations revolves around where it was based during Operation *Acme*. There has been speculation over the years that XW664 operated from an airfield in southern Chile, with the latter government's permission. San Félix, one of the small Desventuradas islands, which lie 530 miles (850km) off the Chilean coast, is regarded as the likely operating base for these "secret" R.1 missions. Although

ABOVE: Nimrod R.1 XW666 in the waters of the Moray Firth immediately after its ditching on May 16, 1995.

certainly not conclusive proof, XW664 did return to the UK four days after the last sortie was flown from San Félix on May 18, 1982.

In July 1990 a Nimrod R.1 and its 28-man crew claimed a world record by reaching a combined total of 266,569 flying hours. But this significant event was soon to be overshadowed by the R.1's involvement in a high-profile conflict when it took part in the Gulf War. In August 1990, all three of No 51 Sqn's R.1s arrived at RAF Akrotiri in Cyprus, from where they operated during Operation *Desert Shield* (August 1990–January 1991), the build-up to Operation *Desert Storm* (January–February 1991). Two of the R.1s, XW664 and XW666, later operated from within the Gulf theatre but, as with all things surrounding the R.1, details on exact locations remain hazy.

THE RISE OF DAMIEN

Chapter 13 of the Book of Revelation in The Bible teaches that the number six is the number of man; a common man is born in his

sin. The number of God's creation was seven, therefore six has fallen short of the glory of God. The reason the number six is considered satanic is that it is the mark of the beast, which is widely understood by theologians as representing Satan. Those familiar with the 1970s *Omen* series of films will know that the character of Damien Thorn, complete with his birthmark of "666", is depicted as the Antichrist, the son of Satan. With typical RAF black humour, Nimrod R.1 XW666 was nicknamed "Damien" by the personnel of No 51 Sqn.

Flight Lieutenant Art Stacey was an experienced Shackleton pilot when he joined No 51 Sqn in 1991. After four years with the unit he was promoted Pilot Leader, and it was in this role that he was tasked, along with his crew, with an air test at RAF Kinloss on the Moray Firth in Scotland in the spring of 1995.

During a routine sortie the aircrew of an R.1 would consist of a complement of 29: two pilots; a flight engineer; one navigator and

TOP: Nimrod R.1 XW665 in the later "hemp" scheme. *Vic Flintham*

ABOVE: The same aircraft at No 51 Sqn's base at RAF Wyton in the 1970s, photographed in its original grey maritime colour scheme. *Terry Panopalis*

ABOVE: "Damien" awaits another sortie at Wyton in October 1988. By this time the Nimrod fleet had adopted the hemp colour scheme with pale grey undersides and toned-down national roundels. Note also the squadron's flying goose emblem painted in a circle on the Nimrod's dorsal fillet. *Terry Panopalis*

25 others of mixed trades and specialisations. Crammed into the back of the Nimrod, these would include Russian and Arabic speakers and many others. This particular air test, however, required a smaller aircrew of seven, including copilot Flt Lt Pat Hewitt, flight engineer Flt Sgt David Rimmer and navigator Flt Lt Dick Chelu. Also aboard was a flight safety team of Air Electronics Operators comprising Stu Clay, Andy Lawson and the junior member of the team, Steve Hart. By the time this air test had concluded, Stacey would be in hospital – and a member of an exclusive brotherhood, as he explains:

"In almost 10,000 flying hours my most memorable day's flying has to be the day I qualified for membership of the Goldfish Club – an exclusive club open only to aircrew who have survived an aircraft ditching and subsequently been rescued from the sea. I became eligible to join on Tuesday, May 16, 1995".

From this point on, Art Stacey takes up the story himself...

A BEAUTIFUL MORNING

"I woke up that morning and it was a beautiful day; there wasn't a cloud in the sky and just the gentlest of breezes. Although permanently stationed at Waddington, I was at Kinloss with six squadron colleagues to conduct a post-major-overhaul air test on XW666.

Having just returned from Cyprus the previous Friday after a three-week stint there, I really didn't want this detachment, as short as it was. However, I had been assured by the squadron that as Pilot Leader I was the only one qualified and available. Although the French expression *fait accompli* had been used, the English expression 'Joed' sprang to mind.

In my haste to get to Kinloss I soon discovered that I had forgotten to pack a Service hat, an omission I became aware of just before leaving the Mess to walk down to Ops for briefing. We left the Mess at about 0900hr, and as we left I noticed hanging in the cloakroom an old and very well-worn 'chip-bag' hat. 'That will do' I thought. If the

owner was still alive – which I very much doubted if the state of the hat was anything to go by – I would have it back on its peg within a few hours with a signed bar-chit inside as explanation and recompense for any inconvenience caused. I forgot to ask the hat if it could swim!

We had a Met brief on what the weather was doing; there wasn't any. Although my plan was to land back at Kinloss we chose Lossiemouth as our diversion airfield; standard procedure for all aircrew, military and civilian. I then briefed the crew so they were aware of what lay ahead for the flight. Take-off was to be at 1100hr; the flight was scheduled to last four hours and in that time we would climb to 15,000ft (4,500m), settle down and begin the air test. During the test flight we would be flying at up to 35,000ft (10,500m), at which we would proceed to shut down engines and relight them, as well as checking things like whether the flaps were in working order.

The briefings, crew-in, start-up, taxy and

take-off were all normal, and as we climbed up to FL150 and turned out over the Moray Firth to start the air test I recalled the words of an old and much-respected former instructor of mine who, on beautiful days such as this one, would turn and utter the immortal words, 'almost a shame to take the flying pay today'.

The weather was marvellous, with unlimited visibility, a light breeze and, most importantly, a sea state of less than one with a swell of no more than a couple of feet. We could see for miles and the area around Kinloss and Findhorn Bay looked absolutely magnificent.

PROBLEMS BEGIN

We had just started the air test checklist when the problems started. Dave Rimmer, the flight engineer, had the checklist on his lap and was checking the engines' anti-icing system. He started with No 1 engine and watched the temperature rise, before switching it off. He then did the same with Nos 2 and 3, but it would be No 4 that would be the cause of our problems. The air-start valve light illuminated on the centre console. This in itself was nothing to worry about as, to my knowledge, it had happened a dozen times before on Nimrods and had always been a false alarm. It was more of a nuisance than an emergency. On this occasion, however, it was not a false alarm.

Above No 4 engine was a loom of wires; over the years, with the vibrations, the insulation that covered the wires had worn. Unbeknown to us, two wires were now touching; one of those wires went down to the engine anti-icing system, with the other going to the starter motor. We later learned that more than 20 years previously, an RAF engineer had been looking at the nut that held the turbine assembly in its titanium shroud within XW666's Rolls-Royce Spey engine, and had expressed concern that this particular nut was not strong enough; if too much stress was applied to it then there was a chance it would shatter. The turbine assembly would then be free to rotate itself off its mounting and come

into contact with the engine. If that was to occur it would cause a catastrophic explosion.

The short circuit had supplied power to No 4 engine's starter motor. The turbine within the starter, under no load, with the engine already running, wound up to more than 100,000 r.p.m. in a few seconds, and in doing so imposed stresses on that £5 nut whose job was to hold the starter turbine in place. Just as that clever engineer had forecast, the nut failed and allowed the spinning turbine to clear the starter motor casing before coming into contact with the engine. Needless to say the catastrophic explosion did occur, which blew the lower casings off the engine and penetrated the adjacent fuel tank. Fortunately the tank was still full. Two hours later it would have been empty except for vapour and the outcome would have been dramatically different.

Back on the flightdeck we didn't know that all this was going on only feet from where we sat. The first indication we had that something was really wrong was when the fire-warning, both aural and visual, for No 4 activated. The copilot and engineer began actioning their checks and I began to turn the aircraft and commenced a descent back towards land and Kinloss.

The fire spread rapidly through the engine and was quickly followed by a fire-warning – false as it turned out – for No 3. All four fire extinguishers were quickly used, to no avail – the contents going overboard, although we didn't know it – and one of the three safety team down the back, Steve Hart, began reporting on the state of the fire. Grey smoke first, quickly turning to black, then the first flames and numerous reports of panels breaking away and the wing appearing to be melting. Steve then reported that flames were

coming out of the thrust-reversers. With thousands of pounds of fuel being driven out at 350 m.p.h. (560km/h), we resembled a blowtorch.

Steve's accuracy of reporting was nothing short of inspired. I saw the fire through his eyes and made the most dramatic and important decision of my 30-odd years of flying, based on someone else's reports.

The copilot transmitted the international distress call, 'Mayday, Mayday, Mayday' and informed Lossiemouth air traffic control (ATC) of our problems. We needed to land as soon as possible, but we first had to dump fuel because we had taken off with about 25 tons for the 4hr flight; far too much weight for the undercarriage.

Having heard the explosion and felt the whole aircraft shudder, and with reports coming from the back, I thought the Nimrod was about to blow up. We were descending at 300kt and I could see Kinloss in the distance, but in our path was Lossiemouth, ten miles (16km) closer and with a north-south runway. Because we were coming in from a northerly direction, we were perfectly lined up for an approach into Lossie. I informed Lossiemouth ATC that we intended to divert and make an emergency landing there.

PREPARE TO DITCH!

I hadn't thought about having to ditch the aircraft and had fully intended to make the airfield. However, as the minutes passed and we got closer to land – and closer to the sea – I began to fear that the wing would collapse and I would lose control of the Nimrod, so I decided to tell the crew to prepare for a possible ditching.

Ditching an aircraft, particularly

*Needless to say the catastrophic **explosion** did occur, blowing the lower **castings off the engine** and penetrating the **fuel tank.***

LEFT: The Nimrod R.1s were progressively upgraded throughout their careers, with the addition of wingtip pods to house additional electronic equipment and finlets on the tailplane to improve handling. Seen here touching down at Wyton, XW664 was despatched to the South Atlantic in 1982 and reportedly undertook night missions in Chilean airspace in support of operations against Argentina during the Falklands conflict. *Vic Flintham*

a large aircraft like the Nimrod, is not an option you take lightly but, if there is no other way, then ditch you must. Everything was in our favour to give us as good a chance of a successful ditching as possible; the sea was like a millpond and the weather was still perfect. With the Nimrod's engines built into the wings and not underslung like on most large aircraft, this gave us a better chance, provided I could keep the wings level, of not somersaulting once we impacted the water.

In preparation for ditching, at about 1,000ft (300m) I allowed the aircraft to slow down and requested 20° flap. Fortunately the hydraulic lines to the flaps had already gone, with the result that the flaps failed to lower. I say fortunately because had they done so we would have been left with asymmetric flap owing to the damage sustained. And although again we didn't know it at the time, we had no starboard aileron. The hydraulics to that had also gone. So I had no option but to go for a flapless-configuration ditching. Unfortunately nobody had foreseen this eventuality and therefore no trials had been conducted; it was not even practised in the simulator and there were no speeds written down anywhere. We were literally going into uncharted waters.

Because of the flat-calm sea state and the aircraft's flapless nose-high attitude I found it extremely difficult to judge my height during the last 100ft (30m) or so. The radar altimeter helped, but my eyes were firmly outside to ensure my wings were level. We finally found the water at 127kt, 2kt higher than I planned. Not bad under the circumstances, looking back on it!

The engineer described the actual ditching as the biggest log-flume in the world. Personally I don't remember much about the events after we touched. We bounced twice, I've since learned, and as we slowed we pivoted about 80° around the port wing and came to rest roughly parallel to the shore about three miles (5km) off.

After the noise of the ditching, the silence when we came to a halt was almost deafening. There was about a foot of water and fuel in the cockpit and without my headset, lost in the impact, I just shouted for everyone to get out. I don't think anyone on board needed telling twice. We exited through the port overwing escape hatch and boarded the dinghy on the wing. Of the two wing-root mounted dinghies, one had obviously burnt through, but the other had inflated on impact and was floating, upside down, about 400yd astern of us. I can honestly say that I didn't really get wet. My flying boots got a little damp and I always feel guilty when speaking to other members of the Goldfish Club and hearing of their feats of survival and endurance in open dinghies in the North Atlantic in winter.

SALVATION

As we pulled away from the still-floating fuselage, I recall the all-pervading smell of fuel and praying that a stray spark would not trigger an explosion. However, the good old waters of the Moray Firth had put out the fire that we had been unable to. Within seconds we heard the 'whoosh-whoosh' of

ABOVE: On ditching, XW666 broke into two major sections and, after Art Stacey and his crew had evacuated the aircraft, began to sink. The forward fuselage and inner wing sections remained in one piece and were salvaged... *via author*

ABOVE: ...as was the starboard outer wing section. *via author*

the approaching rescue helicopter, and within 10min we were all aboard and on our way to hospital for the injured – the scruffs' bar for the remainder.

As for injuries, I sustained compression fractures of the spine, as did Andy Lawson, one of the three safety team. He also sustained a broken ankle, a broken rib and a chipped pelvis when the rails holding his seat came apart, and Andy-plus-seat went spiralling down the fuselage, finally ending up upside down with his head below water and trapped by his shoulders. Fortunately Stu Clay, the smallest member of the crew and the final member of the safety team, provided proof of what adrenalin will do by lifting Andy, plus his seat, out of the hole, dislocating his thumb in the process. In doing so he may have set a new British all-comers record for the straight arm lift!

Dave Rimmer broke a finger and gashed his hand. Dick Chelu, the navigator, slept though the whole affair after giving me an initial steer to the runway threshold and walked away unscathed. And finally Pat, my copilot, has since had an operation on his upper neck to repair damage caused during the ditching but not diagnosed immediately.

ABOVE: The cockpit was removed from the fuselage and remains on display at the South Yorkshire Aircraft Museum at Aeroventure, near Doncaster. *via author*

With the exception of poor old Andy, who was eventually medically discharged from the RAF, we all gradually managed to return to flying and without exception wore the distinctive winged-goldfish with pride.

And the hat? I regretfully have to report that it failed to vacate the aircraft before she sank and now resides on the bed of the Moray Firth approximately three miles off Lossiemouth. Much to my amazement the owner of the hat, a very junior navigator on one of the Kinloss squadrons, contacted me shortly afterwards; after apologising profusely for losing his hat for him, and despite his protestations, I bought 20 tickets for the Christmas draw in his name. None of them won a prize!" ●

Acknowledgments
The Editor would like to thank Vic Flintham and Chris Gibson for their invaluable help with the preparation of this article.

BELOW: Flight Lieutenant Art Stacey (third from left) receives his Air Force Cross, awarded for acts of courage, valour or devotion to duty by officers but not in active operations against the enemy. Other crew members also received commendations, including Flt Sgt Steve Hart, awarded the Queen's Commendation for Bravery in the Air. *via author*

And finally...
Merlin magic Farnborough

In 1962 the SBAC Show at Farnborough celebrated 50 years of British military aviation with a special display of vintage aircraft. KENNETH BROOKES had a prime position by the runway and took these magnificent – and previously unpublished – photographs.

The 1962 SBAC Show at Farnborough offered something slightly different from the usual rip-snorting high-adrenalin state-of-the-art jet fighter displays to which visitors had grown accustomed over the previous decade. The ear-shredding military hardware – Hunters, Lightnings, Gnats, Scimitars, Sea Vixens etc – was there of course, as were other representatives of the British aircraft industry, from Ken Wallis's diminutive gyrocopter to the RAF's

capacious turboprop-powered Argosy. What was different, however, was the addition on the public days of a special vintage display celebrating the 50th anniversary of the formation of the Royal Flying Corps in April 1912.

Taking part in the commemorative display was a selection of nine aircraft representing the considerable achievements of British military aviation – not forgetting those of the Senior Service too of course – over the previous five decades. The aircraft were:

Royal Aircraft Factory S.E.5a D7000 (flown by Gp Capt Pat Hanafin); Bristol F.2B D8096 (Mr J.I. "Willie" Williamson); Hawker Hart "J9933"/G-ABMR (Duncan Simpson); Fairey Swordfish LS326 (Lt-Cdr Peter "Lofty" Wreford); Gloster Gladiator "K8032"/ G-AMRK (Peter Varley); Hawker Hurricane PZ865/G-AMAU (Bill Bedford); Supermarine Spitfire LF.VB AB910/G-AISU (David Morgan); Fairey Fulmar N1854/ G-AIBE and de Havilland Mosquito T.3 TW117.

ABOVE: Fairey Fulmar N1854 was the first production example and made its first flight in January 1940, after which it was used for trials, including deck landing trials aboard *HMS Illustrious*. After the war it was returned to Fairey and registered G-AIBE. In 1972 it was presented to the Fleet Air Arm Museum, where it resides today as a static exhibit. *Kenneth J.A. Brookes*

The last two were flown by Lt-Cdr Trevor Spafford and Civilian Anti-Aircraft Co-operation Unit pilot John Oliver respectively, the pair lining up together on the runway's "piano keys", where keen photographer Ken Brookes was in his usual position waiting with Kodachrome-loaded camera for the perfect moment. Ken explains:

"Those were the days when we could go right to the edge of the runway to get dramatic pictures. It stopped when an aircraft crashed on the other side of the runway and a famous American aviation photographer ran across the runway to get close-ups.

After that they kept us back to a line halfway between the runway's edge and the public line".

In 1962 Ken was perfectly positioned to capture the pair of Rolls-Royce Merlin-engined "old boys" as Oliver and Spafford performed last-minute checks and engine run-ups before launching into a lively display in front of 82,000 people; the Mosquito rolled off its marks on the runway first, the Fulmar following hot on its heels.

So it was that Ken Brookes was in the right place at the right time to capture these magnificent images of the splendid and nostalgic parade of vintage aircraft at Farnborough in 1962. Even if only for a short while, the usual high-pitched whistle of the turbojet, the screaming afterburner, the efficient hum of the turboprop and the beating of turbine-powered rotor blades were all replaced by the majestic roar of three Rolls-Royce Merlins. ●

BELOW: Ken Brookes's superb image of de Havilland Mosquito T.3 TW117 and Fairey Fulmar N1854 on the runway at Farnborough on September 7, 1962. Built at Leavesden in May 1946, TW117 was put into storage, where it remained until July 1947. After serving with various second-line units, it was put into storage again in April 1954, where it remained until March 1960, when it joined No 3 Civilian Anti-Aircraft Co-operation Unit at Exeter Airport. Coded "Z", the Mosquito was still serving with No 3 CAACU when it was flown by John Oliver as part of the vintage display at Farnborough in 1962. It was retired and handed over to the RAF Museum Collection in June 1963, and was used for the filming of *633 Squadron* at Bovingdon the following month. It was subsequently put on display at the RAF Museum at Hendon, before moving to the Norwegian Air Force Museum in Oslo, where it is currently on display. *Kenneth J.A. Brookes with thanks to Stuart Bourne/QAPI*